Twenty-Four Stories From Psychology

To Cathy

Without her love and encouragement,
this book would never have been completed.

Sara Miller McCune founded SAGE Publishing in 1965 to support the dissemination of usable knowledge and educate a global community. SAGE publishes more than 1000 journals and over 800 new books each year, spanning a wide range of subject areas. Our growing selection of library products includes archives, data, case studies and video. SAGE remains majority owned by our founder and after her lifetime will become owned by a charitable trust that secures the company's continued independence.

Los Angeles | London | New Delhi | Singapore | Washington DC | Melbourne

Twenty-Four Stories From Psychology

John D. Hogan

St. John's University

Los Angeles | London | New Delhi
Singapore | Washington DC | Melbourne

FOR INFORMATION:

SAGE Publications, Inc.
2455 Teller Road
Thousand Oaks, California 91320
E-mail: order@sagepub.com

SAGE Publications Ltd.
1 Oliver's Yard
55 City Road
London EC1Y 1SP
United Kingdom

SAGE Publications India Pvt. Ltd.
B 1/I 1 Mohan Cooperative Industrial Area
Mathura Road, New Delhi 110 044
India

SAGE Publications Asia-Pacific Pte. Ltd.
18 Cross Street #10-10/11/12
China Square Central
Singapore 048423

Printed in the United States of America

Library of Congress Cataloging-in-Publication Data

Names: Hogan, John D., 1939- author.

Title: Twenty-four stories from psychology / John D. Hogan, St. John's University.

Other titles: 24 stories from psychology

Description: First Edition. | Thousand Oaks : SAGE Publications, Inc., [2019] | Includes bibliographical references and index.

Identifiers: LCCN 2019012454 | ISBN 978-1-5063-7825-1 (pbk. : alk. paper)

Subjects: LCSH: Psychology—History.

Classification: LCC BF121 .H594 2019 | DDC 150.1—dc23 LC record available at https://lccn.loc.gov/2019012454

This book is printed on acid-free paper.

Acquisitions Editor: Lara Parra
Production Editor: Rebecca Lee
Copy Editor: Cathy Kottwitz
Typesetter: Hurix Digital
Proofreader: Ellen Brink
Index: Molly Hall
Cover Designer: Ginkhan Siam
Marketing Manager: Katherine Hepburn

19 20 21 22 23 10 9 8 7 6 5 4 3 2 1

CONTENTS

PREFACE

I've been a college professor for my entire professional career and have taught courses in the history of psychology for roughly half that time. Although course content is governed by a syllabus, I have the freedom to go off on tangents or to explore additional topics as long as they are relevant. This book is partly about those tangents.

While there are many excellent textbooks available in psychology, they can also be frustrating. Too often the text will introduce an intriguing character or set of circumstances only to have the subject quickly discarded as the narrative moves on to another topic. I'm left wanting more.

The inclination to brevity is not surprising. Most textbook authors are required to cover an enormous amount of material in a relatively small space. But in shifting so quickly from topic to topic, something is lost. Information is often presented in such schematic fashion that much of the complexity and rich detail is ignored. The researchers themselves are rarely given much space. History of psychology texts tend to be the exception, but even they have a lot of traditional ground to cover.

This volume is a more leisurely trip through two dozen topics in the history of psychology. It makes no attempt to be a complete history. The selection is mostly a collection of personal choices, topics that caught my attention—or that of my students—for one reason or another over the years. For instance, my choice of the opening chapter on the witch hunt in Salem, Massachusetts, in 1692 came right out of the classroom. The story of the witches is not found in most psychology texts, but when the subject came up in class one day, my students were riveted. The level of interest was simply too good to pass up. We've continued to discuss the topic periodically ever since.

Not all the choices were made that way. Phineas Gage is often mentioned in textbooks, but there is little information about his years after the accident. I became so fascinated by his story, I took a trip to Cavendish, Vermont, to visit the site of the accident. The visit made the story more tangible to me. Another story, that of Little Albert, is a mainstay of virtually all texts, but again, the rich aftermath of the story, including the criticisms as well as the attempts to identify Albert, with its fascinating twists and turns, is typically found only in professional journals.

Several of the selections are controversial. The prominent British psychologist Cyril Burt was accused of fraud after his death, and his contributions were banished from most historical accounts of the discipline. But later writings have suggested that despite his quirks, he may not have been quite the villain depicted earlier. On the other hand, the research of Stanley Milgram was controversial from the day he first published it more than 50 years ago. Even today, it brings up questions of deception in research and the potential harm to research subjects.

In some cases, my point was simply to tell a familiar story in a more complete way, such as the story of Ivan Pavlov. In other cases, the intention was to clarify the usual way in which the story was told. And, finally, some chapters were chosen to highlight stories that have been ignored but have more value and interest than usually assigned to them. The approach tends toward the biographical. My hope is that such an emphasis will make the history come more alive for the reader.

The volume takes into account some of the more recent concerns in the history of psychology. For instance, in earlier publications, the contributions of women have been underrepresented or even ignored. And although it is true that women did not make contributions on the same order as men in the early days of psychology, that does not mean their history should be ignored. In fact, their absence may be the strongest argument for including them. The same argument can be made for other underrepresented groups.

As students we're usually taught that science is an objective enterprise, taking place on some abstract plane, out of reach of ordinary human concerns. That belief has gone through some modification in recent years. While most scientists make every effort to be as objective as possible in their research, it is also true that scientists are human beings—people with opinions and biases, all of which may have an impact on their approach and the research questions they ask. In understanding more about the people who conducted the research, we may be better able to understand the science itself.

These chapters are written with the introductory student or layperson in mind. No special knowledge of the science and practice of psychology is required. At the same time, none of the material is "dumbed down" in the sense that it leaves out important parts of the story or avoids controversies. While there may be some benefit in reading the chapters chronologically, each chapter is written to stand on its own. As with most endeavors of this sort, my hope is that these stories will lead the reader to seek out more information about the topics under consideration.

The history of psychology is a history of attempts to understand the human condition. It is filled with errors and dead-ends and occasional victories. For all of that, I've found it to consist of some of the most intriguing stories I've ever known. I hope the reader will find these stories equally intriguing

John D. Hogan
Tarrytown, NY

ABOUT THE AUTHOR

John D. Hogan, PhD, is a longtime professor of psychology at St. John's University, New York, where he has taught both graduate and undergraduate courses in the history of psychology. He received his master's degree in counseling psychology from Iowa State University and his doctoral degree in developmental psychology from Ohio State University. He has written more than 200 chapters, articles, encyclopedia entries, and book reviews for various publications, and has presented an equal number of talks at local and professional meetings. He is the author/editor of three previous books.

He has been active in a range of professional associations including service as president of Division 1 of the American Psychological Association (APA, the Society for General Psychology), president of the APA Division of International Psychology, and president of two divisions of the New York State Psychological Association. He has also held leadership positions in the Eastern Psychological Association and the Psychology Section of the New York Academy of Sciences. For thirteen years, he was the history and obituary editor for the *American Psychologist*, the flagship journal of the APA.

PRESCIENTIFIC
PSYCHOLOGY

CHAPTER ONE

THE WITCHES OF SALEM, MASSACHUSETTS

1692

In early 1692, in a rural area of the Massachusetts Bay Colony known as Salem Village, two local girls began to act strangely. They suddenly developed fits and made odd noises, sometimes contorting their bodies into strange postures. At other times, they complained of being pricked by pins while they shouted out or hid under furniture. Local leaders and a physician were consulted. Ultimately an explanation was found for the girls' strange behavior—witchcraft.

The news spread and the fear of witchcraft soon consumed several neighboring communities. In short order, villagers were flinging accusations of witchcraft back and forth at one another. Within months, scores of people were labeled witches. Local magistrates became involved and formal charges were made. Before the long episode was over, nineteen people had been hanged and one man was pressed to death; more than a hundred others had been imprisoned where they were held under appalling conditions. At least five of the accused died in prison.

The shocking facts of the case are not in dispute; the initial behavior of the children as well as the accusations and testimony at the trials have been well documented. However, the events of those painful months continue to defy satisfactory explanation and remain the subject of discussion and debate to this day.

BACKGROUND AND THE INITIAL EPISODES

Incidents of witchcraft had been reported in Europe and colonial North America before the events at Salem. In fact, there had been several notable "outbreaks" of witchcraft in Europe, particularly in England, France, and Germany, beginning in the 1500s. For the accused, the result of being identified as a practicing witch could be severe. The King James Version of the Old Testament Bible (Exodus 22:18) counsels: "Thou shalt not suffer a witch to live." Indeed, thousands of people were put to death as witches in Europe during the 16th and 17th centuries, most of them women (Demos, 2008).

Many religious people of the time believed that God was active in every aspect of their lives, guiding them on a daily basis but also punishing them for inappropriate behavior. In the same way, they considered Satan to be an active and daily source of evil. Any event for which there was no obvious explanation, from crop failure to the death of an infant, might be attributed to God or the Devil. The role of witches was to carry out the orders of Satan. Sometimes they would work through animals, known as *familiars*. Once witches agreed to serve the Devil, usually after signing the "Devil's book," they might be possessed with unusual powers, such as flying through the air or changing shape or demonstrating great physical strength. They had an endless reservoir of potential gifts. In fact, possession of these abilities in themselves might be evidence enough to identify an individual as a witch.

Although witchcraft was punishable by death in colonial North America, there had been only a few reports of such sentences being carried out prior to the Salem episodes. A few years earlier, in Boston, an elderly woman, Goody Glover, was accused of tormenting children. She confessed to being a witch during her trial and even demonstrated her methods for causing the children to suffer from fits. After determining that she was sane, the court ordered her execution, which was carried out on November 16, 1688. Some of the individuals involved in her trial were later involved in the trials in Salem. In fact, the Boston trial may have served as a kind of preparatory learning for the Salem trials. Still, the events in Salem presented a unique set of issues, one of which was its wide scope. In the end, the executions in Salem more than doubled all the colonial deaths for witchcraft up to that time.

In 1692, Salem Village was a small rural community roughly 15 miles north of Boston. It was located to the north and west of Salem Town, a more prosperous and active area. A port city, Salem Town was one of the earliest settlements in the Massachusetts Bay Colony. The two communities were very different and frequently in conflict. (Today Salem Village is part of the town of Danvers; Salem Town is known simply as Salem.) The residents of the Village were mostly deeply religious Puritans. For many of them, religious beliefs dominated every aspect of their lives.

The behaviors leading to the accusations of witchcraft first emerged in mid-January 1692 with two young girls who were living in the home of the Reverend Samuel Parris. They were his daughter, Betty Parris, age nine, and his niece, Abigail Williams, age eleven. Reverend Parris was himself a controversial figure. Not everyone in the Village was pleased with his presence there. He was considered both inexperienced and judgmental, neither of which added to his popularity. Many of the locals chose not to belong to his congregation and he clearly was unhappy with them. This rift in the Village is sometimes seen as a contributing factor to the events that followed.

After the girls began exhibiting their odd behavior, Parris and his wife Elizabeth soon became convinced they were witnessing something out of the ordinary. The children were taken to a local physician, William Griggs, for an evaluation. After lengthy consideration, Griggs also concluded that their symptoms were outside the range of normal medical problems and suggested that the Devil might be the cause of their behavior. This kind of "medical" judgment was not unusual for the time. Medicine and spiritual issues were frequently conflated. Physicians who could not find a physical basis for an ailment were quick to invoke the power of Satan. Parris consulted with other ministers in the area and they came together to pray for relief for the girls and for divine guidance. Before long, however, two other girls in the Village, Elizabeth Hubbard and Ann Putnam, began exhibiting odd behavior as well. Soon after, even more instances of peculiar behavior began to erupt in the community.

ACCUSATIONS AND DEATH SENTENCES

When the girls were first questioned, they were silent. Eventually, however, they identified several individuals who were the sources of their affliction. Prominent among those they accused were Tituba, a slave in the Parris household, believed to be from the West Indies; Sarah Good, a woman from a very poor family; and Sarah Osborne, known for her indifference to attending religious services, a serious issue in the Salem community. Each of them was an outsider in the Village in one way or another. Following formal complaints by several of the villagers, all three women were brought in for public questioning by the local magistrates, John Hathorne and Jonathan Corwin.

Sarah Good was the first to be questioned. She denied any involvement with witchcraft, even under the difficult questioning of John Hathorne. (Decades later, one of Hathorne's direct descendants would become famous as a novelist—Nathaniel Hawthorne.) It seemed clear from the outset that Hathorne considered Sarah Good to be guilty. Eventually, Hathorne brought the afflicted children before her, and the children immediately identified her as their tormentor. She again denied the charge, but this time she argued that the children's tormentor was Sarah Osborne. When Osborne was questioned, she also denied any involvement with the Devil although she too was identified by the children as their tormentor. Even Osborne's family had to admit that she had not been to a church meeting in more than a year. It was Tituba's testimony, however, that proved to be the most explosive (Schiff, 2015).

Tituba, by reason of her dark skin color and background, was the most different of the accused and therefore a natural object for their accusations of witchcraft. After first denying that she was a witch, Tituba admitted that the Devil had appeared to her. Moreover, she agreed that both Sarah Osborne and Sarah Good were witches—she had seen evidence of it. She testified that a group of witches had actually met at the home of the Reverend Parris, although without his knowledge. Further, she admitted to "signing the Devil's book" along with others who lived in the area. Following

▶ **Image 1.1**   Martha Corey is accused of being a witch

her testimony, several residents of the Village who were present at the hearing began to experience fits. Their behavior was interpreted as further evidence of the presence of witches in the community. The accused were jailed and subjected to further interrogation. Sarah Osborne, who had been bedridden before the accusations, died within two months, still in prison.

The questioning and incriminations continued. Now the accused included two upstanding members of church congregations, Martha Corey and Rebecca Nurse. It was clear that even church membership and devotion did not ensure against accusations of witchcraft. As more indictments were made, those accused would sometimes make further accusations, naming others in the community. When John Proctor protested the charges against his wife, he became the object of allegations. Dorcas (Dorothy) Good, the 4-and-a-half-year-old daughter of Sarah Good, was accused of appearing before the girls and biting them in retaliation for her mother's imprisonment. As a result, she was incarcerated for several months. Although she was eventually released from prison, her father later said that she was never able to function normally again. She spent the rest of her life dependent on others (Hill, 2002).

The number of accused grew to 40 and then to 60. The prisons were becoming overcrowded. Betty Parris, one of the young girls who made the initial accusations, was removed from the proceeding by her parents. The constant questioning had grown too much for her and she was showing signs of mental instability. The examinations had now relocated from Salem Village to Salem Town where they were conducted by Deputy Governor Danforth and a number of additional magistrates. But there was a problem with moving forward. At the time, the Massachusetts colony had been operating without an official government, and the locals did not have the authority to try cases of witchcraft. The English governor had been ousted from office in 1689 and a replacement governor had not yet been appointed. The local officials deemed it unwise to proceed further until the official authority had been restored. It was soon in coming.

Word reached the colony that Sir William Phipps had been appointed as governor under a new charter. Soon after his arrival, the new governor arranged for a special Court of Oyer and Terminer (to hear and determine), which was convened in Salem Town in June 1692. Finally, a process was in place. If, after questioning, there was enough evidence of witchcraft, the cases were brought to grand juries and eventually to trial. Sometimes the indictment and trial took place on the same day.

Many forms of evidence were used to identify witches. Direct confession of witchcraft was one of the important pieces of evidence; the observation of

▶ **Image 1.2** A Salem witch trial

Time Life Pictures/Mansell/The LIFE Picture Collection/Getty Images

superhuman feats on the part of the accused, such as flying or lifting heavy objects, was another. One of the more controversial types of evidence was referred to as *spectral evidence*. Usually this consisted of the victims seeing their tormentors, or perhaps just their shape or outline, often while the victim was being tormented. Another form of spectral evidence consisted of a deceased person appearing and identifying the witch as the cause of his or her death. Unusual spots or growths on the body, such as a wart, might be evidence of being in league with the Devil. Such spots were interpreted as sites for nourishing the Devil (Schiff, 2015). The signs used to identify witches—and there were many more—were common knowledge in the community.

The first person to be executed was Bridget Bishop. She was indicted and tried on June 2 and hanged on June 10, 1692. Bridget Bishop had been accused of being a witch before—she even had a local reputation as a witch. Several local people swore she had appeared to them at night in their own homes, terrifying them by her appearance. Even her own husband testified against her. Two men stated that when they took down a wall in a home in which she had lived, they found dolls with pins stuck in them. Although there was no certainty that the dolls belonged to Bridget Bishop, the use of poppets (or puppets) was well known as the kind of "black magic" that witches commonly used as a way to torment their victims (Schiff, 2015).

In a matter of weeks, five more women went to trial—Sarah Good, Elizabeth Howe, Susannah Martin, Rebecca Nurse, and Sarah Wildes. All five were convicted and sentenced to death by hanging. Their executions took place on July 19, 1692. And still the accusations and trials continued. On August 19, 1692, five more people were hanged. On September 22, 1692, an additional eight more were hanged. All of the executions took place from early June to late September. Eighty-year-old Giles Corey, one of the accused, refused to plead at his indictment, protesting the practices of the court. He was subjected to a form of torture in which increasingly heavy stones were placed on his body in an effort to force him to make a plea. Instead, he died from the torture without ever making a plea.

It is difficult to know the great sadness that must have accompanied the deaths of so many innocent people, some of whom were mothers with young children. Not one of those executed had admitted to being a witch. Curiously, not one of those who admitted to being a witch was executed. Tituba, who was so central to initiating the long episode, also escaped execution. She and her husband, John Indian, disappear from the historical record completely soon after the trials.

The Court of Oyer and Terminer was dismissed in October 1692, and during January 1693 a new Superior Court of Judicature was established. This court acted differently. Although dozens of indictments were still being brought by the grand jury, fewer than half continued on to trial. At trial, only a few were condemned but none of those convicted were executed. In May of 1693, the governor issued a general reprieve and it is estimated that 150 or more of the accused were released from prison. (Despite their release, they still might have been required to pay jail fees before they were given their freedom.) Anyone who was convicted after the hangings of September 1692 inevitably escaped execution. It seemed the tide had finally changed. The long terrible episode was over.

FICTIONAL ACCOUNTS

Several novels have been written based on the events at Salem, as well as several poems, but the most popular portrayal is a theatrical one. In 1953, Arthur Miller's play *The Crucible* was produced on Broadway. Although it is a highly fictionalized account of the events in Salem, it used the names and attributes of many of the authentic principal players. Miller, the acclaimed playwright of *Death of a Salesman*, which had opened only a few years before, was understood to be writing about more than the Salem witch trials themselves. He saw in them a parallel for the accusations of communist infiltration into the U.S. government made by the House Un-American Activities Committee under the leadership of Wisconsin Senator Joseph McCarthy. Even today, the phrase "witch hunt" is virtually synonymous with McCarthyism. But it may also be applied to any situation involving supposed moral outrage and unsubstantiated accusations without due process. Today *The Crucible* continues to be produced throughout the world and is standard reading in many high schools and colleges.

UNDERSTANDING THE CAUSES OF THE EPIDEMIC

It didn't take long for residents of the area to question what had happened. In 1696, a dozen jurors signed a statement expressing their contrition at the outcome of the trials. Soon after, several of the accusers confessed that they had acted inappropriately and begged for the forgiveness of the families involved. They blamed Satan as the source of their accusations. One of the judges, Samuel Sewall, publicly admitted his errors and asked that he be forgiven for his sins. Even the government offered an official pardon for those executed and compensation for the survivors or their families. But what had happened that caused the officials of Salem Village and Salem Town to arrive at such a conclusion in the first place?

Modern historians emphasize the importance of context and historical period in trying to explain any historical event. By those standards, the appearance of witches of Salem should be seen as attributable, at least in part, to the effects of living in a community that was isolated, deeply religious, convinced of the existence of witches, and knowledgeable about the powers and attributes of witches. Cotton Mather (1663–1728), a prominent Puritan minister, wrote extensively about witches, supported the trials, and even showed up at some of the executions. In those pre-Enlightenment days in America, science and objectivity played no role. The judicial process, which by contemporary standards showed a strong bias against the accused, was another failure in the system. One of the original judges, Nathaniel Saltonstall, excused himself from further trials, dissatisfied with the way the trials were conducted, but he was clearly in the minority.

Are all of these contextual elements, even taken together, enough to explain the events of that period? In 1976, Linnda Caporael, a graduate student at the time, proposed a different mechanism to explain the events of Salem. In an article in the prestigious journal *Science*, she suggested the possibility of a physiological explanation. Caporael, now an academic who researches the links between biology and culture, argued for the possibility of ergot poisoning as a potential explanation, or at least a contributing factor (Caporael, 1976).

Ergot is a fungus that prospers under certain weather and other growing conditions and is particularly likely to be found on rye crops. Rye was a very common form of grain in New England at the time and was quite popular in the area of Salem. One of the active ingredients in ergot contains chemicals related to the drug LSD (lysergic acid diethylamide), and it has some of the same psychoactive properties as LSD, including physical and hallucinogenic symptoms. Caporael argued that not only were many of the behaviors of the girls and other citizens of Salem consistent with ergot poisoning but also that weather conditions and local geography supported this position.

In the case of the girls, she argued that their behavior was, by all accounts, consistent and dramatic. No one present at the time thought that the girls were simply faking it. A physiological explanation might make more sense considering that so many locals described images and events that can only be characterized as supernatural. Further, she argued, the other cases of witchcraft that had been reported in colonial New England simply did not take on the hysterical tone that was found in Salem. There was something different about this experience.

For some observers, her explanation offered a more reasonable cause of the Salem events than the social-psychological ones then being offered. However, criticism of her essay came quickly. Psychologists Nicholas Spanos and Jack Gottlieb pointed out that the pattern of so-called poisoning did not fit the expected pattern for a staple like rye which would have been used in so many of the homes. Further, the girls seemed capable of turning their odd behavior on and off at will, an ability that would be inconsistent with ergot poisoning (Spanos & Gottlieb, 1976).

Caporael had her supporters, but the arguments against her thesis appeared to win the day. Other physiological explanations have been offered, including encephalitis and even Lyme disease, but none of them were strong enough to supplant the more generally accepted explanation of a social-psychological phenomenon.

IN THE FINAL ANALYSIS

Most contemporary historians accept an explanation for the events at Salem that combines a variety of features. The young girls who began the episode were inexperienced and young and, given their isolation, probably highly suggestible. Some have concluded that the girls were simply seeking attention, and this may have contributed to their behaviors, at least at the beginning. On the other hand, the number of accusations made by the girls and later by other villagers was extraordinary. For instance, Abigail Williams ultimately contended that she was being tormented by 44 different individuals. Other villagers made an even greater number of accusations. Some villagers later contended that they testified under duress, with threats of imprisonment by the magistrates. There is also speculation that there was gain to be made by accusing others in the Village of being witches. For some, the gain was economic (e.g., inheritances); for others, it was simply a matter of settling old personal debts.

To add yet another contextual element, Salem Village was not far from a war zone to the north, which was deeply involved in the little known King William's War, also called the second French and Indian War. Entire families, even villages, had been wiped out in the conflict, and some of the individuals in the Village had escaped the fighting in the north with their lives. It is fair to say that the villagers existed under a state of threat and tension and likely experienced what we would now call post-traumatic stress disorder. As a result, they were vulnerable to a variety of psychological threats (Norton, 2002). When the existence of witches was confirmed by those in authority, with no one to disconfirm their existence, it is understandable that the idea could spread rapidly.

It is more difficult to account for the hallucinatory kinds of experiences, the so-called spectral incidents that many of the villagers experienced. The reports of the villagers were numerous and often very specific. Still, the power of the mind to create and distort has been verified again and again throughout modern history. Such disorders, transient or not, are now recognized by all mental health authorities. Moreover, with the number of accusations that had been flung back and forth, some of the villagers may have been under substantial pressure to demonstrate that they were not witches. One way to do that was to remove themselves from the line of fire by corroborating the signs of witches in others.

We can never be certain of the causes of those events in Salem so many years ago. Several commentators have referred to it simply as an example of mass hysteria. In some ways, it can be seen as a "perfect storm" during which a variety of influences came together to produce a tragic outcome, unlikely ever to be repeated. Whatever the specific cause, it remains a valuable lesson in the power of time, place, and social influences. Even more, it presents a tantalizing reminder of the extraordinary range of behaviors of which humankind is capable.

REVIEW/DISCUSSION QUESTIONS

1. What were some of the environmental and cultural influences in Salem Village that supported a belief in witches?

2. How was it possible to identify witches? What were their outward signs?

3. In your view, what is the most likely explanation for the odd behavior of the girls?

4. Why were the residents so willing to accuse others of witchcraft?

5. What finally brought the executions to an end?

6. Can you identify any parallel incidents in recent history? In world history?

CHAPTER TWO

VICTOR, THE WILD BOY OF AVEYRON

The existence of "feral children" seems like an anachronism in the modern world. How is it possible that such children could exist? By definition, feral children were raised in the wild, without human supervision, and with little or no human contact. The Swedish botanist, Linnaeus (Carol von Linné, 1707–1778), who developed the modern system of classifying animals, formally placed feral children in a separate category of human existence. Mowgli, the jungle boy, a principal character in Rudyard Kipling's *Jungle Book* stories and other writings is one of the best fictional examples. (Mowgli has even served as a main character in Disney movies.)

For scholars of the Enlightenment, feral children held the promise of significant value, not simply creatures of casual interest or entertainment. It was thought that they might provide answers to some of the most significant questions that humans ask about themselves. How much of human behavior and development is innate? How would a child untouched by formal education or traditional social norms view the world? Would it be possible to socialize such a child? Most important for many people of the time was the question: Does a feral child, raised without human contact, possess thoughts about God? And, if so, what kinds of thoughts?

There have been dozens of reports of feral children throughout history, but most of the cases were questionable or even fraudulent. Some experts have doubted whether any child could possibly fulfill the requirements for being a true feral child—that is, a child raised in the wild with little or no human contact. Such children would be unlikely to survive infancy, and even if they did, it would be very difficult to provide concrete evidence of such a history. However, despite the skepticism, there have been a few cases in which the requirements appear to be at least partially fulfilled, such as a child who has lived in the wild for an extended period during early development without any significant oversight from other humans.

One such child was Victor, the wild boy of Aveyron (known in his native France as *l'enfant sauvage*). While his case was far from being the first reported example of a feral child, it is one of the best documented. Moreover, the man who became Victor's principal caretaker developed a detailed plan to socialize Victor and to help him enter the mainstream of human existence. He even kept a journal of Victor's progress, enabling future generations to revisit the case in some detail. Some professionals have identified it as one of the earliest cases of a clinical intervention.

THE FIRST SIGHTINGS

The story of Victor began in 1797 when peasants in the south of France spotted a naked boy running through the nearby woods. Often seen foraging and rooting for food, he was captured several times over the next few years but always managed to escape. Once, when he was captured in July 1799, he was entrusted to the care of an elderly widow who gave him clothing and offered him food. After eight days, he escaped again, but this time he did not return to the forest. Instead, he wandered within a circumscribed area where he was frequently seen by local inhabitants, wearing the remnants of a shirt that the widow had made for him. Sometimes, he even stopped at farmhouses where he would be fed. Finally, in January 1800, he appeared at the workshop of a dyer in the village of Saint-Sernin and began his entry into the civilized world. There is a marker in the village square commemorating the event.

Victor (though he was not yet called that) was 11 or 12 years old when he made his final entry from the wild; he would begin his journey through puberty soon after. He was small for his age, between 4 feet 1 inch and 4.5 feet tall, depending on the account. His round face had some scars and marks, perhaps from small-pox. His body was also covered with scars, animal bites, abrasions, and scratches, all of them attesting to his lengthy stay in the wild. Notable was a thick scar across his voice box. It has been

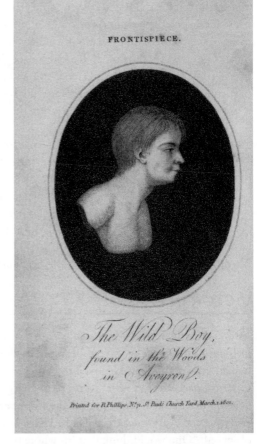

FRONTISPIECE.

The Wild Boy, found in the Woods in Aveyron.

Printed for R.Phillips, N°.71, S.t Pauls Church Yard, March.1.1801.

Album / Alamy Stock Photo

▶ **Image 2.1** Victor, the Wild Boy of Aveyron

speculated that some of the scars were the result of abuse by humans—perhaps parents or caretakers—and that the scar across his neck could only have been caused by a knife, likely a bungled case of infanticide (Yousef, 2001). He appeared to be deaf and did not speak, perhaps the result of severed vocal cords. There is no evidence that he ever lived with animals or was raised by them, as is sometimes suggested.

Shortly after entering the village, he was moved to an orphanage 25 miles away where he stayed for 5 months. While at the orphanage, there was a report that he was temporarily given the name Joseph, but there were never any official documents verifying that. Not surprisingly, he became a person of great interest among the locals. One of the officials in his area wrote a description of him and sent it to a Paris newspaper. Before long, Victor had become a celebrity. Fanciful pictures of him were published in the newspapers. Eventually, he would be brought to Paris and, because of the publicity, he was well known before he even arrived.

At the orphanage, Victor was cared for by Pierre-Joseph Bonnaterre, a scientist and Catholic priest. Bonnaterre attempted to find Victor's parents, advertising his presence in the orphanage as best he could. Several parents of missing children came to see Victor, hoping he might be their missing child, but no one ever claimed him. (The effects of the French Revolution, beginning in 1789 and lasting a decade, had uprooted many families.) Bonnaterre said that he was prepared to believe one particular story about Victor's parentage, but he wouldn't supply the details because it involved living people. Instead, he wrote this rather provocative statement:

> According to some very recent information given me by people in whom I have confidence, and according to stories passed around in the canton of _____, this boy is the child of a certain D_____ N_____ from M_____. They say he was born of a legitimate marriage, but the inhuman parents abandoned him after about six years because he did not have the gift of speech. (as quoted in Shattuck, 1980, p. 23)

No other possible parental connections ever surfaced.

VICTOR IN PARIS

After 5 months in the orphanage, Victor was brought to Paris. He had changed in the months since his first appearance at the orphanage. Among other things, he had grown quite fat. He loved to be tickled and he laughed easily. He was also toilet trained, surely a relief to those in charge of his daily care. He appeared to develop brief attachments, but for the most part he seemed indifferent to almost everyone and everything around him. There was an exception. One of his caretakers observed: "One would think that his whole being was focused in his stomach; it is the center of his life" (Shattuck, 1980, p. 27).

When Victor was brought to Paris, he was examined by a commission that included Philippe Pinel (1745–1826), the great French physician and psychiatrist. Pinel had developed a reputation for introducing humanitarian care to institutions for the mentally ill and feebleminded. He would later become known as the "father of modern psychiatry." Not surprisingly, his evaluation of Victor was taken very seriously. Pinel was particularly interested in Victor's senses. He had observed many developmentally disabled children in institutions and found that they frequently had sensory deficits.

This same limitation appeared to be true of Victor. He seemed to have little awareness of pain and was indifferent to varying temperatures—he was known to run around naked in the snow. And he didn't respond to loud sounds. But this lack of response was unlikely due to a genuine hearing deficit. Victor would be suddenly attentive when a key was turned in a lock, and he would react when a potato was dropped into a pot of boiling water. Clearly, he heard things, although he did it selectively. Still, Pinel saw Victor's sensory deficits as a telling sign. Victor was no feral child, he declared. After examining him, he wrote a report stating that nothing could be learned from Victor—he was an "incurable idiot" (Candland, 1993).

Pinel's verdict was a damaging blow, made all the more potent because it was delivered by such a well-regarded expert. It seemed, then, that Victor would be of no value in answering any basic questions about the nature of man. It was doubtful that he would ever learn to speak. Given that conclusion, what were they to do with Victor? He was not a docile creature; his sheer presence seemed to evoke hostility from some quarters. Other inmates at the Institute for Deaf-Mutes where he lived had occasionally attacked him. It seemed likely that he would be sent to an asylum for the insane and feebleminded to spend the rest of his days, an outcome both unpleasant and life threatening. Despite some progress, many institutions at the time remained difficult and dangerous places with a high mortality rate. But then Victor had a stroke of good luck.

▶ **Image 2.2** Jean-Marc Gaspard Itard

There had been a medical emergency at the Institute where Victor lived. Twenty-seven-year-old Jean-Marc Gaspard Itard, a physician whose training was largely "on the job" during the French Revolution, was called in to provide treatment. The director of the institute was so impressed with Itard's work that he invited him to work full-time with the inmates at the institute, and Itard accepted the invitation. As it turned out, he would go on to devote his entire professional life to working with the deaf. He is now considered one of the founders of special education.

TEACHING VICTOR

Philippe Pinel had warned Itard that Victor was unteachable. Although Itard was greatly impressed by Pinel and his accomplishments, he nonetheless disagreed. Itard was convinced that with the proper training, Victor's abilities could be substantially improved. He had several goals in mind for Victor, including making him more sensitive to his environment, encouraging him to develop a social life, and teaching him to communicate in various ways. He was particularly interested in teaching Victor to speak (Candland, 1993).

Given the first impression that Itard had of Victor, it is a wonder that he had any interest in working with Victor at all. Itard wrote that Victor was

a disgustingly dirty child affected with spasmodic movements, and often convulsions, who swayed back and forth ceaselessly like certain animals in a zoo, who bit and scratched those who opposed him, and who showed no affection for those who took care of him, and who was, in short, indifferent to everything and attentive to nothing. (Itard, 1962, p. 4)

Itard was able to secure a government grant to assist in his work with Victor. He also enlisted the help of a woman, Madame Guérin, who lived in an apartment at the institute with her husband. She was about 40 at the time and would spend the rest of her life caring for Victor. But caring for Victor proved to be a difficult and sometimes futile endeavor. Victor was not interested in many of the things that Itard expected he would be. Itard had intended to use toys as a means of educating him, but Victor showed no interested in toys. Still, he *did* learn things.

Victor became very finicky about cleanliness and being bathed. Where once he delighted in running naked in the snow, now he became truculent if the water in his daily bath was not hot enough. He formed emotional attachments, particularly to Madame Guérin and Itard. If guests bored him, he would go to the closet, get their hat and gloves, and push them toward the door. All this happened within the first 3 months of his time at the institute. By the end of 9 months, Itard wrote that Victor was "an almost normal child, who doesn't talk."

VICTOR'S MENTAL ABILITY

Victor had displayed abilities soon after his capture that differentiated him from a retarded child. When Victor lived with Father Pierre Bonnaterre, before he was brought to Paris, the priest conducted several experiments with him. In one of them, Bonnaterre held a mirror in front of Victor to see if Victor would recognize himself. This was a common procedure at the time to evaluate low-level mental abilities. Victor passed the test easily.

Victor appeared to be obsessed with potatoes, and Bonnaterre took advantage of Victor's obsession. As a test, Bonnaterre encouraged Victor to look into the mirror while, simultaneously, he held a potato in back of Victor so that it would be reflected in the mirror. At first, Victor tried to reach into the mirror for the potato. The priest repeated the test several times with the same result. Each time Victor tried to reach into the mirror to grasp the potato. But the priest later wrote that when he tried the test one last time, Victor suddenly reached back over his shoulder, without turning around, and snatched the potato out of the priest's hand, displaying excellent visual–motor coordination.

Itard's approach to education was strongly influenced by the philosopher and physician John Locke (1632–1704). A British empiricist and one of the most influential of the Enlightenment thinkers, Locke believed that knowledge is acquired primarily though the senses. Consistent with that belief, Itard tried to incorporate various senses into his lessons with Victor whenever possible. He made cutouts for letters of the alphabet and had Victor run his hand over a particular letter while Itard produced the sound associated with the letter.

At one point, Itard presented the cutout letters for the French word *milk—LAIT*—to Victor five or six times, each time giving him milk. Victor seemed to make the association between the letters and the food. A week later, when they were going to visit the home of a friend of Itard, Victor took the letters with him. When they arrived at the friend's house, Victor laid the letters out on a table in the proper order. The friend gave Victor some milk. It appeared that Victor had made a major breakthrough. He had not only taken the letters to a new setting, he understood that someone else would know the meaning of the letters.

Although Itard was initially impressed with this behavior, he later concluded that the letter combination was simply an accident, with no specific knowledge behind it. Victor used the word *lait* for anything that gave him pleasure. In 1803, however, Itard was still optimistic about his pupil. He wrote:

> I shall report only that, after several months, Victor knows how to copy the words whose meaning he already knew. Soon after, he learned to reproduce them from memory and finally to use his writing, crude as it was and still is, to express his needs, to ask for what he wants. By the same means, he can grasp the needs and wishes of others. (as quoted in Shattuck, 1980, p. 138)

In effect, Itard was suggesting that Victor had learned to read and write, although in primitive fashion.

DIAGNOSING VICTOR

All the evidence suggests that Victor was not retarded, at least not in the traditional sense. Among other things, his abilities appeared to be very uneven. What were the other possibilities? Could he have been autistic? His lack of speech and asocial qualities would be consistent with a diagnosis of autism. Bruno Bettelheim, in his book *The Empty Fortress* (1967), discussed the case of Victor and concluded that Victor was indeed autistic. Since the publication of that book, however, many of the ideas that informed Bettelheim's diagnosis have become outdated. Harlan Lane, the American psychologist and linguist who wrote a lengthy account of Victor, came to the conclusion that Victor's symptoms were the result of his isolation in the wild, presumably during critical periods in his development (Lane, 1976).

The critical period hypothesis that Lane cites derived its initial importance primarily from the work of ethologists Konrad Lorenz and Nikko Tinbergen, both of whom would later become Nobel laureates. Eventually, it would become an important explanatory mechanism for a host of social scientists and clinicians, including psychiatrist John Bowlby and psychologists Mary Ainsworth and Harry Harlow. The central thesis of the critical period hypothesis is that there are distinct periods in development during which the capacity to learn certain skills are at their peak. The capacity is not simply "readiness" but something more biologically driven. If the critical period is "taken advantage of," meaning if the subject has the appropriate environmental experiences during this period, the learning in question can proceed at an optimal rate. If not, the ability or skill may be limited or lost forever.

One of the examples that is frequently used to illustrate the critical periods hypothesis is language learning. It has been argued that a critical period for language exists for approximately the first 12 years of life during which language learning is relatively easy. When that period ends, the ease of learning a new language is significantly reduced. In a similar way, researchers such as Harry Harlow, have demonstrated that early isolation of rhesus monkeys can have a profound effect on later social and emotional development. (Harlow's work is discussed elsewhere in this volume.) Many other examples have been presented in support of critical periods in humans. Could Victor's early isolation have stunted his ability to learn language, as well as to interfere with appropriate social and emotional development?

SPEECH AND SOCIALIZATION

The ability that Itard was most interested in developing in Victor was speech. For him, speech was the key to socialization. If Victor could talk, he could also tell everyone what had happened to him, as well as reveal his personal thoughts and feelings. Itard developed several techniques for teaching Victor language, perhaps the most famous being the use of cutout letters, mentioned earlier, a technique that would later be adopted by others. Although Victor's sound production was never strong, he was able to differentiate among the letters, if only in a rudimentary way.

One frequently made observation is that Victor lived for more than five years in an institution that housed approximately 100 deaf-mutes who communicated with each other in sign language. Yet Victor was never taught sign language. Some critics have felt this was a grave mistake (Lane, 1976). Itard, who had become the chief physician at the institute and worked for 40 years with deaf-mutes, never learned sign language himself. Apparently, he thought of it as an inferior form of communication. More recent work has shown that sign language can, in fact, be a rich form of communication. Moreover, was it possible that Victor was never going to be able to speak as a result of damage to his vocal cords? He was never able to produce a full range of sounds. The scar across his neck was at least partial evidence that the attempts to successfully teach him speech may have been limited from the start. (Itard thought that Victor's limited ability to vocalize was more likely due to disuse, rather than physical damage.) One can only speculate about the possibilities if Victor had been taught sign language.

Shattuck points to a related area of concern in Victor's development. He was given virtually no social experience with people his own age. Such experience is known to be a crucial piece of successful development. Still, it is questionable whether that experience would have helped. Most of the time Victor showed little regard for other people, including his caretakers, those who provided his most basic needs. It's unclear how he would have responded to agemates.

THE EXPERIMENT ENDS

Itard was initially delighted with the progress of his student. But, by 1806, after five years, Itard gave up his active teaching of the boy. Victor's care was turned over to Madame Guérin completely. She continued to receive a fee from the government to care for Victor, who spent the rest of his life living with her. Although he was largely out of the public eye during this period and little is known about his daily life, on one occasion Victor was visited by a writer for a French publication who hoped to provide the public with an update on "the wild boy." He reported that

Victor's condition had deteriorated significantly. Victor died in Paris in 1828, at approximately age 40; some accounts say of pneumonia. But there are no extant records related to the cause of death or to his place of burial.

Itard was disappointed in the outcome with Victor. Looking back on his work with him, Itard wrote,

> A large portion of my days for six years was sacrificed to this demanding experiment. The boy, who was called the Savage of Aveyron, did not gain from my attentions all the advantages I had hoped. But the numerous observations I was able to make, the instructional procedures suggested to me by the intractability of his organs, were not entirely lost, and later I put them to more successful use in dealing with children whose muteness arose from less insurmountable causes. (Shattuck, 1980, p. 78–79)

Itard died in 1838, 10 years after Victor's death.

LESSONS FROM VICTOR'S TREATMENT

Though Victor's progress was very limited, his case contributed directly to Itard's development of methods for teaching the deaf and mentally disabled. Later, one of Itard's students, Édouard Séguin (1812–1880), a young French physician, would further refine these techniques. Séguin eventually moved to the United States where he became renowned for his work with the developmentally disabled. He began several schools devoted to them and later became president of an organization that was the predecessor for the American Association on Mental Retardation. He died in New York City and is buried there.

Another person influenced by Séguin also had a significant educational impact. In the early 1900s, an Italian physician studied the work of Itard and Séguin and used it as the basis for developing her own system of teaching both normal and handicapped children. Her name was Maria Montessori (1870–1952), and her approach to teaching would eventually become known and respected throughout the world. (Montessori's life and work are discussed in Chapter 10 of this volume.) Several of the methods and materials developed by Itard and Séguin can be found in her schools today.

Victor's story has generated a great deal of interest over the years. In addition to the two reports written by Itard, there were several others by his contemporaries. There have been at least two major books about Victor, as well as a movie, titled *The Wild Child* (1970). In the silver screen version of Victor's life, the great French director Francois Truffaut played the part of Itard (in addition to directing the film). Unfortunately, the movie takes many liberties with the story, streamlining the events and sacrificing accuracy for dramatic effect.

In the final analysis, Victor's earliest history and the cause of his difficulties remain unclear. Since so much time has passed since his discovery, it appears unlikely that we will ever know the circumstances that led him to that forest in Aveyron. Still, his case provided a framework for future research, education, and care of children who suffered from a wide array of developmental barriers. Although Victor himself never seemed to benefit much from Itard's teaching, his life gave rise to techniques that have benefitted countless others.

REVIEW/DISCUSSION QUESTIONS

1. What are "feral children"? Do you think such children have ever existed?

2. Why were Victor's contemporaries so interested in feral children?

3. Itard worked in an institute for the deaf. Why didn't he attempt to teach sign language to Victor?

4. What was so unusual about Itard's training materials that Montessori incorporated many of them into her system?

5. How would a contemporary clinical psychologist characterize Victor's behavior? What would be Victor's likely diagnosis?

CHAPTER THREE

PHINEAS GAGE
The Man With a Hole in His Head

Phineas Gage was the 25-year-old foreman of a construction crew preparing the path for a railroad track in the late summer of 1848. By all accounts he was reliable and friendly, both a good worker and a pleasant companion. But in an instant his life was changed through a terrible accident that would haunt him until his premature death at age 36.

Gage's accident also had ramifications for scientists who were trying to understand the relationship between the brain and behavior. Although the implications of his accident were not immediately appreciated, his case became a common fixture in basic textbooks in psychology, neurology, and related fields. His case has also been used to demonstrate the role of the brain in determining personality. But the account of the accident has also been filled with errors and exaggeration, sometimes making it difficult to separate the facts from fiction.

THE ACCIDENT

Late in the afternoon of September 13, 1848, Phineas Gage was working with his crew near Cavendish, Vermont, preparing the way for a new track bed for the Rutland and Burlington Railroad. The crew was using explosives to blast away rock. It was a slow process that required precision in determining where to bore the holes and estimating how much explosive powder to use. Gage would place a fuse in the hole, followed by gunpowder, and then fill the rest of the hole with sand. Gage had a long iron rod, a tamping iron, which he used to pack down the sand. This last operation was necessary to ensure a powerful explosion; the smaller the area containing the explosive powder, the greater the force of the explosion.

The tamping iron was Gage's own creation, 3 feet 7 inches long, with a diameter one and a quarter inches at the blunt end and tapering to a rough point at the other. A blacksmith had prepared it especially for Gage. It was an imposing object and more than half the height of Gage himself, who stood about 5 feet 6 inches. Usually, after Gage tamped down the sand to his satisfaction, he would light the fuse, and everyone would run for cover. The ensuing explosion, if successful, would break down the rock into pieces small enough for the work force to handle and remove. That was the way it was supposed to happen. But this time, something went terribly wrong.

Eyewitnesses varied slightly in their descriptions about what happened next. It appears that Gage poured gunpowder into the hole in the rock but had not yet covered it with sand when something distracted him. As he turned his head slightly away from the rock, the tamping iron dipped into the hole and created a spark setting off an explosion. The tamping iron then became a projectile, with the sharp end entering Gage's left cheek, moving through his head, and exiting through the top of his skull. The rod itself was later found more than 30 feet away, encrusted with brain matter. Gage was thrown on his back by the force of the explosion but, to everyone's astonishment, he remained conscious. He was completely aware of what had happened to him and even engaged his fellow workers in conversation.

Gage's coworkers helped him walk to an oxcart that took him into town about three-quarters of a mile away. His destination was the tavern where he had been boarding on the town's main street. Within a half hour, he was examined by a physician, Dr. Edward Williams, who found it difficult to believe the story that Gage and his coworkers told him. How could Gage still be alive if an iron rod had passed through his head?

About an hour later, another physician arrived, Dr. John Martyn Harlow. Williams and Harlow brought Gage to his room and began tending to his wounds. In addition to the obvious head injuries, he had also suffered some burns on his hands and arms. After a further evaluation of their patient, the physicians didn't have much doubt about what had happened. The hole in Gage's cheek was readily apparent as was the hole in his skull. In fact, Harlow could view Gage's brain through the hole.

The physicians cleansed the wounds, carefully removing the tiniest of the skull fragments and maneuvering the larger pieces back into place as best they could. Neither had ever witnessed such an injury before and they did not have much hope for Gage's recovery. Gage was now vomiting blood and becoming weaker. Harlow, who lived a short distance away from the tavern, returned again and again to tend to Gage. His goal was only to make him more comfortable. He didn't expect him to survive.

Gage's mother, who lived about 30 miles away in Lebanon, New Hampshire, where Gage was born, was notified of the accident. She and Gage's uncle arrived early the next morning, surprised that Phineas was still alive. Everyone around Gage seemed to understand how serious his injuries were—except for Gage. He spoke of going back to work the next day or perhaps the day after.

He would soon find out the unrealistic nature of his plan. After resting for only a short time and seemingly on the road to recovery, Gage developed a fever and his pulse quickened. Despite all the efforts of Dr. Harlow to cleanse his wounds, Gage had developed an infection. This was a common occurrence in the days before antibiotics and the results were often fatal. The fever persisted, then worsened, with Gage sometimes drifting in and out of consciousness.

Harlow tried all the tactics he could think of to help Gage, including the use of purgatives, bloodletting, and restricting Gage's diet. Other symptoms developed along with the fever. At one point, Gage's pulse went up to 120, higher than it had ever been. It appeared that Gage would never recover. One of the locals suggested that Harlow should terminate treatment so that his patient wouldn't have to suffer any further. The local undertaker even measured Gage for a coffin.

But Harlow was now on a mission and would not give up. He continued to treat Gage with all that was available to him. Finally, after more than two months, all of Gage's symptoms appeared to have abated. His strong constitution had won out. Soon after, toward the end of November, Harlow deemed Gage well enough to travel and he was able to return to the family home in New Hampshire.

Harlow visited Gage in New Hampshire shortly after the New Year and found Gage walking about, seemingly symptom-free. He was not quite as strong as he had been before, but his physical condition had improved considerably. Although he had lost sight in his right eye, his cheek had healed over, and the top of his skull had begun to heal too, although a part of the brain was still visible through a small opening. Gage was eager to return to his job on the railroad, but now he had a new set of problems.

The railroad declined to hire Gage back at his old position. Something had happened to him that went beyond his physical injuries. He had previously been a good worker—industrious, social and friendly, and well organized. Now he had become argumentative and short tempered, and his language had become vulgar. He was not the leader that he once was. He had difficulty planning, and his friends no longer cared to be with him. His personality had changed so much that Dr. Harlow would later write, "He was no longer Gage." This was a surprising development and one that would cause great difficulty for Gage himself. Moreover, there were far-reaching implications of Gage's injuries for the scientific community.

GAGE'S ACCIDENT BECOMES MORE WIDELY KNOWN

Gage's case immediately generated interest, mostly because of the horrific nature of his accident, and several stories about him appeared in local publications. One of the people who became attracted to the case was Dr. Henry Bigelow, a physician, soon to be a professor of surgery at Harvard Medical School. At first, Bigelow was skeptical about the stories he had heard. It just didn't seem possible that Gage could have survived an object as large and destructive as the tamping iron passing through his head.

To satisfy his curiosity, Bigelow wrote to Harlow, asking for further details. He also asked Harlow to collect descriptions from others about what had happened. The details Bigelow received began to convince him. Eventually, Bigelow arranged for Gage to visit Boston so that he could examine him. Bigelow paid all the expenses. By the time Bigelow had completed his examination of Gage, he was no longer skeptical. In fact, he had become a strong believer. He even wrote several short articles about Gage and the accident.

Several months after examining him, when Gage's wounds had healed even further, Bigelow presented his case at a meeting of the Boston Society for Medical Improvement. Using a skull that he had prepared to resemble Gage's injury, Bigelow was able to demonstrate to other physicians how Gage's survival was possible, assuaging many of their doubts. Bigelow's support went a long way to establishing the legitimacy of the case. Some began to speculate that the Gage case might offer some insight into a current debate about the brain and its function.

FRANZ GALL AND PHRENOLOGY

The understanding of how the brain works was primitive in the mid-1800s. The existence of neurons was unknown, for instance, as was the electrochemical nature of brain function. Instead, one of the central disagreements of the time involved the degree to which the brain acted as a whole or, conversely, had areas devoted to specific functions. We now know that, to a degree, both of these are true: the brain has some general, overall functions as well as some functions assumed by specific regions.

Franz Gall (1758–1828), a German physician, had developed a belief system about the brain's functions that became known as *phrenology*. Gall was a well-regarded anatomist and was probably more important than anyone in convincing fellow scientists that the brain was the source of psychological functions. Phrenology was Gall's attempt at describing this relationship.

Gall asserted that many psychological functions could be traced to very specific areas of the brain. He believed that the development of these areas reflected dominant personality characteristics whereas less developed regions reflected less dominant characteristics. Therefore, personality could be determined by "reading" the bumps and indentations on the skull. Although phrenology did not have strong support from scientists of the time, it remained very popular with the general public. Gage's case had the potential to shed light on this ongoing debate.

When Gage was brought to Boston in late 1849, members of the medical profession were allowed to examine his head and even to view the tamping iron, which he usually carried with him. It was clear to most of them that the story of Phineas Gage was not a myth. Those who remained skeptical about the details accepted the general nature of the accident. Bigelow had arranged for a life mask to be made of Gage's face and skull so that his visage, including the external signs of his injuries, could be preserved for future generations. Many years later, two portraits of Gage would be discovered—one

▶ **Image 3.1** Phineas Gage with his tamping iron

a daguerreotype (Wilgus & Wilgus, 2009), the other a photo. Each depict Gage, dressed in a formal outfit, looking proud and holding the tamping iron.

For those who believed that the brain acted as a single unit, the Gage case represented a setback. If the brain was a single unit, how was it possible that Gage's brain could have suffered so much damage and still retain its earlier function? Later, when the phrenologists learned of Gage's change in personality, they used that information to support their own position.

THE CHANGE IN PERSONALITY

While early interest in the case focused mostly on the physical trauma that Gage had suffered, later interest concentrated more on his personality change. This part of his story was more difficult to document than the physical aspects of the case. There were no objective measures of Gage's personality before the accident, which made a clear comparison difficult. Much of the reported change relied on anecdotal reports and hearsay. Some of it may have been exaggerated.

Descriptions of Gage before the accident depict him as energetic, shrewd, and a smart businessman. Others described him as the best foreman the railroad had contracted. Harlow noted some periods of disorientation and even intellectual lapses a few weeks after the accident but wrote nothing specific about Gage's personality. He wrote that Gage's memory remained excellent. However, following the earliest period, Harlow's written descriptions began to change. He noted that Gage had become obstinate and sometimes childish. His friends had difficulty subduing him. Harlow wrote an even more damning retrospective appraisal of Gage in 1868 in which he outlined the reasons that Gage was not hired back at his old job. Harlow described him as impatient, unwilling to heed advice, grossly profane, and, again, obstinate and childish. In short, he had changed radically (Macmillan, 2002).

GAGE'S LATER YEARS

Most of what can be verified about Gage following his time in Boston is based on reports from his mother and from Harlow. Little information about Gage can be found in the public record. For instance, it was rumored that he was seen begging in Boston on several occasions, but there is no independent verification of that behavior. What appears to be true is that Gage became restless after his visit with Bigelow in Boston. He had always been engaged in hard work, much of it physical, and he was eager to continue it.

For several years Gage drifted in the New England area, exhibiting himself and his tamping iron up and down the East Coast. He even appeared at a museum that had been organized by the famous P. T. Barnum in New York City. For more than a year he worked at a livery stable and as a stagecoach driver in Hanover, New Hampshire. But then a very different opportunity presented itself.

A stagecoach line was being developed between Valparaiso and Santiago in Chile, a distance of 75 miles. Gage was offered a position as a driver. He left Boston in August 1852 and spent the next seven years in Chile. While there is no record of his service there, it is likely that the demands of the job were considerable.

Stagecoaches in Chile in that period typically employed six horses, a challenge requiring many skills. The driver not only had to interact with the passengers, but he also had to take care of the horses. According to Gage's mother, her son had developed a particular affinity for working with animals, and he was a successful driver. The fact that Gage could work at such a demanding job for as long as he did has been offered as evidence that his dramatic personality changes were not permanent (Macmillan & Lena, 2010).

While her son was in Chile, Phineas Gage's mother had moved to San Francisco to be closer to her daughter, and it was in San Francisco that Gage made his next appearance. According to Gage's mother, he experienced several bouts of illness while in Chile. By mid-1859, his health issues had become more serious and he returned to the United States by ship to San Francisco, ill and in need of help. He attributed his illness to seasickness; he pointed out that he had also been very ill on his initial trip to Chile. And, indeed, sea sickness might have been part of his health issues.

Gage seemed to regain some of his health for a brief period, and he was even able to secure work on a farm. But while dining at his sister's home one evening, he suffered a seizure. Gage's ability to work became more unsettled after this incident. Several more seizures followed. The assumption has always been that his seizures were related to his accident. The physical damage to his brain was finally expressing itself in less subtle ways, perhaps because of scarring or other brain changes associated with age.

Gage continued to work occasionally, usually in farming or with animals, but he could not sustain a single place of employment, and his health continued to deteriorate. The time between his seizures grew shorter and shorter. He moved into his mother's house and after only a brief period there, he suffered a series of quick seizures. Finally, Gage's increasingly frail body could take no more. He died on May 20, 1860, at the age of 36 and was buried in San Francisco's Lone Mountain Cemetery (later renamed Laurel Hill Cemetery). Most accounts indicate that his tamping iron was buried with him, although this has been disputed. The cause of death was listed as epilepsy.

AFTER HIS DEATH

Gage's story might have ended there except for Dr. Harlow, the physician who tended to him after the accident. Harlow had been in contact with Gage during his early years in Chile but had lost contact with him. When he finally wrote to Gage's mother, she informed him that her son had died several years before. It was then that Harlow made an unusual request.

His interest in Gage's case had remained strong. Now, with the death of Gage, he had the opportunity to add more information to the case study. Would Gage's mother permit her son's body to be exhumed and his skull removed so that it could be more carefully examined? Such an examination might help to clarify exactly the kind of brain injury that Gage had suffered. She agreed, attesting to her confidence in Harlow's intentions and, perhaps, also understanding the importance of her son's injuries to science.

Gage's skull and his tamping iron soon found their way to Harlow's home in Woburn, Massachusetts. It was immediately apparent from the skull that some additional healing had taken place after the accident. The hole in Gage's head had begun to mend although it was still not completely closed by the time of his death.

After examining the skull for several months, Harlow held a gathering at the annual meeting of the Massachusetts Medical Society in 1868 to display the skull and present a follow-up on the unusual case. It was here for the first time that he outlined some of the psychological difficulties that Gage had suffered as a result of his injuries. This aspect of the case had been minimally examined in most of the earlier reports, and indeed, not much attention was paid to it immediately after this report.

When Harlow was finally finished working with the skull, both it and the tamping iron were deposited in the Warren Museum of the Harvard University Medical School. There they remain, along with the model of Gage's head, both a real and a symbolic reminder of Gage's struggle to conduct a life after suffering such a cruel misfortune. But Gage's story was still not complete. The fact that his skull and even his tamping iron were saved for posterity has led to further study.

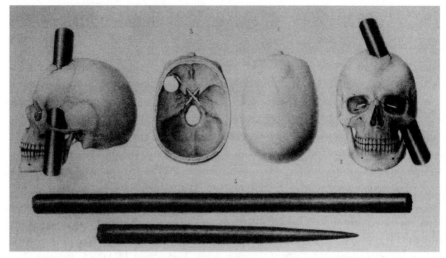

▸ **Image 3.2** The skull and tamping iron of Phineas Gage, U.S. National Library of Medicine/Science Photo Library

Everett Collection Inc/Alamy Stock Photo

THE LEGACY OF PHINEAS GAGE

When Gage's mother agreed to have her son's body exhumed and his skull removed, she could not have anticipated the important role her decision would play in the history of brain-related sciences. The cemetery where her son's remains were interred—and where her remains were ultimately interred as well—was later demolished by the city of San Francisco to make way for a new highway. The remains of both mother and son were moved to a common burial ground and their identity was eventually lost. If a later scientist had been interested in exhuming Gage's body, it would not have been possible. But thanks to his mother's decision, his skull and tamping iron remain available for study today.

The implications of Gage's case became apparent to physicians and surgeons soon after his case was publicized. If Gage could live so long after such a horrendous accident, then surely it was possible to operate on the brain successfully, for instance, to remove a tumor. The possibility became even stronger once medicine adopted aseptic procedures. In addition, using Gage's case as a starting point, physicians began to use personality changes as guides in a rudimentary approach to diagnosis. Diagnosing brain disorders on the basis of personality changes has serious flaws, and brain surgery experienced many failures before it became the success it has become today. Yet both diagnosis and brain surgery ultimately benefitted enormously from the case of Phineas Gage.

PSYCHOSURGERY

One of the more negative developments attributed to the Gage case is that of psychosurgery, that is, using surgery to directly address psychological characteristics rather than physical ones. Although there were a number of such surgeries before the 1930s, the work of Egas Moniz (1874–1955) had the greatest impact. Moniz, a Portuguese neurologist, introduced a form of surgery in 1936 known as a prefrontal leucotomy (later referred to as a lobotomy) in which the frontal lobes of the patient were either disrupted or severed from the rest of the brain, usually in an effort to reduce the symptoms of severe mental illness. Walter Freeman (1895–1972), a physician, along with neurosurgeon James W. Watts (1904–1994), was responsible for introducing a form of this surgery to the United States. Freeman is believed to have operated on several thousand patients, some of them as young as seven years old, over the course of his career. Moniz eventually won a Nobel Prize for his work before his procedure and those of Freeman were discredited. Did the Gage case play a role in encouraging such procedures as some critics have charged?

It seems likely that Moniz or Freeman or any physicians practicing such surgery would be familiar with the case of Phineas Gage. It is simply too rudimentary to the history of brain science for it to have been unknown to them. And it is true that the Gage case centered on damage to the frontal lobes. But the evidence from Gage would appear to contradict the goal of Moniz and Freeman. Gage exhibited behaviors that society found unsatisfactory after damage to his frontal lobes. That would hardly be a reason for surgeons to operate on the frontal lobes. Moreover, there is no direct evidence that Moniz or Freeman or anyone else used the Gage case as grounds to support their approach to psychosurgery, except to point out that patients could survive damage to their frontal lobes.

PHINEAS GAGE TODAY

Modern medical technology has grown significantly since Bigelow was able to take Gage's tamping iron and demonstrate the likely path that the iron took through Gage's skull. Computers can not only simulate the skull and the internal parts of the brain, but they can also provide probabilities for the most likely path or paths that the iron took. These modern studies reveal that Gage was very lucky. That seems like an odd thing to say for someone who experienced severe physical trauma, but the point is that it could have been far worse. For one thing, the iron must have missed the major speech areas of the brain since it was known that Gage exhibited no apparent problems with either understanding or producing speech after the accident.

Even with modern technology, however, the precise path that the tamping iron took was not easily determined. When the rod exited his skull, it took related bone with it. Even the precise point of entry has been debated. A husband and wife team of neuroscientists, Hanna and Antonio Damasio, have tried to clarify many of the remaining questions about Phineas Gage. Their research focused on using CT scan technology and computers to plot out likely paths that the rod could have followed. Based on known information about Gage's condition, they were able to identify several possibilities. They concluded that the assumed damage to the left frontal cortex would be consistent with symptoms noted in other victims with frontal lobe injury. However, in the end, we will probably never know the precise path the tamping rod took. The inconclusive evidence from the skull, combined with known individual differences in the brain, will continue to raise doubts about any suggested model (Damasio, Grabowski, Frank, Galaburda, & Damasio, 1994).

The interest of the Damasios, and other researchers, is not simply historical curiosity. Patients who suffer frontal lobe damage through tumors or injury may also experience personality change, though perhaps not as dramatic as that of Phineas Gage. The Damasios have been particularly interested in studying the emotional changes that accompany brain injury. At the same time, they're trying to understand the role that emotion and the brain play in our intellectual activity. In their view, what we call intellectual activity and emotional activity are connected, and that connection is in the brain. In a real way, their studies began with the case of Phineas Gage and they have continued to use that knowledge to investigate brain behavior at the University of Southern California (Damasio, 1994).

THE MEMORIAL

Over the weekend of September 12–13, 1998, a memorial event was held in Cavendish, Vermont, to celebrate the 150th anniversary of the famous accident to Phineas Gage. His skull and tamping iron were on display, as were a number of documents related to the case. Tours were arranged to relevant locations in the town, such as the site of the tavern where he had stayed. (The tavern itself no longer exists.) A series of symposia were presented related to the accident and to the frontal lobes in particular, once again pointing to the Gage case as the first to clearly establish the relationship between the brain and personality. Finally, a plaque was placed in the Cavendish Town Green to commemorate the event and testify to the fact that after so many years, the case of Phineas Gage still matters.

REVIEW/DISCUSSION QUESTIONS

1. The injury to Gage was horrific. How did he manage to survive?

2. In what way did Gage's personality change after the accident?

3. Phrenology was popular around the time of the accident. How would a phrenologist interpret Gage's postaccident behavior?

4. What impact did Gage's case have on the development of brain surgery? On prefrontal lobotomies?

5. Why does the Gage case continue to hold so much interest?

NOTE

The book by Malcolm Macmillan (2002) cited earlier (see References) was the major source for this chapter. It not only contains a thorough and detailed review of the case, with copies of original documents, but also analyzes the myths that have developed regarding Phineas Gage. Macmillan and others have created a Phineas Gage Information Page on the University of Akron website with updated material and additional information.

PART TWO

THE EARLY YEARS

CHAPTER FOUR

HYPNOSIS AND HYSTERIA

Mesmer, Charcot, and the "Country Bumpkins"

By 1880, the neurologist Jean-Martin Charcot (1825–1893) had become one of the most esteemed physicians in Europe. As director of La Salpêtrière, a huge medical complex in Paris, he was the first to identify several important neurological disorders, including multiple sclerosis. But later in his career, he changed the focus of his work from neurology to the study of hypnosis and hysteria, the latter a common diagnosis of the time. His work in abnormal psychology would eventually earn him the title "Napoleon of the neuroses."

During the same period, a French country doctor by the name of Ambroise-Auguste Liébault (1823–1904) was exploring the medical uses of hypnosis with his patients. His surprising success caught the attention of Hippolyte Bernheim (1840–1919), a physician who taught at a nearby university. Initially skeptical, Bernheim observed Liébault in practice and quickly became a convert. The two joined forces to promote a view of hypnosis that posed a direct challenge to the work of the much better-known Charcot.

An intellectual battle between Charcot and his associates—sophisticated Parisians—and the supposedly less sophisticated upstarts from the province of Nancy raged for years. Each side developed strong supporters before the controversy was finally resolved. The debate not only resulted in a better understanding of the nature of hypnosis, but it was also instrumental in changing the public view of hypnosis from a questionable technique used by charlatans to a legitimate medical intervention. The road to legitimacy was not an easy one, and its early path involved a particularly flamboyant practitioner by the name of Franz Mesmer.

MESMER AND HYPNOSIS IN THE NINETEENTH CENTURY

The 1800s were a period of tremendous scientific discovery when many new ideas about the world and the nature of man were introduced. Animal magnetism, the precursor to modern hypnosis, was considered one of the remarkable discoveries of the age. Franz Anton Mesmer (1734–1815), a German-born physician, was probably more responsible for its visibility than anyone else. After graduating from medical school, he began a private practice, but he also married a wealthy widow, which allowed him to pursue whatever other interests he chose. Of particular interest to him were scientific developments. He first became aware of animal magnetism when he learned of the extraordinary cures attributed to a local priest and university professor, Father Maximilian Hell (a curious last name for a priest, to be sure).

With the aid of an assistant, Father Hell had created a series of magnets which he used to treat medical ailments. He would place the magnets on various parts of the body of the afflicted person, and the patient would often feel an abatement of symptoms. Intrigued by the apparent results, Mesmer began working with Father Hell to learn more about his procedures. As they worked together, Mesmer began to develop a set of beliefs about human magnetic fields, a combination of Father Hell's work and Mesmer's doctoral dissertation (Ellenberger, 1970).

Mesmer, a graduate of the University of Vienna, had written his dissertation on planetary forces and their effect on humans. As a result, he was familiar with the history of magnets as curative agents (although his dissertation was later found to be plagiarized). He believed that everyone was surrounded by a magnetic field. When that field was distorted or interrupted, physical ailments could arise. Further, he believed that it was possible to realign the magnetic field of individuals and that the realignment had a strong potential for curing their maladies.

When Mesmer first began using magnets for medical purposes, he required his patients to swallow a mixture that included metal filings. Although he was successful with this approach, he came to believe that magnets and metal filings were not necessary

to effect a cure. Instead, he postulated that some individuals possessed innate magnetic properties and could promote cures largely through their touch. Not surprisingly, he believed his own body was a source of strong magnetic forces.

At first, his approach was seen as scientific, and he had many apparent successes. But with success came criticism, and Mesmer soon found himself under the watchful eye of the local medical establishment as well as the clergy. When one of his young and highly visible patients experienced a relapse, he was accused of being a fraud.

▸ **Image 4.1** Franz Mesmer

Culture Club/Hulton Archive/Getty Images

The criticism became so strong that he was forced to leave Vienna under a cloud of suspicion. He moved to Paris in 1778, where some of the criticism followed him. However, he persisted in his work and eventually achieved even greater celebrity. His apparent ability to "cure" many disorders, aided by his constant self-promotion, brought people flocking to his door.

Mesmer established a salon in one of the most exclusive areas of Paris where he treated patients both individually and in groups. He installed a *baquet*, a tub containing water and iron filings, around which patients would gather. After they settled in, they would begin to hear the eerie sounds of a glass harmonica, a new instrument that Mesmer had learned to play. Shortly after, Mesmer would appear in a robe and proceed to touch the individuals gathered with a wand. Many would then experience a "crisis" during which they might suffer from convulsions and faint. But when they emerged from the crisis, their symptoms were often diminished or sometimes gone completely.

Although the general public became very accepting of him, the scientific community of Paris was more critical. In 1784, the French Academy of Sciences appointed a committee to investigate magnetism and its power to cure. The committee—which included the then-ambassador from the United States, Benjamin Franklin, among other notables—found the technique to be without merit. The committee concluded that Mesmer's results were due more to imagination (what we would now call a placebo effect) than to anything else. With that pronouncement, Mesmer's celebrity began to diminish. Eventually, he moved back to Germany and sank into obscurity (Wyckoff, 1975).

A few individuals continued to experiment with hypnotism, further modifying Mesmer's ideas. Several physicians were able to demonstrate its usefulness in dentistry and surgery, especially as an anesthetic in a time before other forms of anesthesia had been developed. But their successes were largely criticized or ignored. Through the efforts of a Scottish physician, James Braid (1795–1860), the name of the phenomenon evolved from magnetism and mesmerism to the currently used term *hypnosis*. Braid also tried to bring the phenomenon into the scientific arena for empirical study. By this time, however, hypnotism had become the province of stage performers and held little interest for most scientists. When Charcot began to investigate its properties, the technique was not held in high regard.

JEAN-MARTIN CHARCOT

The son of a coach maker, Jean-Martin Charcot was determined from his earliest years to achieve a high status in life. A gifted student, and later a gifted physician, he also married a wealthy widow whose money assured him of a secure place in the upper rungs of French society. As a young intern he had worked at La Salpêtrière, an enormous medical complex of more than 40 buildings that housed thousands of women, most of them destitute and many of them elderly. At the time, the institution was little more than a poorhouse. In 1862, as a full-fledged physician, he returned to La Salpêtrière when he was appointed medical director of one of its large sections. A hard worker, he would eventually become the director of the hospital. Ultimately, he successfully transformed the institution from a dreary passive complex into a vibrant teaching and research hospital (Owen, 1971).

Charcot was well ahead of his time as a neurologist and was a trailblazer in the field. He was one of the first to describe the characteristic symptoms of multiple sclerosis; his work also led to a better understanding of Parkinson's disease and amyotrophic lateral sclerosis (Lou Gehrig's disease), among many other disorders. Sometimes referred to as "the father of modern neurology," he was unquestionably one of the leading neurologists of his time, and a figure of great celebrity in France (Ellenberger, 1993). However, it was not his neurological work that made him such a strong participant in the psychological and psychiatric literature. It was Charcot's focus on hysteria and hypnosis, beginning around 1880, that would become his legacy.

HYSTERIA

The view during Charcot's time was that most forms of mental illness were incurable. However, it was important to observe patients in order to gain a greater understanding of the mechanisms and course of the illness. La Salpêtrière provided a perfect opportunity for Charcot to conduct his research on mental illness. The large number of poor and older women who inhabited the institution could be observed for as long as he wanted, with the opportunity for autopsies after death. Charcot was particularly interested in a strange malady of the time called *hysteria*, which defied most medical and neurological explanations.

The diagnosis of hysteria had been around since early Greek times. The name itself derived from the Greek word for *womb* and was initially attributed to a "wandering womb." For that reason, only women were believed to be victims of the disorder. Later physicians would question exactly how a womb could "wander," but the connection to sex remained. Charcot acknowledged that women suffered from hysteria more frequently, but he also identified men who he believed suffered from the disorder.

Through the years, hysteria developed a long list of symptoms, and some physicians began to suspect that it was a false diagnosis, closer to malingering than to an actual disease. Charcot viewed it differently. He believed all psychiatric problems ultimately had an organic basis. Hysteria, as such, was due to an inherited disposition and the outward manifestation of a deteriorating nervous system. Moreover, he saw it as closely tied to the capacity to be hypnotized, a tendency that he also saw as related to a deteriorating nervous system. In 1882, he presented a paper to the Academy of Sciences outlining specific stages in an individual undergoing hypnosis. With this act alone, he restored respectability to a phenomenon that had been discarded as fakery.

Often described as a vain and autocratic man, Charcot didn't seem to care that he was not trained in psychiatry. He was dogmatic in his positions even when he had little backing for them. Disagreements with him were not welcome. At the same time, he was judged to be an excellent lecturer. On Friday mornings, he would make a weekly presentation, always to a packed auditorium. He would use blackboards and even demonstrations from his patients at La Salpêtrière to drive home his point. Sometimes he acted out symptoms himself.

His presentations had a very theatrical quality to them, involving a stage and special lighting. One of his students wrote of a presentation during which Charcot demonstrated different degrees of head tremor. The patients on display were fitted with hats with long feathers, which shook in unison with the patient. But the feathers magnified the effect, allowing viewers to detect small differences between patients. It was clear that in addition to being an excellent neurologist, Charcot was also somewhat of a showman. However, his shift to hypnosis and hysteria, as well as the theatrical nature of his presentations, made him many enemies.

Students came from all over the world to study with Charcot, including a young neurologist from Vienna—Sigmund Freud. As a practicing physician, Freud had concluded that many of his patients were not suffering from a neurological disorder at all but something that could not be explained by his medical training. Freud obtained a four-month fellowship from late 1885 to early 1886 to study with

Imagno/Hulton Fine Art collection/Getty Images

▶ **Image 4.2**   Charcot demonstrating hypnotism and hysteria

Charcot and attend demonstrations with his patients. What he saw amazed him. Charcot could make blind men see. Paralyzed limbs suddenly became useful simply by Charcot demanding that patients comply with his wishes. It was a remarkable demonstration of the power of the mind.

Although Freud disagreed with Charcot about the nature of hypnosis, he always considered his experience with him to be invaluable. Over his famous couch, Freud kept a copy of the painting by Andre Brouillet depicting Charcot at La Salpêtrière demonstrating his hypnotic techniques. In the ultimate tribute, Freud named one of his sons Jean-Martin, after Charcot.

During his time in France, Freud also met with Charcot's critics, Ambroise-Auguste Liébault and Hippolyte Bernheim, and learned about their approach to hypnosis. Later, he translated one of Bernheim's books on the uses of hypnosis in therapy into German. When Freud returned to Vienna, he initially incorporated hypnosis into his treatment method. Eventually he found that his free association technique produced better results, and he discarded the use of hypnosis completely. Still, he considered his time with Charcot and the Nancy School to be pivotal in his development of psychoanalysis.

AMBROISE-AUGUSTE LIÉBAULT AND HIPPOLYTE BERNHEIM: THE "COUNTRY BUMPKINS"

Ambroise-Auguste Liébault had settled in the village of Pont-Saint-Vincent, near Nancy, after completing his medical studies at the University of Strasbourg. Animal magnetism had been an interest from his early student days. In his practice, he explored the phenomenon further by offering his patients a choice: They could receive traditional medical treatment at the usual rate, or they could choose "magnetizing" at no charge. Little by little, his patients were drawn to magnetizing. The method was eventually so successful that virtually all of his patients chose it, challenging the economic base of his practice.

As a result, Liébault changed his payment rules, requesting compensation for his services but leaving the amount up to the patient. Liébault's success in curing patients is at least circumstantial evidence of the degree to which medical symptoms of the time were often psychogenic in origin. In 1866, Liébault published a book on his medical work with magnetism, but it went largely unnoticed. Still, he had developed a local reputation among his patients, and it was his local success that caught the attention of a nearby medical professor, Hippolyte Bernheim.

Bernheim was the director of the hospital in Nancy. Initially skeptical of Liébault's work, he visited with him and soon became a strong promoter of the uses of hypnosis. He used his position at the hospital to hypnotize male patients and observe the results. His honesty in depicting his failures as well as his successes enhanced his image as trustworthy and reputable. Eventually, he would attract students from many other countries, including the United States. In time, he became the spokesman for the Nancy School.

The principal distinction between the philosophy of the Nancy School (i.e., Liébault and Bernheim) and that of Charcot involved the very nature of hypnosis. Charcot believed it to be a sign of a deteriorating nervous system. In his view, only patients suffering from hysteria could be hypnotized; it was the pathology of the disorder that made an individual susceptible to hypnotism.

On the other hand, members of the Nancy School saw hypnotism as a completely normal phenomenon. Individuals might differ in their capacity to be hypnotized, but susceptibility to suggestion was not necessarily abnormal. Bernheim's book, *Suggestive Therapeutics: A Treatise on the Nature and Uses of Hypnotism* (*De la Suggestion et de son Application à la Thérapeutique* [Second Edition], 1887), went a long way in bringing the position of the Nancy School to prominence.

FLAWS IN THE SYSTEM: ALFRED BINET AT LA SALPÊTRIÈRE

Charcot conducted few of the regular hypnotic sessions himself; most were relegated to assistants. One of those assistants, Alfred Binet (1857–1911), would later become famous as the creator of the first workable intelligence test, but his time under Charcot was less successful. Binet and another assistant, Charles Féré (1852–1907), believed they had discovered an entirely new phenomenon related to hypnosis. While the subjects were hypnotized, Charcot's assistants found that with the use of magnets, they could transfer sensations from one part of a patient's body to another part. Using a similar technique, they believed they were able to reverse feelings or moods.

One of the most famous patients at the institution was a young woman by the name of Blanche Wittmann (1859–1913). She is generally known as "Wit," the name used in publications referring to her. Binet and Féré would pass magnets over Wit's body, literally attempting to reverse her mood—and they were successful! When Wit experienced a depressed mood, Binet and Féré could make her joyful and energetic with the passing of magnets. The effect seemed so astonishing that Binet and Féré acknowledged their surprise in a publication. This publication caught the watchful eye of the Belgian scientist, Joseph Delboeuf.

Delboeuf had been critical of Binet before, and this new publication made him suspicious again. One day, he traveled to Paris to observe for himself. He quickly saw the error that Binet and Féré could not see. Wit was highly suggestible; it was one of the qualities that made her such an excellent subject for hypnosis. When Binet and Féré were looking for a change in Wit—a mood change, for instance—they expressed their wishes openly. She, in turn, happily complied. When Delboeuf tried to duplicate the experiments that he had seen, but blinded the subjects from his expectations, he found no effect. He concluded that the Paris school was in error.

Delboeuf's criticism was particularly devastating to Binet. Although initially defensive, he eventually realized that Delboeuf was correct. The magnets had nothing to do with Wit's mood changes; it was all about her suggestibility. Binet quit La Salpêtrière never to return. He had been humiliated and would rarely speak of his time there. When he returned to psychology some years later, he had become very sophisticated about methodology and very sensitive to the effects of suggestion. He would carry that sophistication into all of his later trailblazing work in psychology. Binet's work with Blanche Wittmann would eventually lead Charcot to question his beliefs about hypnotism and hysteria.

THE SUCCESS OF THE NANCY SCHOOL

Despite his reputation in neurology, Charcot was the subject of much criticism over his foray into psychiatry. As he neared the end of his career, professional opinion had clearly shifted in favor of the Nancy School. Evidence later surfaced that many of Charcot's demonstration subjects had been coached beforehand by assistants to give responses that would support his position (Crews, 2017). No one accused Charcot himself of purposely misrepresenting his results. Still, his authoritarian personality prevented a clear and honest picture of his work from emerging.

Despite his belief in the organic nature of mental illness, Charcot assumed that many of his hysterical patients had experienced early trauma in their lives and it was a combination of genetic disposition and trauma that made them susceptible to hysteria. He believed these hidden forces would act on current behavior. Hypnotism became a way of unlocking some of their causal memories. One of Charcot's most prominent students, Pierre Janet (1859–1947), later took his ideas and developed them further, anticipating many aspects of dynamic psychiatry that would follow, including aspects of Freud's psychoanalysis.

At the very end of his life, Charcot was exploring the link between hypnotism and the power of suggestion in general, such as that found in faith healing. Afflicted with a heart condition and suffering from *angina pectoris*, he received anonymous letters taunting him about his impending death. Whatever his accomplishments, they did not protect him from enemies. Charcot died in his sleep, at age 67, while on a vacation trip to visit churches in the center of France. Despite his medical accomplishments in the field of neurology, his lasting legacy has been his role in bringing a more complete picture to the study of hypnosis and hysteria. In the end, even he had to admit that it was the Nancy school that was correct, not his own Paris school.

REVIEW/DISCUSSION QUESTIONS

1. What role did Franz Mesmer play in the development of hypnosis? How did he view the phenomenon?

2. Charcot believed that hypnosis and hysteria were connected. What was the link?

3. What evidence did Charcot have to support his position on hypnosis? What evidence did Liébault have to support his position?

4. Sigmund Freud visited both parties in the dispute. Which side did he ultimately agree with? Why?

5. For many years hypnosis was relegated to theater presentations. How did it become "respectable"? How do contemporary psychologists view the phenomenon of hypnosis?

CHAPTER FIVE

THE MYSTERIOUS CASE OF ANNA O.

When Sigmund Freud visited the United States in 1909 to lecture at Clark University in Worcester, Massachusetts, he gave significant credit for the invention of psychoanalysis to his mentor, Josef Breuer, a well-respected Viennese physician 14 years his senior (Freud, 1910). More than 25 years earlier, Breuer had treated a patient identified as Anna O., who had set the wheels in motion for the development of psychoanalysis. In the years that followed, Freud was less willing to give Breuer credit. On the contrary, he would criticize him for not understanding the very same case.

Although Anna O. had never been Freud's patient, Breuer had discussed the case with Freud at length, and Freud was intrigued. In 1895, the duo published a book, *Studies on Hysteria*, which is considered the first important work in psychoanalysis. Anna Freud, Sigmund's daughter, often said that she and psychoanalysis were born the same year; indeed, she was born in 1895, the year of the *Studies* volume. The opening case study in the volume was titled "Fräulein Anna O."

During his first Clark lecture, Freud described some of Anna O.'s symptoms, which began in mid-1880, when she was 21 years old. They included bouts with limb paralysis, nausea, strange eye movements, an uncontrollable cough, difficulty with language, and states of confusion, all without an apparent organic basis. In the absence of a clear physical cause, she was given a diagnosis of "hysteria," a form of emotional disturbance not uncommon for the time.

Although some physicians then considered hysteria to be nothing more than malingering, it had been increasingly recognized as a genuine disorder, albeit a mental disorder. In fact, it had become so common—as Freud pointed out in his lecture—that no competent physician would fail to make the diagnosis. But there was something different about the case of Anna O.—her treatment. Perhaps it is best illustrated with an example.

One of Anna's symptoms had been particularly odd. Despite the intense heat of the summer and a driving thirst, she found herself unable to drink. Whenever she brought a glass to her lips, she forced herself to push it away. This went on for six weeks. Fortunately, she was able to eat fruit which helped to relieve her thirst. One day, while under light hypnosis, she told Breuer of an incident involving the pet dog of her English companion. She remembered entering a room to find the dog drinking out of a glass, a situation she found disgusting. At the time, she had said nothing to her companion out of politeness. But after relating the incident to Breuer, she expressed her anger about the incident. She then asked for a glass of water, drank a large quantity of it, and awoke from the hypnotic state with the glass to her lips. The symptoms never returned (Freud, 1910).

Freud pointed out that no one had ever been cured of a hysterical symptom in this way before. It was not the use of hypnosis that was unusual. Indeed, the use of hypnosis with hysteria had become relatively common. But the typical procedure was for the physician to suggest under hypnosis that a symptom would disappear. In this case, however, it was Anna O., the patient herself, who was able to remove the symptom by locating its underlying cause. Breuer dubbed it the *cathartic method*. Freud noted that Breuer went on to treat some of Anna O.'s other symptoms with equal success. Freud was cautious to say that not all symptoms were based on a single event, as this one was. Rather, some of them involved a combination of similar events. Nonetheless, the mechanism was clear. When Freud began using the method in his own practice, his results mirrored those of Breuer.

Freud concluded that the symptoms of hysteria were vestiges or residue of past events, often traumatic ones. He called them *reminiscences*. The emotions associated with the events had originally been denied a normal outlet. As a result, they later manifested themselves in somatic symptoms. Inevitably, there was a gap associated with the original cause and the symptoms. As a result, the memory of the past event was not available on a conscious level. The lapse was restored only when the source of the original symptom was revealed. Freud later wrote that it was when he first heard the story of Anna O. from Breuer that he became fully aware of the great power of the unconscious.

BREUER'S CASE STUDY

According to Breuer's original account in *Studies on Hysteria*, Anna O. was a markedly intelligent young woman, who was highly imaginative, with strong willpower, but also full of kindness and regard for other people. She had been caring for her father, who was seriously ill, when she began experiencing difficulties of her own. At first, she suffered mostly from exhaustion, but she was eventually debilitated enough that she had to give up the care of her father. However, she soon developed a variety of other symptoms, beginning with intense coughing. Later she developed visual disturbances, paralyses, and language disturbances. It was during this period that she came under Breuer's care (Breuer & Freud, 1957).

By most measures, her symptoms were very unusual. During one 2-week period, she was completely mute. At another time, she spoke a mixture of four or five languages. Still later, she would speak only in English. As Breuer worked with her, visiting her at home almost daily, she began to show some progress. By April 1881, she was able to leave her bed for the first time in almost four months. But

▶ **Image 5.1** Josef Breuer and his wife Mathilde

shortly after that, her father died, and she developed a whole new set of symptoms. Now, she hallucinated, showed signs of great anxiety, and began to exhibit suicidal impulses. Breuer said it was almost as if she had two different personalities, one of them slightly depressed but near normal, the other clearly abnormal. This would later give rise to thoughts that she was suffering from a "split personality," now called *dissociative identity disorder*.

Breuer continued to treat her through occasional hypnosis while also encouraging her to talk about whatever came to mind. It was an arrangement that they had worked out together. He kept very detailed notes and progress was slow. However, little by little, she began to show signs of improvement. She referred to her treatment as "chimney sweeping" or "the talking cure," the latter a phrase that is still sometimes applied to psychotherapy (Ellenberger, 1993). Both Freud and Breuer strongly suggested that Anna O. was eventually cured through the cathartic method. This was a landmark event. An entirely new form of treatment had emerged from her care. The "talking cure" had become a reality.

ANNA O.'S IDENTITY IS REVEALED

The story of Anna O. remained an anonymous case history for many years and became the prototype for a cathartic cure. Some people questioned the original diagnosis of hysteria—at least one early writer thought that Anna O. was schizophrenic—but for the most part the case study was accepted as it was presented. Although four other case studies were discussed in detail in *Studies on Hysteria*, it is almost always the case of Anna O. that is described in textbooks. The case is considered one of the foundations of psychoanalysis; in a very real sense, Anna O. was the first psychoanalytic patient. And since her story had played such a central role in the new therapy, she remained a subject of interest through the years.

Later, little rumblings began to emerge regarding the case. In 1925, Carl Jung revealed an interesting piece of information about Anna O. in a seminar in Switzerland. Jung had been a close friend of Freud, beginning in 1908, and was the heir apparent to the leadership of the international psychoanalytic movement. Jung had accompanied Freud from Europe on his visit to Clark University, where both received honorary doctoral degrees (Rosenzweig, 1992). But Freud and Jung had a famous falling out in 1914 and never spoke or communicated with one another again. It was more than a decade after communication between them had ceased that Jung commented on the case of Anna O. He said that Freud had confided to him that, in fact, Anna O. had not been cured. It was a remarkable statement regarding one of the foundations of psychoanalysis (Ellenberger, 1970).

As time went on, there were a few other questions about the outcome of the case but nothing so damaging as to challenge Anna O.'s central role in the founding of psychoanalysis. Then, in 1953, Ernest Jones (1879–1958), in the first volume of his biography of Freud, revealed that Anna O. was actually Bertha Pappenheim (1859–1936), the daughter of a prominent and wealthy orthodox Jewish Viennese family. The Pappenheim family was not pleased at this revelation. Anna O./Bertha herself never commented on her treatment with Breuer. Before her death, she destroyed all of her papers related to this period of her life. But according to Jones, Freud told him that Breuer had developed a strong countertransference toward Anna O., and Breuer's wife had become jealous.

Notions of transference and countertransference had come later in the development of psychoanalysis when Freud began to appreciate the powerful dynamics that took place between the therapist and client. He realized that, over the course of therapy, clients often use the therapist as the central emotional touchstone in their lives. The client can develop feelings toward the therapist analogous to those toward his or her mother, father, spouse—any emotionally important figure in the client's life. The interactions between client and therapist reflect those emotions and can vary along the entire spectrum of emotional responses. They may even include what appears to be love.

Countertransference also involves a potential emotional link between therapist and client, but this time it emanates from the therapist. Freud suspected that there were many transference and countertransference issues in the therapeutic relationship between Anna O. and Breuer. One of the reasons for the strong countertransference was the fact that Anna O./Bertha was very attractive, and that Breuer's mother, who had died when he was very young, was named Bertha. Breuer sometimes saw Anna O./Bertha twice a day for hours at a time. It is also worth noting that he never used the cathartic method with any of his other cases (Micale, 1993).

According to Jones, after Breuer decided to end the treatment, he found that Anna was in the midst of a hysterical childbirth, the result of a phantom pregnancy that had been developing without Breuer's awareness. Breuer then fled Anna's home

▶ **Image 5.2** Anna O./Bertha Pappenheim

in a cold sweat, and the next day, he left with his wife on a trip to Venice where their daughter, Dora, was conceived. Jones went on to say that Anna was institutionalized at a sanitarium that he named and that she remained ill for many years.

Nearly two decades after Jones's book, Henri Ellenberger, a Swiss historian whose work focused mostly on medical and psychiatric issues, became interested in the story of Anna O. He decided to research the case further for his book *The Discovery of the Unconscious* (1970). His first task was to confirm that Anna O. was indeed Bertha Pappenheim. All of the dates that he could find for her and her family matched exactly those in the story of Anna O. What he could not reconcile were several of the stories that Ernest Jones told about Breuer. Apparently, Jones had accepted Freud's comments to him uncritically—and perhaps embellished them a bit. For instance, Jones's assertion regarding the timing of the conception of Breuer's last child, Dora, was inaccurate. The dates didn't match. There was no evidence that Breuer and his wife had visited Venice that year. In addition, there had never been a sanitarium in the location where Jones stated that Bertha Pappenheim had been institutionalized.

But Ellenberger didn't stop there. He did some sleuthing. He found a photograph of Bertha Pappenheim taken in 1882. After he examined the photo under special lights, he found on it the name of a German town: Constanz. He determined that near Constanz, in Kreuzlingen, there was a famous sanitarium—the Bellevue Sanitarium. Further investigation revealed that Bertha Pappenheim had been a patient at Bellevue from July to October 1882, and in her file was a copy of a case history. It appeared to have been written by Breuer himself. There was also a follow-up report written by one of the doctors at Bellevue.

The case history offers a more complete account of Bertha Pappenheim than was known before. For instance, it reveals that she was not permitted to see her father for several months before he died and that her mother lied to her about her father's health, telling her that he was improving, even after he had actually died. Ellenberger concluded that Jung's comments were confirmed: Anna O. had not been cured, and certainly not by a cathartic method. Rather, by the end of treatment at Bellevue, she had become dependent on morphine and retained many of her former symptoms. Furthermore, Ellenberger concluded that Jones's account of the false pregnancy and hysterical childbirth could not be confirmed, and in fact did not fit into the chronology of the case.

DID FREUD LIE?

The research by Ellenberger inevitably leads to an important question: Did Freud know the real outcome of the case? It seems certain that he did. As it turns out, Freud's fiancée—later his wife—Martha Bernays, was a friend of Bertha Pappenheim. When Pappenheim's father died, Martha's father was put in charge of the estate. Before their marriage, Freud had written to Martha keeping her up to date on Bertha Pappenheim's condition and institutionalization. He knew about her morphine addiction and continued symptomatology long after her treatment with Breuer had ended. The evidence even intimates that Freud added a little self-serving information (really speculation) about why the treatment with Breuer had failed.

Freud suggested in letters to several people that Breuer had not been able to handle "the sexual element" that lay at the base of Bertha Pappenheim's problem. Without addressing that issue, according to Freud, there could be no cure. Could the story of the phantom pregnancy have existed only in Freud's mind or through one of his famous "reconstructions"? When Breuer admitted Bertha to the sanitarium, he noted that she was remarkably undeveloped "in the sexual realm." He had made the same comment in his original case study of her. It seems unlikely that he would have lied, given his responsibility in admitting her. And if he had lied, the truth would have soon been discovered (Breger, 2009).

It is worth noting that Freud and Breuer became estranged after the publication of *Studies on Hysteria*. They had once been very close, particularly at the beginning of Freud's career, with Breuer referring patients to him and even lending him money. There seemed to be a genuine and strong bond between them. However, in later years, Freud minimized the role of Breuer in the development of psychoanalysis, even suggesting that it was Breuer's limitations as a therapist that prevented him from having an accurate understanding of the case.

For Breuer, the case of Anna O. represented a turning point. He never used the cathartic method in his practice again. Contrary to Freud's intimation that Breuer became afraid of the method because of some of the sexual elements that might surface, the evidence is that Breuer simply found it too time consuming, Moreover, both he and Freud must have known that the case history contained in the volume left readers with the impression that Anna O. had been cured. Without a cure, the case study loses most of its impact. It appears that Freud used a simplified and inaccurate version of the story to promote his theory in his famous lecture at Clark University.

The impact of Freud and psychoanalysis continued to grow after 1909. The United States seemed particularly fertile ground for its growth. Psychoanalysis not only became the most important form of psychotherapy for many years, but it also had an enormous impact on popular culture, academia, and the arts. Even today many people identify Freud as the "face" of psychology—to the great consternation of psychologists with different scientific bents and theoretical persuasions. Despite all the challenges made to the approach—including its focus on long-term treatment—it continues to survive, even thrive. Most of its practitioners will point out that today's psychoanalysis is very different from the original, although many of its underlying beliefs remain unchanged. For all of its checkered history, it is impossible to deny the contributions it has made to the treatment of needy individuals or the insights it has given us about human behavior.

ANNA O.'S LATER YEARS

But what happened to Bertha Pappenheim? It turns out, a fair amount is known about her later life. She was hospitalized four more times during the 1880s and continued to suffer from a variety of severe symptoms. However, her symptoms appear to have abated by the end of the decade. At that point, she moved to Frankfurt with her mother, where they had many relatives. Although Bertha and her mother had had a difficult relationship, particularly during the period when Bertha's father was dying, they eventually became reconciled.

In Frankfurt, Bertha initially busied herself writing children's stories, eventually writing more political essays. A play she wrote showed increasing evidence of her interest in feminism. She began a career as a social worker with particular concern for orphans and abused children. She founded and ran an orphanage for Jewish girls and later led a campaign against prostitution, particularly when it involved young Jewish women. Some psychoanalysts find evidence for Bertha's sexual problems in her need to "save" prostitutes.

As a feminist, she spoke strongly against the educational and social limitations that were placed on women, particularly young women. Her own life had been a striking example of a highly intelligent young woman whose expected role in society was to prepare only for marriage. She never married. She also never spoke openly about her identification as Anna O., and she apparently had an abiding dislike for things psychoanalytic. She died in 1936. In 1954, she was honored with a postage stamp by the Federal Republic of Germany for her work as a pioneer social worker.

Many questions remain about Anna O. One of the items most frequently discussed is her diagnosis. At various times, scholars have argued that she suffered from schizophrenia, multiple personality disorder (now called dissociative identity disorder), or drug addiction, among other diagnoses (Rosenbaum & Muroff, 1984). It is doubtful that there will ever be unanimous agreement on this point. By way of introduction to the story of Anna O., one author simply wrote, "Every society has its therapeutic myths . . . and our society is no exception" (Borch-Jacobsen, 1996, p. 1). Most teachers use the story as an effective introduction to psychoanalysis.

In the end, the case of Anna O. likely falls into the category of a "founding myth." Did Freud actively contribute to the myth, knowing that it was fundamentally false? Perhaps to feed his own ambitious agenda (Breger, 2009)? With the information available now, it is difficult to reach any other conclusion.

REVIEW/DISCUSSION QUESTIONS

1. Anna O./Bertha had an odd mix of symptoms. How would she be diagnosed today?

2. Why is her case considered so important to psychoanalysis?

3. Explain the cathartic cure? How does it work?

4. Did Freud lie about the outcome of the case? What is the evidence?

5. What became of Bertha Pappenheim after her experience with Breuer?

6. Does the story of Anna O. have any impact on the contemporary value of psychoanalysis?

CHAPTER SIX

CLEVER HANS, THE WONDER HORSE

Beginning in the summer of 1904, a horse with surprising abilities was put on display in Berlin. The horse was called Hans, and among other feats, he could correctly answer mathematical questions by tapping out the response with his foot, identify scarves of different colors, and answer questions by shaking his head "yes" or "no." Was it possible that an animal could actually think? That was certainly the impression he gave.

Genuine thinking was traditionally thought to be an ability unique to human beings. But the question of animal intelligence had become more prominent with the publication of Charles Darwin's *The Descent of Man* in 1871. In it, Darwin argued for continuity between man and lower animals in a variety of realms, including the senses and emotions, and such faculties as love, memory, attention, curiosity, imitation, and reason. Was the difference between animal and human intelligence truly one of degree, not kind? And could Hans be a particularly strong example of animal intelligence? The possibility that animals might be capable of human-like thinking had implications that were staggering.

Wilhelm von Osten (1838–1909), a 65-year-old retired mathematics teacher, had worked with Hans for several years before exhibiting him. Von Osten had long believed that the intelligence of animals was underestimated, and he planned to use Hans to illustrate his point. Hans was actually the second horse that von Osten attempted to train. Another horse, also named Hans, had died earlier. Von Osten said he instructed the horses as he might instruct high school students.

When von Osten began exhibiting the horse to the public, crowds began gathering almost immediately. Most observers found the ability of the horse to be both genuine and impressive. Still, some had questions about the horse's ability. Was there trickery involved? Could this be a case of thought transference between trainer and animal? Frustrated that people questioned the horse's intelligence, von Osten asked for a formal investigation to prove that Hans's thinking was genuine. In the end, there were two investigations, the first absolving von Osten of any attempt at deception. However, when the second more detailed investigation was completed, the conclusions were devastating to von Osten and appeared to undercut all of his work.

Different takeaway lessons have been proposed for the case of Hans. Most have focused on the methodological issues involved in the study and how easy it is to fall into the trap of seeing what we want to see, a phenomenon known as confirmation bias (Heinzen, Lilienfeld, & Nolan, 2015).

THE VENUE AND THE REPERTOIRE

The demonstrations with Hans took place in a courtyard surrounded by apartment houses on Griebenow Street, in Berlin, Germany. It was there, on the fifth floor in one of those apartments, that von Osten, a bearded and white-haired bachelor, lived alone. When von Osten was satisfied that Hans was ready for display, he took out a small newspaper ad inviting the public to witness a demonstration of the mental powers of a horse.

Soon a routine was established, and Hans was exhibited on an almost daily basis starting at noon. Some people came to the courtyard simply to observe, but all were free to ask questions. Observers were frequently cautioned by von Osten if they gave too much of the answer away.

Von Osten didn't charge anyone to witness the demonstration. Adding to his credibility, he declined significant financial offers after Hans became famous. His only apparent compensation was the satisfaction that his training had paid off as he predicted and that he was making a contribution to science.

Das lesende und rechnende Pferd, mit seinem Lehrer HERRN von OSTEN (Berlin)

▶ **Image 6.1** Wilhelm von Osten and Clever Hans

Interest spread to other parts of Berlin and beyond. Newspaper articles were written about Hans, and pictures of the horse even appeared on post-cards and liquor labels. A number of notables visited the demonstrations to observe the wonder horse for themselves. Among them was C. S. Schillings, a well-known zoologist and explorer. His endorsement of Hans and his abilities helped to bring scientific respectability to the case (Heinzen, Lilienfeld, & Nolan, 2015).

Hans had an extensive repertoire. He answered most questions by tapping his right hoof the appropriate number of times, although occasionally he might stomp down on his left hoof as well. Simple addition or subtraction was child's play to him, but more complex problems didn't pose much difficulty either. For example, he could add fractions with different denominators, first taping out the numerator and then the denominator of the final answer. Hans used his head to answer "yes" or "no" to questions, shaking it up and down or sideways to indicate his response. Using a blackboard with letters that von Osten had prepared, Hans could spell out words or phrases by tapping out the number assigned to a particular letter of the alphabet. He could even count the number of children playing on nearby rooftops.

When asked to identify a particularly colored scarf from a group of scarves, Hans would grasp the appropriate colored cloth in his teeth. Knowledge of the calendar was still another behavior in his repertoire, with Hans able to indicate the day of the week on which a particular date fell. Perhaps, most amazingly, he could indicate when a musical scale was in error and even suggest the missing element.

Although Hans had a very high percentage of correct answers, his responses were not error-free. However, when Hans made an error and was asked to correct it, he did so quickly and almost always with positive results. The demonstrations would often go on for many hours and it was reasonable to assume that at least some of the errors came about because the animal was fatigued.

Karl Krall, Denkende Tiere, Leipzig 1912, Tafel 2

▸ **Image 6.2** Clever Hans in the courtyard

Locals found his behavior astonishing. Experts in animal behavior as well as other professionals who were brought in to observe his behavior were equally baffled. As far as anyone could determine, Hans could engage in feats of thinking that are usually associated with humans alone. Von Osten himself saw Hans as an example of an animal who was not merely trained but who could engage in genuine thinking. To bolster his case, he claimed to have taught Hans only basic mathematics and that Hans had learned to multiply and divide on his own. Von Osten contended that Hans was not unique. Other horses could be taught to think in the same way if properly trained.

Still, not everyone agreed. Several theories were proposed to explain Hans's unusual abilities, including the belief that he was responding to surreptitious hand or eye movements. One critic thought there were electrical grids in the sand giving prompts to the animal. Others saw Hans's success as a case of mental telepathy between von Osten and Hans. Ultimately, von Osten became so upset with the negative comments made in the press and elsewhere that he asked a local educational group to investigate Hans and his abilities.

THE INVESTIGATIONS

The German Board of Education responded to von Osten's request by appointing a commission headed by psychologist and philosopher Carl Stumpf (1848–1936) to investigate the abilities of the horse. At the time, Stumpf had an appointment in the Department of Philosophy at the University of Berlin and also headed its Institute for Experimental Psychology. He was one of the most distinguished German psychologists of his era. Stumpf appointed 10 other people to the commission, including a circus manager, a zoologist, and a physiologist. The task of the commission was to determine if any fraud was involved in the case.

The commission investigated the horse's behavior over the course of several days. Various tasks were assigned to Hans, including mathematical problems and questions about the days of the week. During one period, the members of the group were assigned to carefully watch different parts of von Osten's body looking for signs that he might be signaling Hans. When the investigation was complete, the commission issued a report. It concluded that the abilities displayed by Hans were not due to fakery. They could find no evidence that von Osten was signaling the horse in any way. However, they did not reach a conclusion about the source of Hans's abilities. Unfortunately, some newspapers reported that the commission had verified that the horse was indeed unusually intelligent, a conclusion that was embarrassing to members of the commission, as well as to Stumpf.

In order to explore the question of Hans's intelligence further, Stumpf assigned a student of his, Oskar Pfungst (1874–1932/1933), to the problem. One writer has suggested that the appointment of Pfungst to conduct further research may have been an attempt by Stumpf to claim the topic of animal intelligence as part of the discipline of psychology (Kressley-Mba, 2006). It was early enough in the development of the discipline for such an attempt to be made.

Pfungst brought a new level of investigation to the issue. Going about his assignment methodically, he organized a series of controlled observations. He even set up a tent in the courtyard so that he would have better control over possible extraneous cues from the environment. Blinders were prepared for the horse in order to limit his vision, when necessary. The blinders prohibited Hans from seeing either his trainer or anyone else asking a question. Some of the questions Pfungst used were selected so that no one present knew the answer. This was done by hiding the stimulus material from the view of everyone but the horse or by posing the question in parts so that no one present had access to the complete question.

After making extensive observations, Pfungst reached several conclusions. Consistent with the commission's report, he could find no evidence of fakery. The trainer, von Osten could be annoying, but there was no reason to doubt his honesty. However, Pfungst found that the horse was unable to perform with any degree of accuracy when he wore the blinders that prohibited him from seeing his trainer or anyone else asking the question. Without the blinders, Hans's accuracy was approximately 89%; with the blinders, his accuracy dropped to 6%. Moreover, even with the blinders absent, Hans was not able to respond accurately if no one in his immediate view knew the correct answer. Across all of the experiments, when no one present was aware of the correct answer, Hans's accuracy was 10% or less. When the answer was known by those present, Hans's accuracy was typically between 90% and 100% (Fernald, 1984).

It was clear to Stumpf that Hans could not think in any real sense of the word. Rather, he was responding to cues in the environment. Among them, Stumpf concluded, were subtle cues that came unknowingly from his trainer, von Osten. But clues also came from others who were present. Pfungst observed that when Hans was confronted with a problem, he would typically try to look toward his trainer or the questioner. If he could see neither, he would become frustrated and sometimes aggressive, a type of behavior that was not typical for him. Pfungst ended up with several animal bites during this phase of testing. (When Hans became aggressive, the testing was usually discontinued, at least momentarily.)

Pfungst concluded that the subtle cues for Hans typically involved small bodily changes, such as a slight movement toward Hans or a change in body posture. For instance, the trainer would often lean slightly forward indicating that the tapping was to begin. When it was time for the tapping to stop, the trainer might stand more erect and there would be a slight reduction in bodily tension. As subtle as the cues were, the horse had learned to read them.

Pfungst found a final part of the experiment the most telling of all. He learned that he could control the number of taps made by Hans by changing his own body posture. By leaning forward in a certain way, he could cause the taps to begin. He could even increase the rate of tapping by varying his body posture. When he made his posture more erect, the tapping would stop. The mystery of "Clever Hans" appeared to be solved (Pfungst, 1911). But the case posed new questions, and not only for animal researchers.

WHAT HANS LEARNED

One explanation for Hans's behavior suggested that horses are particularly sensitive to body posture as part of their evolutionary heritage. As a result, Hans was a receptive subject for the tasks required of him. But how much did the training contribute to his sensitivity? In working with Hans, von Osten had employed many of the same techniques used to train circus animals. Scientists such as B. F. Sinner would later conduct research using these same techniques.

One of the methods used to train circus animals is called *molding*, in which the animal is gently coerced into the desired behavior. For instance, an animal might be made to tap its foot by rewarding the animal as it approached the desired behavior in small, incremental steps—a method of approximation. Rewards would be offered each step of the way as the animal moved closer to the desired behavior— that is, the use of reinforcement. Both approximation and reinforcement would be standard tools for later behaviorists. It is worth noting that von Osten is believed to have underfed Hans slightly and that the horse was always ready for a food reward, often a carrot or a piece of bread, which von Osten provided during the course of the demonstrations.

Pfungst employed a method that was a variation on the "double-blind" procedure. In a typical double-blind experiment neither the experimenter nor the participant knows the experimental condition into which the participant has been placed. One of the effects of such a method is to reduce the possibility of experimenter or observer bias. Pfungst designed a test in which none of Hans's usual trainers were present, and none of those present knew the answer to the questions posed to Hans. When those conditions were met, Hans could no longer answer questions accurately. This type of experimental error—that is, cueing the experimental subject to the correct answer—has become known as the "Clever Hans phenomenon" or "the Clever Hans effect," a situation that is now known to operate in a wide range of experimental disciplines (Sebeok & Rosenthal, 1981).

Pfungst wrote a detailed account of his experience with Hans that was published in March 1907, with an English version in 1911. When the results were announced by Pfungst, von Osten was understandably upset. Years of his work were shown to be for naught. He refused to allow Hans to undergo any more testing. Candland (1993) reported that von Osten was not upset with Pfungst but rather blamed Hans for deceiving him, even causing him to become ill.

When von Osten died in 1909, the horse was willed to a friend, Karl Krall, a wealthy jeweler, who had an interest in animal communication. Despite the Pfungst report, Krall believed that animals could think, and he continued to work with Hans and other horses.

HOW COULD OBSERVERS HAVE BEEN SO WRONG ABOUT HANS?

The great lesson from Hans continues to be the important role that bias may play in scientific experiments and the methods that science must employ to protect against it. But how could so many people be so wrong about Hans? Everyone seemed to agree that von Osten was an honest man. And surely there were skeptics among the crowds who came to see the demonstrations who would have pointed out any obvious deceptions. It is worth remembering that Hans had been put through an extensive training period. Hans was no longer just a generic horse but one that had been taught very specific behaviors.

Heinzen, Lilienfeld, and Nolan (2015) offer a detailed critique of the entire Hans experience. They begin by noting the principle of parsimony, an approach that argues for the simplest level of explanation before assuming a higher level one, for instance that Hans was responding to cues in the environment rather than actually thinking. They list some of the unlikely views that observers must have accepted about Hans if they believed that he engaged in genuine thinking, including the fact that he could understand both French and German.

They also note that von Osten's body cues had grown so subtle that they were unseen by the assembled crowds and were not even recognizable by von Osten himself. As noted earlier, von Osten, and other questioners, would inevitably lean slightly forward in anticipation of Hans beginning to tap—offering a cue for Hans to begin his tapping. And when Hans reached the correct number of taps, von Osten (and others) would inevitably lean back—the cue for Hans to stop. Moreover, whenever Hans made a mistake, von Osten had a ready answer. Hans was tired or stubborn or even bored. As it turns out, Hans was indeed quite clever, but not in the way von Osten and others concluded.

After his work with Hans was completed, Pfungst conducted a series of parallel tests with humans. His experiments make clear that Clever Hans effects are quite as likely to occur in research with humans as with animals. For this reason, care is usually taken in most areas of psychology, from perception, cognitive psychology, and social psychology, to make experiments double-blind so that neither the experimenter nor the subject knows what condition the subject is in and thus what his or her responses are predicted to be.

As for Pfungst himself, he enjoyed a brief period as a minor celebrity, writing articles and giving lectures. Despite his work, there is no evidence that he received his advanced degree from the Berlin Institute. And yet he is the real hero of the Hans story—pointing out the important role that the investigator may play in the outcome of research while simultaneously demonstrating the power of the scientific method. In the process, Pfungst provided a cautionary tale for all the sciences that remains as useful today as when he first presented it more than 100 years ago.

REVIEW/DISCUSSION QUESTIONS

1. The case of Clever Hans really begins with Darwin's *The Descent of Man*. Explain.

2. What does it mean to anthropomorphize animals? How often do we engage in it? Can you think of any specific examples?

3. How was Hans able to deceive so many people for so long? What role did his trainer, von Osten, play in the deception?

4. Psychologists have cited the study of Clever Hans as support for the behaviorist position. Explain.

5. How was the mystery of Clever Hans eventually unraveled? How does the solution relate to confirmatory bias and double-blind experiments?

NOTE

The Heinzen et al. (2015) volume cited in this chapter (see References) is a clearly written overview of the Hans case with an additional message about sloppy scientific thinking and its pitfalls. The authors conclude with an intriguing chapter on the "Clever Hans effect" in everyday life, from drug sniffing dogs to "scared straight."

CHAPTER SEVEN

FRANCIS GALTON
Explorer, Eugenicist, and Accidental Psychologist

Francis Galton (1822–1911) was one of the most notable polymaths of the Victorian era, making important contributions in a range of areas. While still in his 20s, he mapped out a previously unexplored part of Africa. Later, he helped develop basic information on fingerprinting, elements of which remain in use today. And he was one of the early weather forecasters, correctly noting that weather systems are predictable, at least to some degree. But when his half-cousin Charles Darwin published *On the Origin of Species* (1859), Galton found a new cause that dominated the rest of his life.

Galton saw in Darwin's work important implications for the human race, specifically the possibility of improving mankind through selective breeding, an effort he called eugenics. In service of that goal, he invented several statistics and laid the groundwork for the modern intelligence test. And although he was not formally a psychologist, his impact on the field, particularly on American psychology, was profound. Ultimately his work in eugenics would lead to one of the most passionate controversies in the history of science and one that is still being played out in various forms today.

CHILD GENIUS

Born into a Quaker family in Birmingham, England, in 1822, Francis Galton was the youngest of seven children. Both sides of his family were well off and accomplished, and it was apparent from childhood that Francis was destined for great things. As the youngest in the family, Francis was doted on by his older siblings. His sister Adele took a particular interest in his intellectual development and drilled him constantly, adding content and ambition to his precociousness (Fancher, 1985). On the eve of his fifth birthday, Francis composed a bit of braggadocio that has often been used to attest to his genius. In it, he described his abilities in both language and mathematics that were so beyond the typical child of his age, a psychologist later estimated his IQ to be 200, an extremely rare and high level of functioning (Terman, 1917).

The Galton family took note of his precociousness and encouraged him to show off for visitors. Not surprisingly, young Francis developed a high opinion of himself and his abilities. He was brought back to reality when he attended college and found the demands to be much more than he expected. His disappointment was so great that he suffered a nervous breakdown. Although he eventually completed his degree, he did so without particular distinction. However, there was a positive aspect to this setback. The breakdown instilled in Francis a lifelong interest in the subject of intelligence, and it was there that he would make his most important contribution to psychology—although it would not come immediately.

TRAVEL AND ADVENTURE

Francis could hardly have predicted where his life was headed based on his early adult years. He had originally intended to be a physician, a goal supported by his father. After studying for a year, he took time off to travel and later enrolled at Cambridge, still planning on medicine for a career but also interested in broadening his knowledge. The trajectory of his life changed with the death of his father at age 61. The inheritance that Francis received made it unnecessary for him to pursue a profession. Since Francis had never felt passionate about practicing medicine in the first place, the choice to abandon it was easy. Instead he opted for travel and adventure, interests that would eventually turn him into a noted explorer.

A year after his father's death, Galton began one of his first great adventures—a trip to Egypt and a voyage part way down the Nile. The trip was done in style and included the services of a faithful manservant, Ali. Before turning home, Galton also explored parts of the Near East. Still in his mid-20s, his life was assuming that of an aimless youth, with much drinking, carousing, and adventure. But Galton was beginning to question his goals in life. Was he living up to the standards of his family? He realized there was a way to satisfy his desire for travel and adventure but still engage in a noble undertaking.

In the 1840s, many parts of the world remained unexplored—blank areas on maps. Galton decided he would become an explorer. But what would he explore? The interior of Africa beckoned him almost immediately. He made the trip "official" by obtaining the sanction of the Royal Geographical Society. It helped that he had friends in high places. In April 1850, he set sail from Plymouth, England, to Cape Town, South Africa. The dangers that Africa presented were real and significant. Beyond the terrain itself, they included Dutch settlers who were hostile to the British and native tribes at war with one another. In his travels earlier, Galton had already shown physical courage and the capacity to endure significant hardship. His time in Africa would further test him.

His plan was to explore interior areas of the country that no White man, with the possible exception of a few missionaries, had ever visited. He first traveled by boat 1,000 miles north of Cape Town. Galton's original entourage consisted of nine mules and horses, seven servants, and a male Swedish traveling companion. The entourage would eventually grow considerably larger with the addition of oxen and local guides (Brookes, 2004).

RETURN TO ENGLAND

Despite the dangers, Galton kept careful notes of all he observed. He had a passion for detail that would serve him well. When he finally returned to England after more than two years, his descriptions of the natives and their habitat so impressed the members of the Royal Geographic Society that some felt he had brought a new level of sophistication to exploration. As a consequence, the Society awarded him one of its two gold medals for that year, a very high honor. Galton had become a national hero, with a significant reputation, while still a young man.

Soon Galton began to explore in another direction. Now age 30, his thoughts turned to marriage. The object of his affection was Louisa Butler, an Anglican from an accomplished academic family. Surprisingly, they seemed to have little in common. She was religious; he was not. She was interested in the music and the arts; again, he was not. From his description, Galton seemed more interested in marrying into her eminent family than marrying Louisa.

But marriage seemed to provide Galton with even more energy. Not only did he and Louisa travel extensively throughout England and the continent, he completed writing a book on his earlier travels, *Narrative of an Explorer in Tropical South Africa* (1853). Written in an adventurous style, the book proved a success not only with mainstream readers but also with the Royal Geographic Society. But the book has a significant drawback for modern readers. It is filled with racist comments about the natives he encountered in Africa,

▶ **Image 7.1** Francis Galton

a view that would have been common and unexceptional in Victorian England but that is highly inappropriate to modern sensibilities. That year, Galton was invited to become a council member of the Society, yet another honor.

His next publication, *Hints to Travelers* (1854), first a journal article and then a small book, listed equipment that every traveler and explorer should employ. It eventually became the most popular publication of the Society. *The Art of Travel* (1855) described survival skills for the adventurous, some of them quirky and questionable, others still useful today. Galton would later give lectures to military men describing some of these same survival tactics.

In short order, Galton became immersed in the daily activities of the Royal Geographic Society. In 1856, only in his mid-30s, he was made a fellow of the Society. But exploration was not his only interest. One of the other areas to which he devoted much time was an attempt to understand weather patterns. Weather forecasting was in its infancy when Galton began collecting data on it. Eventually he would set up a system inviting reports from different areas of Europe, establishing a foundation for modern weather forecasting (Gillham, 2001).

CHARLES DARWIN AND THE ORIGIN OF SPECIES

When Charles Darwin published his *Origin of Species*, Francis Galton went through a significant change. He proclaimed it was the beginning of a new phase in his mental development. Darwin's volume was devoted primarily to descriptions of plants and animals and contained very little about the human condition. But Galton saw the implications for humankind immediately. If animals were able to change through natural selection, wasn't it possible to help the process along for humans? With the proper selection, he saw the prospect of breeding better human beings. All that was required was to identify the individuals who were the most able mentally and physically and encourage them to marry. Perhaps the government could provide some kind of financial encouragement. Although the details were still to be worked out, and Galton would not give a name to his plan for several more years, the basic outline of eugenics was in place.

Galton set out to prove his thesis through several publications. He noted that eminence tended to run in families to a remarkable degree. While this result could be equally explained by environmental factors, Galton chose to focus on heredity almost exclusively. In *Hereditary Genius* (1869) he laid out his strongest arguments using family histories of eminent men from a variety of professions. He maintained, for instance, that eminent judges had more prominent relatives than could be found by chance. Moreover, the possibility of eminence decreased as the biological relationship to the prominent judge became more remote (Forrest, 1974). In addition to his emphasis on the power of heredity, Galton's criteria for eminence were suspect. Some of his choices seem odd when objective selection criteria are applied, and some of the individuals he left out appear to have been demonstrably more accomplished.

In his quest to provide a framework for his thesis, Galton made use of the new and original work on statistical deviation by a Belgian scientist, Adolph Quetelet. Originally working with the chest measurements of more than 5,000 soldiers, Quetelet found that chest sizes, when presented graphically, arranged themselves in the shape of a bell, with the bulk of scores clustering in the middle of the distribution and a decreasing number of scores at each of the ends. Subsequently, Quetelet found that a similarly-shaped distribution would result from very different measures, such as height and weight. Galton concluded that Quetelet's curve would apply to intellectual measurement as well, thereby providing visual support for his beliefs about the extremes of intelligence. The distribution is now known as the *bell curve* or *normal distribution*.

UNDERSTANDING HEREDITY

For all his talk about hereditary genius, Galton, like other scientists of his day, had little understanding of the way heredity worked. Folklore explanations attributed many childhood characteristics to experiences of the mother while pregnant, such as eating the wrong foods or being frightened by an animal. The most common scientific beliefs at the time derived from the theory of Jean-Baptiste Lamarck (1744–1829) who argued that characteristics acquired by parents during their lifetime could find expression in their children. But none of these explanations was sufficient to explain the obvious differences and similarities found in families. Darwin himself had a theory proposing that specific particles in the body contained the elements of heredity. Galton tested the theory by transfusing blood between rabbits but found no evidence to support Darwin's theory. Later, both he and Darwin continued the experiments with unsatisfactory results (Gillham, 2001).

THE QUESTIONNAIRE METHOD

When scholars challenged Galton's views on the dominance of heredity, Galton took a new approach—he asked members of the Royal Academy to fill out an extensive questionnaire on their backgrounds and lives. Although this may seem like the most benign activity to modern sensibilities, it was in fact an innovation. Galton had pioneered a new technique for personal data collection. The results of his survey appeared in *English Men of Science* (1874), and although the identity of those who took the survey were originally anonymous, some of them are known today, including the modest self-assessment of Charles Darwin. Galton's volume, rough as it was, introduced a new phrase to the lexicon—nature versus nurture. He called it a "jingle of words," but it was a "jingle" that stuck and whose impact continues to be debated to this day.

Although the responses seemed to temper Galton's belief in the power of heredity—he acknowledged that it was possible that the environment could play a strong role in development—he nonetheless concluded that heredity was the overriding determiner. But how was he to prove it? By 1875, he had adopted still another weapon for his arsenal—the study of identical twins. By gathering information on identical twins reared together and others reared apart, he felt confident that he could sort out the relative contributions of nature and nurture. Of course, finding twins who had been separated early enough to make his point was not going to be easy.

He was also looking for objective, easy-to-measure characteristics that would separate the brightest individuals from the rest of the flock. Head size was a possibility. Others had suggested it as well. Sensory acuity and reaction time seemed like additional possibilities. He became obsessed with measurement of human characteristics in all forms but particularly that of intelligence. Many of his ideas about intellectual measurement would come together in 1884 with the opening of the International Health Exhibition.

The exhibition took place in South Kensington, only a short distance from his home. It was composed of a variety of health-related products and home improvements, including a model for a flush toilet. Galton's space consisted of a narrow passageway, 6 feet wide and 36 feet long. After paying a small fee at the entrance, visitors would be led through the corridor as a series of measurements were taken—from height, weight, and lung capacity to sensory discrimination, color perception, and beyond. Everyone participating was given a copy of the results; Galton kept a duplicate copy for himself. By the time the exhibition and its sequel closed, Galton had collected measurements on more than 9,000 people, an enormous amount of data. Moreover, he had created an "anthropometric record" of the people of London at a specific time in history.

Francis Galton's First Anthropometric Laboratory at the International Health Exhibition, South Kensington, 1884–5.

▶ **Image 7.2** Galton's laboratory at the International Health Exhibition

Statistics was still in its infancy when Galton began his work. He would help develop it into a more mature scientific tool. And one of his most important statistical contributions would emerge from his exhibition data. He plotted up the heights of more than 200 pairs of fathers and sons. What he saw immediately was a visual relationship between the two—not perfect, but a relationship nonetheless. As the heights of fathers increased, so did those of sons. This simple plotting was the beginning of a rudimentary form of a tool that some view as the most important statistic of all, the correlation coefficient. Later, associates of his would refine the concept mathematically. Today correlations are calculated for such wildly disparate topics as predicting school success to developing hypotheses about the causes of cancer. It has become an incredibly useful tool for a vast array of disciplines. The importance of Galton's contributions did not go unnoticed. In 1886, the Royal Geographic Society conferred on him its Gold Medal.

FINGERPRINTS

In yet another of his forays into human measurements, Galton began to explore the use of fingerprints as a form of identification. Handprints had a long history in Japan and China as a way of sealing a contract, much like a signature might be used today. The technique became less cumbersome and more refined as it was adopted in the West. But despite the promise of being able to identify individuals even when they denied their identity—something that might be very useful in criminal cases—the technique was not widely accepted or used. Galton saw what had to be done to make the use of fingerprinting more acceptable (Brookes, 2004).

Building on the work of two earlier aficionados of the technique, Galton set about to prove that fingerprints not only vary considerably among people but also that they are constant over the life span. Moreover, he was able to develop a system for classifying them, a necessity if fingerprinting was going to have any practical value. Working intensely over a period of several years, he was able to satisfy himself on all the above counts. He had brought fingerprinting to a new level of distinction. His work resulted in a great deal of public recognition, much to the distress of the individuals who had actually pioneered the technique. To Galton's disappointment, he could find nothing in fingerprints that identified eminent individuals or that distinguished between races. His specific method would eventually become outdated, but fingerprinting itself would soon find an important role in the penal system.

Continuing with his passion for measurement, Galton also applied his numerical approach to religion. One of the first things he noted was that pastors didn't live any longer than the general population. That fact raised some interesting questions in him about religion. Galton then explored the efficacy of prayer on ships and whether they survived. Shipping was a dangerous undertaking at the time. It was not unusual for ships to perish, resulting in significant financial disaster along with the obvious personal loss. Galton concluded that prayers directed toward the well-being of ships had no noticeable effect.

THE FINAL YEARS

Galton's beloved wife, Louisa, died in 1897 while they were on vacation in France. After a period of mourning, Galton came back with renewed energy, perhaps more aware than ever that his own days were limited. He was gaining scientific supporters, chief among them Karl Pearson, a mathematician and statistician at University College London. Pearson was also a staunch eugenicist. A research fellowship in eugenics was established at the University of London giving greater status to Galton's proposal. In his will, Galton created a eugenics professorship at University College London with Pearson named as the first occupant. Eugenic societies were erupting all over the world but particularly in Europe and the United States. Germany established a society for racial hygiene that owed many of its ideas to Galton and would have horrific implications in years to come.

By the time Galton reached his mid- to late 80s, all of his siblings had died, and he was suffering from a variety of ailments, including asthma, rheumatism, and gout, all of which limited his capacity for travel. In 1909, at age 87, he was knighted, one of a multitude of honors that he had received. In his last years, Galton, who had avoided reading fiction for most of his life, not only began reading fiction, but he also wrote a novel. Not surprisingly, its central theme was about a society based on eugenic principles. Publishers declined to publish the novel, supposedly because of its sexual passages, and Galton asked that it be destroyed after his death. Most of it was destroyed, including some passages that were described as very erotic (Brookes, 2004).

GALTON'S LEGACY

On January 17, 1911, Galton died in a rented home in Surrey. He was 88 and had been suffering from bronchitis and asthma. Despite the fame he experienced during his lifetime, he is not well known today, at least not among most U.S. audiences. He was very much a product of his time, with all of the biases about class and race that his generation experienced. But he was also remarkable for his time, offering new ideas and working with the fervor of a zealot. As biographer Martin Brookes pointed out, by placing man in an evolutionary context, Galton anticipated modern anthropology, sociobiology, and evolutionary psychology, a remarkable achievement (Brookes, 2004).

Galton's contributions to psychology, particularly American psychology, are not always obvious, but they were in fact enormous. While Wilhelm Wundt of the University of Leipzig is generally considered the founder of experimental psychology, he had a specific agenda in mind. Wundt was looking for attributes of the "common man"—that is, the qualities that all men (and women) had in common. Galton was interested in how men and women differ, what Darwin called variability and what most psychologists refer to as individual differences. Wundt's form of psychology still exists, but it represents only a small portion of experimental psychology. Most current American psychology emphasizes variability.

Galton's work had another, far less commendable, impact. In 1907 in the United States, the state of Indiana adopted sterilization laws, a type of "negative eugenics." Rather than simply encouraging the brightest and most able individuals to marry and reproduce, negative eugenics tries to limit reproduction at the lower end of the intellectual spectrum. Thirty other states soon followed Indiana in adopting sterilization laws. Many—probably most—of the leading U.S. psychologists during the 1920s and 1930s believed strongly in eugenics. It had an appealing simplicity and seemed to be scientifically based. However, in the aftermath of World War II, American psychology experienced a dramatic turnaround.

During the war, Nazi Germany had as one of its ultimate goals the "purification" of the race, resulting in the deaths of millions of Jews, along with Sinti and Roma people, the disabled, gender and sexual minorities, and anyone else who didn't meet their so-called standards. The horrific implications of an unfettered eugenicist approach became clear. Although many of the sterilization laws remained on the books until the 1960s and 1970s, American psychology increasingly moved away from strongly biological explanations of behavior to strongly environmental ones.

The nature–nurture problem that Galton proposed so many years ago continues to have an impact to this day. In fact, it may well be the most fundamental issue in all of psychology. At its best, the discussion of it is sophisticated and balanced. Modern day characterizations of gene–environment interaction alone have moved the discussion miles away from a simple question about which one is more important or how much each contributes. But, sadly, the popular discussion is typically not very sophisticated. Newspapers and other news outlets will still occasionally report that the gene for schizophrenia or alcoholism or some other extreme type of behavior has been found—statements that are no more sophisticated than the simplistic explanations offered during Galton's time.

REVIEW/DISCUSSION QUESTIONS

1. Galton became an expert in several different areas. Is it still possible today for a person to have such expertise and breadth in so many fields?

2. Why was Galton so committed to his position on heredity? What evidence did he develop to support his position?

3. Why did Galton need an intelligence test to extend his work in eugenics?

4. What was the basis for Galton's intelligence tests? How successful were they?

5. Does Galton's idea of breeding people to be more intelligent actually work? Why or why not?

6. Eugenics is sometimes broken down into *positive eugenics* and *negative eugenics*. Explain the difference.

CHAPTER EIGHT

A MAN AND HIS DOGS
The Story of Ivan Pavlov

Ivan Petrovich Pavlov (1849–1936) is one of the more unlikely creators of modern psychology. He was trained as a physician, although he never pursued that profession. For much of his career, he maintained that psychology was unscientific, vague, and placed too much emphasis on internal states. Even when he was recognized by the psychological community for his contributions, he was hesitant to be considered part of them. His quirky personal attributes have only added to his historical mystique.

Pavlov was the recipient of an early Nobel Prize (1904) but not for his best-known work. He spent the first part of his career systematically trying to understand the process of digestion. His observations of salivation among his experimental dogs led him to his later interest, the study of learning. This research consumed the second half of his career and not only established many of the ground rules for understanding the process of learning but also assured Pavlov of a permanent place in the history of psychology.

A DIFFICULT BEGINNING

Ivan Pavlov was born on September 14, 1849, in Ryazan, Russia, the son of an Eastern Orthodox priest; his mother was the daughter of a priest. The family lived modestly, taking in boarders and selling produce from its large garden to make ends meet. Ivan's family had been active in the ministry for several generations, and it was expected that Ivan would eventually enter the ministry himself. When Ivan was 8 or 9 years old, he fell from a high fence and injured himself badly (Todes, 2014). He came under the care of his godfather, the superior at a nearby monastery, and it was from him that Ivan later said he acquired his love of learning and the need for discipline.

Ivan's early studies were at the seminary in Ryazan, where he experienced a traditional education in Latin and Greek. He spoke highly of his early education, which he considered rigorous and fulfilling. Pavlov's childhood coincided with a crucial and transitional time in the history of Russia. The new tsar, Alexander II

(1818–1881), who took over the government reins when Pavlov was 6 years old, not only abandoned the old system of serfdom but opened the country to new ideas, including Western ideas. Science came to be highly valued, holding the promise of a better future based on a system of scientific exploration and discovery. Pavlov was deeply affected by the change, which offered the possibility of a new life for him beyond the priesthood. He began reading works with a materialistic orientation—that is, works that described man and the universe with an entirely "natural," non-spiritual explanation.

Many of the new scientific books were scarce, and Pavlov and other students fought for the opportunity to read them. Pavlov was particularly influenced by the works of Ivan Sechenov (1829–1905), a Russian physiologist, whom Pavlov would later call the "father of Russian physiology." Sechenov was the author of *Reflexes of the Brain* (1863), which introduced much of electrophysiology and neurophysiology to medicine. He believed strongly in the role of reflexes and considered the human organism to be nothing more than a well-built machine. Pavlov was also strongly influenced by the newly available Western scientific literature, particularly the work of Charles Darwin. His career plans were now directed toward natural science, with both Sechenov and Darwin as foundational to his approach (Windholz, 1997).

THE MOVEMENT INTO SCIENCE

During his final year of seminary studies, Pavlov made the decision that he would not complete his studies for the priesthood. Instead he used the time to prepare for the entrance exams to St. Petersburg University. Not surprisingly, Pavlov's father was deeply disappointed, resulting in a rift that never completely healed. However, young Pavlov stuck to his decision and entered a new world in St. Petersburg, the Russian center for intellectuals and science. The first year was difficult for him emotionally, but the following year his younger brother Dmitry joined him at the university and proceeded to arrange for all of their basic needs, such as housing and food, even Ivan's social life. Throughout his career, Pavlov would always have someone to help him with the practical side of life. He needed no help with the scientific side.

Physiology became Pavlov's passion, encouraged by the support and direction of Ilya Tsion, a controversial but brilliant professor at the university who briefly became his mentor. In 1875, Pavlov completed a degree at the university, now certain that he wanted a career in research. In fact, it had taken him a year longer to complete the university requirements because he spent so much time on his research.

He decided to continue for a medical degree at the Imperial Medical and Military Academy, which he completed in 1883, in the hope that the degree would make it easier for him to obtain one of the few university positions available in his field. He had no interest in becoming a practicing physician. Medical school was followed by two years of postdoctoral study at the University of Leipzig. While at Leipzig, he was impressed by how well equipped Western laboratories were, certainly as compared to their Russian counterparts. He also learned a style of running a laboratory that he would later incorporate into his own approach.

Pavlov's mentor, Tsion, was drummed out of academia for a variety of reasons, among them his controversial ideas, his abrasive personality, and the fact that he was a Jew. He was also a hard grader. The latter was a particularly crucial issue for many of his students. Pavlov was left without guidance and a strong person to recommend him. As a result, his early positions were at a lower level than his abilities warranted, and he was poorly paid, a great burden for his wife Serafima (Sara) and their growing family. He would later confess—and his life was the living proof—he was very impractical in his daily living. In one telling example, related by psychology historian Raymond Fancher, Pavlov bought his then fiancée a pair of shoes from his meager salary before she left for a trip. But when she reached her destination, she found only one shoe and a note. Pavlov confessed that he had kept the other shoe on his desk as a reminder of her (Fancher & Rutherford, 2012).

Pavlov spent the bulk of the 1880s toiling in someone else's laboratory, frustrated that he did not have the resources to put his own ideas into action. Then in 1891, everything changed. He was appointed to a position in the Institute of Experimental Medicine as well as to a professorship at the Military-Medical Academy. Now he not only had the financial resources for his family, but he also had the laboratory resources to establish his own research agenda. One of the elements that contributed to his success was his insistence on sterile conditions when conducting surgery on animals, an idea that was controversial at the time.

Despite the impractical qualities of his home life, Pavlov's work was focused and systematic to a degree that approached an obsession. The value he placed on science was enormous, often causing him to ignore social conventions. He was known as a demanding supervisor, frequently yelling at subordinates if he was dissatisfied with their work. But he would also tell his underlings to disregard his outbursts—his behavior was simply in the service of science. In 1893, Alfred Nobel donated enough money to the laboratory to enable Pavlov to double its size. Nobel hoped that Pavlov would investigate some of the health issues that had been plaguing him, including digestive problems. He even offered specific problems for Pavlov to investigate. Pavlov was partially accommodating, but he also used the money to build a two-story laboratory that included all of the amenities that had only been a dream before (Todes, 2014).

RESEARCH ON SALIVATION

Pavlov's choice of dogs as his primary experimental animals was the result of careful deliberation. Dogs were available at low cost, and they also had a digestive system resembling that of humans. Pavlov considered dogs to be particularly intelligent animals and active participants in the research. Over time, he would employ more than one hundred dogs in his laboratory.

Pavlov's early independent research grew out of work that he had been exposed to during his postdoctoral studies. It involved creating an artificial pouch or stomach in his experimental dogs in an attempt to understand the role of gastric juices. The first dog to successfully survive such an operation was named Druzhok (or "Little Friend" in Russian), an animal whose digestive processes Pavlov and his coworkers carefully observed for 3 years. After reaching some tentative conclusions, they followed up their research by verifying the results with a dog named Sultan.

The research was eminently successful, unlocking many of the mysteries of digestion, particularly by clarifying the adaptive capacity of gastric juices. Pavlov summarized his digestive research in *Lectures on the Work of the Main Digestive Glands* (1897), giving credit to his coworkers by name. This was the research for which Pavlov received the Nobel Prize. But in the process of conducting his research, he became aware of a "psychic" component related to digestive processes that he could not explain solely in physiological terms.

Pavlov found that it was not only the presence of food that stimulated the production of gastric juices but also the presence of environmental cues that were seemingly neutral. For instance, his dogs might begin to salivate in anticipation of food when a door was opened or when the usual caretaker approached the dog near to feeding time. Pavlov realized that he was no longer dealing with a response that was strictly physiological. The animal had learned a new response. Further, Pavlov reasoned, it was not the glands themselves that were responsible for the salivation but something in the brain. For him, the study of salivation was actually a way of studying brain function.

Beginning about 1897, Pavlov dedicated the remainder of his life to researching this phenomenon. Rather than using a stomach pouch to gather his data, he was able to operate on the salivary glands of his dogs so that they were exposed, and the saliva could be more easily collected. One of the reasons for his success was that, in addition to his insistence on high antiseptic standards, he was a masterful surgeon, aided by the fact that he was ambidextrous. He did not actually conduct much of the research himself. Rather, he supervised a laboratory with a few permanent workers and a raft of graduate student researchers, several of whose work was crucial to his overall achievements.

▸ **Image 8.1** Ivan Pavlov in his laboratory

The type of learning he researched was later named *classical conditioning*. It was called *classical* because it came to be regarded as the first experimental study of learning. But it was called *conditioning* through a mistranslation. Pavlov described this type of learning as conditional on cues from the environment (Todes, 1997). The mistranslation has stayed. In its current usage among psychologists, *conditioning* has become a synonym for *learning*. When Pavlov received his Nobel Prize in 1904, he devoted most of his acceptance speech to the new "psychic" phenomenon that he was researching, not to his previous work on digestion.

CLASSICAL CONDITIONING

The type of learning that Pavlov researched had very specific characteristics. It began with a reflex or response that was already a natural part of the organism; that is, it was not a learned response. Examples would include a blinking response when a puff of air is directed at the eyes or the well-known patellar (knee-jerk) response when a specific location on the knee is tapped. In Pavlov's research, the focus was on salivation as a natural response to the presentation of food. In this instance, the food would be called the *unconditioned stimulus* or the unlearned stimulus. The salivation would be termed the *unconditioned response* or the unlearned response.

Pavlov's insight was to recognize that repeated association between the unconditioned stimulus and a previously neutral stimulus was the essential element for classical learning. For instance, if a neutral stimulus such as a bell were to be presented along with the unconditioned stimulus, it would take on the properties of the unconditioned stimulus. After a number of pairings, the bell itself would be able to elicit salivation. In the language of the paradigm, it would become the conditioned (or learned) stimulus. The salivation that followed would be termed the conditioned (or learned) response.

Pavlov's research would go much beyond his initial discovery. In the years that followed, he would uncover many basic rules of learning—and forgetting. He demonstrated, for instance, that if the unconditioned stimulus and the conditioned stimulus ceased to be paired, over time the conditioned stimulus would lose its power to elicit the response. In other words, a form of forgetting (or extinction) would take place. If the pairing was reinstituted, the conditioned response would reoccur quickly and strongly, a phenomenon he termed *spontaneous recovery*, suggesting that the response had not really gone away but had only been hidden. Additional research was conducted on the phenomenon of stimulus generalization, a condition under which the dog would respond to a conditioned stimulus that was similar to the stimulus on which it had been trained but not identical to it.

Pavlov and his students were able to demonstrate the phenomenon of discrimination learning by training the experimental dogs to respond to one stimulus but not to another. For instance, they could be trained to respond to a circle but not to an oval. After the successful discrimination was learned, the oval was modified in steps so that it began to resemble the circle. As the oval changed, the experimental dogs became agitated. When it finally became difficult for the dogs to discriminate between the circle and the oval on which they had been trained, they became severely agitated. Some of them wrestled with their harnesses, whined, and tried to leave the experimental situation. Pavlov declared that he had created an "experimental neurosis" and speculated about the implications for human development. It was a topic that he would explore further in his later years. Others would take up the topic after Pavlov's death.

Pavlov produced hundreds of papers from his laboratory, most of them based on research from his workers, many of whom were physicians looking for advanced doctoral degrees. A two-year degree from Pavlov's laboratory would not only increase their stature as physicians but almost surely guarantee them a higher income. Pavlov created an extremely efficient laboratory, assigning topics, overseeing the research, and eventually closely editing the papers that emerged. He used all of the research that emanated from his laboratory to formulate a theory of higher mental activity. He insisted that his theory was entirely physiological, although it is clear that it was a psychological one.

CRITICISMS OF PAVLOV'S RESEARCH

Many researchers found Pavlov's work to represent a crucial turning point for psychology. In their view, he demonstrated that psychology could use completely objective methods to solve many of the problems they posed. In short, he opened up the possibility of psychology as a science on a par with other natural sciences. In Russia, the approach was sometimes referred to as "objective psychology." In America, Pavlov's work was seen as an important pillar for the development of behaviorism, a school of psychology that dominated the discipline for decades.

During his lifetime Pavlov was also the subject of criticism from other researchers. One of his own countrymen, Vladimir Bekhterev (1857–1927), had harsh words for many aspects of Pavlov's work. Bekhterev had developed a theory of associated reflexes that was very much like that of Pavlov. However, he used mild electrical stimulation to achieve his results. He argued that Pavlov's use of salivation as his prime experimental target was fraught with errors. For one thing, in order to measure salivation, Pavlov was required to perform surgery, a difficult procedure if it was to be applied to humans. Moreover, the degree of salivation was dependent on the degree of hunger present, an association that could contaminate the experimental results. Finally, Bekhterev considered salivation to be a relatively trivial piece of behavior.

Pavlov did not take the criticism lightly, characterizing Bekhterev's work as shoddy and unsystematic. Some have argued that if John B. Watson, the father of American behaviorism, had taken his cues from the work of Bekhterev rather than Pavlov, it would be Bekhterev's name that would be better known today.

Pavlov was also criticized by animal-rights groups. They considered his research cruel and asked that it be limited to research that they approved. Pavlov offered a sympathetic response, noting his own love of animals and the deep sorrow he felt when any of them were lost during surgery. However, he pointed out the necessity of animal research in many areas, such as drug research. If animal research was not permitted, he noted, the only choice was to experiment with humans. If criticism from animal-rights groups were not enough, Pavlov's wife was also critical of his research. Serafima was deeply religious and believed that some of her husband's studies were based on a philosophy that undercut a belief in God.

ATTITUDE TOWARD PSYCHOLOGY

Pavlov was not simply a passive critic of psychology; he actively opposed the field in many ways. For most of his professional life, he was a materialist, committed to explaining behavior in purely physiological terms. He argued that when psychologists tried to understand behavior by using such terms as *mind* and *consciousness*, they were not being scientists (Kimble, 1991). He reserved particular scorn for the Gestalt school of psychology. Their global approach to explaining behavior was incomprehensible to him, especially because of its explicit antireductionist stance. For Pavlov, the only way to understand a phenomenon was to break it down into its elements (Todes, 2014).

A psychologist to whom Pavlov was favorably disposed, at least initially, was Edward L. Thorndike, who would become one of America's leading psychologists. Both Pavlov and Thorndike had little use for exploring internal states. Learning was something that began with the environment. However, Thorndike's approach was different in many ways from Pavlov's. Among other things, Thorndike ignored built-in physiological responses; unconditioned stimuli or responses had no place in his system. He concentrated entirely on the power of the environment. Later, his approach would be recognized as another major paradigm for understanding learning. As Pavlov understood Thorndike's system more fully, his evaluation of it and Thorndike grew less positive.

CONTRIBUTIONS TO MENTAL HEALTH RESEARCH

Pavlov had been interested in mental health issues from an early age. Some writers have speculated that his mother's unstable emotional life may have sparked this interest. In the last half dozen years of his life, his interests in mental health became more explicit. With the assistance of psychiatrists, he observed the behavior of patients at various clinics and conducted interviews with some of them. He had earlier detected temperamental differences among his animals, and he considered these differences to be a crucial element in understanding abnormal behavior. Central to his thesis was the balance between excitatory and inhibitory states. In his view, when individuals of a weak temperamental type were faced with difficult environmental circumstances, the result could be a variety of neuroses. In addition, he believed a weak temperamental type provided the basis for schizophrenia to develop.

THE LATER YEARS

With his receipt of the Nobel Prize, Pavlov's fame continued to grow. Eventually, he would run three separate research laboratories. Scientists traveled from around the world to learn his techniques. He was famous and financially secure, with his four surviving children all involved in worthwhile careers. But in 1914, when he was 65 years old, his life began to change dramatically. Russia entered the Great War and suffered enormously as a result. The loss of life was massive, and the country became increasingly poor and unable to meet the needs of its people. Tsar Nicholas II was held responsible for the state of the country and was overthrown in a revolution that promised a redistribution of wealth for all of its citizens. Eventually, the tsar and his entire family were murdered.

Although the war with Germany ended in 1917, civil war still raged. By the time the Bolsheviks (later renamed Communists) obtained absolute power in 1921, the country was in ruins. Pavlov's laboratory could no longer function for the lack of such basic resources as food for his dogs. Pavlov himself suffered. His Nobel Prize money was confiscated, and he was reduced to growing his own food. He wrote to the government, asking to emigrate. At age 70, he felt that he still had a few good years of research left to him and he wanted to complete his mission.

Surprisingly, his letter came to the attention of Vladimir Lenin himself, the premier of the then-Soviet Union. The government decided to provide everything Pavlov needed for his research, so strongly did its leaders believe in him as a symbol of the country (Todes, 2000). From then until his death, Pavlov's laboratory prospered, regaining the facilities it once held as the most highly funded laboratory in the country. The new funds didn't stop Pavlov from continuing to criticize the new government for its lack of religious tolerance and academic freedom, but his fame provided a measure of protection. Later he would grudgingly admit that at least the new government understood the value of science.

Pavlov continued to work well into advanced age. He delved into eugenics, seeing in it, as many other scientists of the time did, an opportunity for science to improve the human race. He became interested in studying the aging process, both in himself and in his dogs. He found that many of his older dogs retained elements of their earlier conditioning, although it was difficult for them to learn new material. He saw this having a direct counterpart in the human condition.

Twice he traveled to the United States to give lectures. On his visit in 1923, he was in Grand Central Station in New York City when he was robbed of all of his travel money. His sponsors for the trip paid his expenses. In 1929, he was a principal speaker at the Ninth International Congress of Psychology held at Yale University, clear recognition of the value that psychologists placed on his work.

At the age of 86, Pavlov contracted pneumonia, his second bout within a year. He died on February 27, 1936, and was making observations on himself virtually up to the moment of death. His death resulted in an outpouring of praise for him and his work, not only in Russia but throughout the world. He had become a major contributor to the science of physiology, but he had also played an important role in changing psychology from a study of conscious states to one that focused on behavior. As a result of his contributions, his name has entered into the general culture in a way that few people have experienced.

REVIEW/DISCUSSION QUESTIONS

1. What did Pavlov bring to the study of learning that was missing before? Describe Pavlov's model for learning.

2. What are some of the elements that contributed to Pavlov's research success?

3. Why did Pavlov initially find himself in agreement with the work of E. L. Thorndike? How is classical conditioning different from other forms of learning?

4. How did Pavlov later apply his principles to the study of abnormal psychology?

5. Why was Pavlov so reluctant to be associated with psychology?

NOTE

The volume by Daniel Todes (2014) cited in this chapter (see References) is the most comprehensive work on the life and work of Pavlov currently available and an excellent resource. It consists of 700-plus pages of text and more than 100 additional pages of notes and bibliography.

CHAPTER NINE

HERMANN RORSCHACH AND HIS (IN)FAMOUS TEST

As a young man studying in the local Swiss *gymnasium*, Hermann Rorschach (1884–1922) was nicknamed *klex* (or inkblot) by his fellow students. The designation reflected both Hermann's artistic talent as well as his interest in a popular game of his youth called *klexography*. Neither Hermann nor his fellow students could have predicted that inkblots would become a prime professional interest of Hermann or that they would secure his place in the history of psychology.

While still a medical student, Rorschach was exposed to the work of two giants in psychiatry, Sigmund Freud and Carl Jung. Each of them was offering exciting new explanations not only for mental illness but for the nature of man itself. Their contributions were part of a form of dynamic psychiatry that was beginning to emerge while Rorschach was still in the early stages of his career. He listened to what they had to say, and although he remained skeptical of parts of their theories, he incorporated many of their ideas into his own work.

The end result of his thinking was the creation of the Rorschach inkblot test, a personality test consisting of ten cards, most in black and white but a few in color. The test owed its existence not only to then-current theories of psychodynamic psychiatry but also to Rorschach's practical work with psychiatric patients. Ever the amateur artist, Rorschach saw meaningful differences in the way people responded to his inkblots, whether they were psychiatric patients or friends.

The test has come to be emblematic of the mysterious powers of psychology and psychologists. Some professionals believe that the way individuals respond to the cards exposes an inner personality, aspects of which may be unknown even to the individuals themselves. Although Rorschach would not live to see it—he died prematurely at the age of 37—his test became one of the most popular and controversial tests in all of psychology. Usually referred to simply as the Rorschach, it has been used in ways that its author never intended. Praised by some for its power to unveil the unconscious, it has been damned by others for its lack of reliability and validity, sometimes described as nothing more than a cheap parlor trick.

Thousands of research papers have been written about the test, and it has been used in a variety of venues outside of therapy, including job selection and forensic evaluations. The name itself has entered the culture in multiple ways, often used to describe any ambiguous situation that reflects personal rather than objective values and impressions. Despite the ups and downs of its popularity, the test continues to be used, helped by strong supporters convinced of its powers. And it remains as controversial as ever.

EARLY LIFE

Hermann Rorschach was born on November 8, 1884, in Zürich, Switzerland, but spent most of his early life in the picturesque town of Schaffhausen, Switzerland. His father was a school teacher and artist; his mother, a housewife. His mother died when Hermann was only 8 years old and his father when he was 18. Raised subsequently by a cold and rigid stepmother, he and his younger siblings, Paul and Anna, were desperate to escape her control as well as the limited financial circumstances in which they found themselves.

Young Hermann was torn between a career as a scientist and a career as an artist. At the age of 19, he chose to enroll at the University of Zürich to pursue medical studies, but art would remain a lifelong hobby. At the time, medicine had little to offer by way of a cure. Physicians were frequently knowledgeable about the course of an illness but helpless to mount an effective intervention. Similarly, psychiatrists were learning to catalogue various mental ailments but could offer mostly limited and ineffective treatments. Fortunately for Rorschach, psychiatry was undergoing a dramatic change, and nearby Burghölzli Hospital in Zürich was one of its centers. Although Rorschach never worked officially at Burghölzli, the University of Zürich and the hospital were closely affiliated, and he was able to benefit greatly from their association (Searls, 2017).

Perhaps the greatest direct influence on Rorschach was Eugen Bleuler, the director of the hospital. Bleuler had taken an approach to the treatment of the patients under his care that was unusual for the time. Generally, patients with serious mental illness were believed to have organic diseases of the brain. Though many of Bleuler's patients were schizophrenic and considered hopeless, Bleuler listened to them, trying to understand both their symptoms and their stories. Rorschach was impressed with Bleuler's attitudes toward his patients. Earlier, Bleuler had invented the modern term for schizophrenia to replace the previous designation, *dementia praecox*, the latter suggesting an early appearing and lifelong disorder, a view of schizophrenia that Bleuler found too negative.

Another important figure at Burghölzli was Carl Jung, a fast-rising star of the psychiatry world with new ideas about the causes of mental illness. Although Rorschach had little direct contact with Jung, he was open to the new psychodynamic ideas being offered by both Jung and the Austrian physician and psychiatrist Sigmund Freud. Indeed, they would have a profound impact on his thinking about mental illness.

In 1906, Rorschach met Olga Stempelin, a fellow medical student and a native of Kazan, Russia. (Historian Henri Ellenberger was able to speak personally with many friends and acquaintances of Rorschach, as well as with Rorschach's wife, Olga. Much of the personal information available on Rorschach can be gleaned from his accounts.) What emerges is a portrait of a friendly, cheerful, and modest scholar. He was tall and blond, with a wide range of interests, but with a particular interest in visual art.

In 1909, shortly after completing his final exams that allowed him to practice medicine, Rorschach visited Russia and stayed for 4 months, working in various venues. He and Olga became engaged, but they didn't have enough money to get married, nor did they want to get married on borrowed money. Instead, Rorschach returned to Switzerland to work at a hospital clinic in Münsterlingen, leaving Olga behind temporarily. Even his return was not without difficulty. Rorschach was stopped at the border and forced to pay a bribe in order to leave the country (Searls, 2017).

ESTABLISHING A CAREER

After Rorschach settled into his new job, Olga joined him, and they were married in a civil ceremony in 1910. The hospital at Münsterlingen served more than 400

Album / Alamy Stock Photo

▸ **Image 9.1**   Hermann Rorschach c. 1910

patients, many of them diagnosed as schizophrenic, and the support staff was limited. But Hermann and Olga seemed content there. Rorschach devised a variety of activities for his patients, including plays and art pursuits. He seemed to have a special ability to relate to his patients. He composed several scientific works based on observations of his patients. He also wrote popular pieces for newspapers, apparently for the money.

Around this time, Rorschach made his first professionally related foray into inkblots. In 1911, he worked with a school-teacher friend, Konrad Gehring, to test children and some of his patients on various inkblots. Rorschach was particularly interested in seeing how the responses compared to Jung's word association test. The testing was unsystematic, and no publications were generated from their tests. But they laid some groundwork for what was to come later.

Several other people had explored the use of inkblots before Rorschach. Justinus Kerner (1786–1862), a German physician, had assembled a group of blots that he felt gave him access to a hidden and secret world. Although Rorschach knew of his work, he appears not to have been directly influenced by it. Alfred Binet (1856–1911), the famous French psychologist, had also conducted research with inkblots, seeing them primarily as a test of imagination. Binet's work became well known among groups of psychologists, and eventually parts of it were adopted by U.S. psychologists. However, Rorschach had something very different in mind for his inkblots.

RUSSIA AGAIN

In December 1913, Rorschach and Olga left for Russia. Accounts vary as to how long they remained, but by the time Rorschach returned to Switzerland, he had lost his position at Münsterlingen and was forced to take a less well-paying position at the Waldau Mental Hospital in Bern. To complicate the situation even further, World War I had broken out in the interim and Olga, who had remained in Russia temporarily, was not allowed to leave the country (Ellenberger, 1993).

When Olga was finally allowed to return from Russia, they decided that Hermann's meager salary and the rooms made available for their living quarters were not enough for both of them. Rorschach applied and was accepted for a position at an asylum in Herisau, Switzerland. It was in Herisau that he completed his family. A daughter, Elisabeth, was born in 1917; a son, Ulrich Wadin was born in 1919. It was here that a new interest began to take up all of his spare time. Rorschach had begun to work on a book that had as its focus the diagnostic value of an inkblot test.

THE TEST

This renewed interest in inkblots appeared to come about because of a published dissertation by a Polish student named Szymon Hens who worked with Eugen Bleuler at the University of Zürich. On a trip to Zürich, Rorschach met briefly with Hens. Although Hens used a large sample for his dissertation, contrasting a normal and emotionally disturbed group, he did little more than count the responses. Rorschach saw so many more possibilities. Despite his other significant duties, Rorschach now devoted as much time as he could to his new project (Ellenberger, 1993).

The first thing Rorschach needed to do was to make a set of inkblots that would be appropriate for the work he had in mind. Far from being random choices, the cards he created employed his knowledge of art although they purposely lacked any sense of artistry. They were symmetrical, but also too detailed to be genuine inkblots. They were meant to be vague and draw the viewer in. Red was chosen as one of the colors because it would stand out more to the viewer. As Rorschach conceived it, the experience for someone responding to the inkblots was supposed to be fun. Initially, he did not see it as a test at all but a way of exploring how different people see things. He soon changed his mind (Searls, 2017).

Unlike Binet, Rorschach did not see his instrument as merely a way to assess imagination. His experience with it suggested that responses could not only differentiate levels of intelligence and other aspects of personality but also subtypes of mental illness. He began exploring ways to score the test. But what kinds of responses were important? What if an individual refused to respond to a specific card? Did that have meaning? Or if an individual responded only to the whole card and not to details? How did individuals respond to the color cards? Was movement implied in their response? There were so many questions that had to be answered. A system of scoring the cards was evolving although it was not based on any theory—it came from Rorschach's experience presenting the inkblots to various people. And he had not yet established norms. These were all shortcomings that would prove more problematic later.

PSYCHODIAGNOSTICS

Despite his efforts to interest publishers in his ideas, Rorschach was met with regular rejection. One of the issues was a financial one. The publishers recognized that the inkblots would be expensive to reproduce. When the book was finally accepted, the number of inkblots had been reduced from 15 to 10, but even that was not the end of Rorschach's difficulties. Publication was delayed for many months due to technical problems, and when the first printing of 1,200 copies appeared in June 1921, the size and color of the cards had been changed. Undaunted, Rorschach used the delay in printing to explore his ideas even further.

His book *Psychodiagnostics* contained the results of his experiments with both normal and disturbed patients using his diagnostic inkblot cards as well as principles of interpretation. The book had barely been published before Rorschach had ideas for changing it. Rorschach's magnus opus was more than a book about his inkblot test and an evaluation of personality. He believed his test was capable of describing the ebb and flow of development through the life span. It could even be used as an anthropological tool that could characterize ways of thinking among races. Ultimately, "he considered his *Psychodiagnostics* a universal key for the deciphering and understanding of human culture and civilization throughout all the world and all the centuries" (Ellenberger, 1993, p. 222).

Not everyone was enthusiastic about his work. When he presented his early ideas to local professional societies, there was little interest. One of the clever things he did that gained him adherents was to engage in blind diagnoses. He asked individuals to administer the test to someone they knew and send him the responses. But they were instructed not to include basic information about the individual tested, even excluding gender and age. Rorschach would then proceed to describe the person psychologically. His hit rate was impressive. One of the people impressed with the results was Eugen Bleuler, Rorschach's former mentor. Ultimately, he became a devoted fan of the technique (Searls, 2017).

When Bleuler spoke favorably of the book, Rorschach thought he was in the clear. However, other responses were not so favorable. In particular, Rorschach was criticized for the subjectivity of the test and its lack of a theoretical underpinning, the latter issue being one that Rorschach agreed with. He knew that many things in his book were tentative and that much more work was required. But when the book proved to be a financial failure as well, he lapsed into depression.

Rorschach had begun to suffer abdominal pains toward the end of March 1922. For a variety of reasons, he did not take any immediate medical action. According to one report, his wife Olga, who was also trained as a physician, thought he was suffering from something minor. When he was finally brought to the emergency room of the hospital a week after first experiencing symptoms, it was determined that he was suffering from appendicitis. Plans were made for surgery although it was recognized that the delay in diagnosis did not bode well. He died on the operating room table the next morning, April 1, 1922, from peritonitis due to a burst appendix. It was only 7 months after publication of his masterwork. He was 37 years old. When he died, he took many of his newer ideas to the grave with him (Ellenberger, 1993).

AFTER RORSCHACH'S DEATH

Rorschach was mourned for his warm personal qualities and for his great skills as a psychiatrist. At first, it appeared that his entire work on *Psychodiagnostics* would die with him. It didn't help that the book, written quickly, was poorly organized and difficult to read. There was another, perhaps greater, issue. Rorschach had worked alone in a nonuniversity position. As such, his work automatically lacked the prestige that would have been afforded anyone who worked in affiliation with a university professor.

Several prominent academic psychologists denounced its methodology, among them such notables as William Stern and Georg Müller. One bright spot occurred a year after Rorschach's death. Ludwig Binswanger, a prominent Swiss phenomenologist, wrote a favorable review of the volume, pointing to its potential use in evaluating patients during the process of psychoanalysis. A few study groups focusing on the test were established in Switzerland, but none of the groups seemed to have much of an impact. The fate of Rorschach's masterwork continued to be in jeopardy.

For many years, the test existed largely in professional limbo. But as World War II approached, it was rescued by a visiting psychiatrist from the United States. David Levy spent a sabbatical in Europe, working with Rorschach's friend Emil Oberholzer. When Levy returned to the United States, he brought with him a copy of an essay by Rorschach and several other pieces of Rorschach material, including the book and the inkblot plates. Eventually, he would spend a large part of his professional life introducing the test and its scoring to an eager U.S. audience (Searls, 2017).

Levy helped develop acceptance of the Rorschach in another way. He had a student by the name of Samuel Beck (1896–1980) who was searching for a dissertation topic. Levy gave him a copy of Rorschach's book, and Beck needed little more encouragement. The study of the Rorschach became Beck's lifelong work.

Bruno Klopfer (1900–1971), an emigre from Nazi Germany, would also become an important leader of the Rorschach in the United States, in direct competition with Samuel Beck. Carl Jung had sponsored Klopfer for a position in Switzerland and Klopfer soon found himself learning and administering the Rorschach, mostly for vocational purposes. A year later, when he came to the United States, he realized that people were eager to learn about the test and he began teaching it. Klopfer eventually became one of the leading authorities on the test. He founded a newsletter titled *The Rorschach Exchange* and, in 1936, was one of the founders of the Rorschach Institute. The main purpose of the Institute was to conduct appropriate research, publish relevant material, and ensure adequate training (O'Roark & Exner, 1989).

The Rorschach arrived in the United States at precisely the right time. Although academic psychology was still heavily invested in an experimental approach, World War II brought a new clinical emphasis to psychology. Returning veterans were in need of mental health services, and clinical psychologists were ready to help them. The Rorschach was welcomed as an additional aid for psychologists who had a limited number of tools available to them. Interest in the Rorschach was also arising in other areas. Psychoanalysis was experiencing a boom, and the Rorschach, with its emphasis on unconscious motivation, tied the two together. Anthropologists were also using it to understand differences in cultures, consistent with their increasing use of psychodynamic principles as an interpretive tool.

Still, a battle continued between the two leading interpreters of the Rorschach—Beck and Klopfer. Beck had a strong empirical grounding and was reluctant to change anything from the original formulation that could not be demonstrated empirically. Klopfer felt free to add any interpretation to the test that fit his own experience. It would take a third party to try to iron out the vast differences between their interpretations. Marguerite Hertz (1899–1992) was one of those who devoted her career to reconciling the conflict. Above all, she stressed the need to standardize the test in every way, including the administration and the scoring (Kessler, 1994).

The individual who would finally bring together many of the competing forces into one system was John Exner (1928–2006). As a graduate student, he became fascinated by the Rorschach and was eventually able to arrange summer internships with both Beck and Klopfer. Later, he developed contacts with the leaders of the other major interpretive systems. Concluding that each of the systems had strengths and faults, he set about to establish a comprehensive system.

What at first had appeared to be a relatively simple task involved Exner for the rest of his life. In 1974, he published *The Rorschach: A Comprehensive System*, which standardized the best elements of the earlier systems. Eventually he conducted highly valued workshops teaching his approach. Additional volumes and editions of his books followed, which included new samples and various refinements. Active in professional associations, Exner kept interest in the Rorschach alive through his presidencies of the Society for Personality Assessment (earlier the Rorschach Institute) and the International Rorschach Society. He was also a curator of the Hermann Rorschach Museum and Archives in Bern, Switzerland (Erdberg & Weiner, 2007).

CURIOUS USES OF THE RORSCHACH

In 1945, a military tribunal was convened to prosecute Nazis involved in war crimes following World War II. The trials are generally known as the Nuremberg trials, named for their location in Germany. In order to determine if the defendants were fit to stand trial, the prisoners were subjected to a series of interviews and psychological tests. The Rorschach was one of the evaluative devices. The results were controversial and not immediately available, though eventually they were published. Overall, they did not demonstrate what had been expected. There was no single personality type that characterized the defendants. They were not psychopathic monsters. Instead, they showed a great deal of variability, several with strong, aggressive personalities, not unlike what might be found in business executives.

An outsider might conclude that the test was painfully wrong, but another interpretation was offered by the Rorschach experts. Perhaps the evil behavior of these men did not lie in their person as much as it lay in their environment and circumstances. Fifteen years later, a related trial took place. Adolph Eichmann, the mastermind behind the slaughter of six million Jews, was captured in Argentina and put on trial in Israel. He also was given the Rorschach, and the administering psychologist concluded that he was an extreme psychopath. But to many, he appeared to be no more than a simple bureaucrat. His defense was that he was simply following orders. Such a defense might seem outrageous, but studies by psychologist Stanley Milgram (discussed in Chapter 23) demonstrated how much individuals are prone to obey authority, even when the results may be injurious to another person. If nothing else, the results of these high-profile cases began to call into question the accuracy of the Rorschach as well as other psychological instruments.

CRITICISMS OF THE RORSCHACH

Psychological tests are typically evaluated on several standards. Have norms been established for the instrument with appropriate comparison groups? Is the administration standardized? How strong are the reliability and validity? Although reliability can be measured in different ways, essentially it refers to consistency of measurement. If there is no consistency, how much faith can be put in the instrument? Validity is the degree to which a test measures what it purports to measure. Validity can also be measured in different ways, but typically it is demonstrated by comparisons to some outside criteria.

In the 1960s, when so many different systems for scoring and interpreting the Rorschach were prominent, it was impossible to achieve any degree of certainty on the reliability or validity of the test. Hundreds of studies were conducted with frequent contradictory results. As a result, several strong supporters of the instrument changed their minds and became critics. With the development of the Exner Comprehensive System, the psychometric properties of the instrument became stronger. Among the advantages of the Exner system were greater standardization and quantification plus the availability of norms and scoring guidelines. Not surprisingly, these changes led to more acceptable levels of inter-rater agreement and general reliability. Most graduate programs began teaching the Exner system, and the previous approaches were deemphasized. However, criticisms of the instrument would again resurface.

Although Exner and his associates produced a substantial amount of literature supporting their method, critics noted that it was done mostly "in house" and not subject to peer review. Moreover, several doctoral dissertations presented results that contradicted aspects of Exner's method. A debate on the merits of the Exner system developed. One aspect of the system subjected to severe criticism was the reliability of its scoring, which some found to be much lower than advertised, even below the standard that Exner himself had established. Another aspect of concern was the tendency of the Rorschach to diagnose psychopathology when there was none. In fact, this was a criticism that had haunted the Rorschach from its earliest days. There were other criticisms as well, including questions about the norms. The net impact was to question the Exner system in a way that it had not been questioned before.

Many validity studies have been conducted to determine the ability of the Rorschach to predict various outcomes, such as success at a job or psychopathology. The results from the Rorschach have not been reassuring. Particularly troublesome have been meta-analyses, which combine the results of multiple studies. More recently, some of its former adherents have admitted that it is not a diagnostic tool and was not meant to be one. All of the evidence suggests that the instrument, whatever its positive characteristics, is deeply flawed (Wood, Nezworski, Lilienfeld, & Garb, 2011).

THE RORSCHACH TODAY

The Rorschach is not as popular today as it once was. Surveys suggest it reached its peak use by psychologists sometime in the 1950s and 1960s. Most other "projective" tests have also declined in popularity, along with the decline in psychodynamic theories of psychotherapy. Many graduate programs in clinical psychology once required two semester-long courses on the administration and interpretation of the Rorschach. Now the test is more likely to be combined into a one-semester course covering all nonobjective tests of personality, if it appears in the curriculum at all. The development of the Exner system gave the test renewed life, but even that has begun to fade. Despite attempts to keep the Rorschach plates out of the hands of the public, they are now available on the Internet. Comments vary as to how much the easy availability has affected the integrity of the test.

Instead of the Rorschach, the evaluation of personality has taken a less subjective route with the use of such instruments as the MMPI (Minnesota Multiphasic Personality Inventory). The administration and scoring of the inventory is objective, and while some interpretation may be necessary, it is minimal. However, the Rorschach is still popular among a substantial number of practitioners. It has become particularly prevalent in forensic evaluations. Even among those practitioners who find the traditional scoring to be questionable, many use it instead to encourage clients to talk more openly about themselves.

It is likely that as the current generation of clinical practitioners retire and die, the Rorschach will become even less popular. A lot will depend on graduate programs and how much emphasis they place on the instrument. But Hermann Rorschach's test will probably not disappear completely. Professional Rorschach societies exist in 20 countries, with publications and enthusiastic supporters.

Still the test remains a curiosity. Rorschach himself never intended the test to be used in the way it is. At his death, he was already making plans to change it. The test survived due to the legions of believers looking to find a way to understand the core of personality, both of people and of cultures—one more attempt to characterize and comprehend human complexity.

REVIEW/DISCUSSION QUESTIONS

1. What was Hermann Rorschach's primary goal in creating the inkblot test? What are the basic assumptions behind it?

2. Different methods of scoring and interpreting the test were developed. Who was responsible for the divergent approaches? How are they different?

3. What have been some of the criticisms of the instrument?

4. John Exner was thought to be the "healer" of the Rorschach. Why?

5. What is the status of the test today? How frequently is it used?

NOTE

Readers who wish to learn more about the personal life of Hermann Rorschach, as well as his test, are encouraged to consult the book by Damion Searls cited in this chapter (see References). It is one of the most comprehensive sources available, and with excellent references. The volume by Wood et al., also cited in this chapter, is equally comprehensive, with substantial research citations. It focuses on the test itself and is mostly critical of the instrument.

CHAPTER TEN

THE CASA DEI BAMBINI
Maria Montessori and Her Method

Even as a child there was something special about Maria Montessori. Born on August 31, 1870, in the small village of Chiaravalle, in the province of Ancona, Italy, she had ambitions well beyond those of most young girls of her time and place. When she graduated from medical school in 1896, one of the first female physicians in modern Italy, she became an immediate celebrity and an icon of feminists. But her reputation would ultimately rest on other accomplishments.

While working with children in an institution for the developmentally disabled, she created materials to help educate them despite their supposed limitations. Later she was offered the opportunity to supervise a school for children in a slum section of Rome. To the surprise of many, she accepted. This school, the *Casa dei Bambini* (or Children's House) became her experimental laboratory. The principles, techniques, and materials that she developed there gave rise to an educational system known as the Montessori method, an approach that was later adopted in countries throughout the world and continues to have an impact more than 100 years after its creation.

BEGINNING A CAREER

Maria Montessori's parents moved to Rome when she was about 12 years old, in part to provide better educational opportunities for her. As a young girl, Maria considered several possible vocations, none of them pleasing to her father, who held traditional views on the role of women. But Maria had no intention of being hampered by the gender expectations of her times. One of her earliest choices was to become an engineer; later she decided to study medicine. Her choice was fraught with obstacles beyond her father's disapproval. Her application to the medical school of the University of Rome was rejected by the all-male faculty. Instead, Montessori took science classes for 2 years at the university, at which point she applied again to the medical school. This time she was accepted.

Once in medical school, male students were reluctant to participate in classes with her and subjected her to a variety of petty annoyances, frequently shunning her. She was not allowed to enter a classroom until all the men were seated. Since it was considered improper for Montessori to dissect a body in the presence of male students, she was required to perform her dissections alone and at night. But Maria persevered, and in 1896 she graduated from the medical school of the University of Rome with honors in several subjects. Even her father was impressed with her success and no longer was critical of her vocational choice (Gutek & Gutek, 2016).

Immediately after graduation, Montessori opened a private practice and began working at the university hospital. Her work at the hospital required her to visit local asylums, and it was there that she became concerned with the plight of emotionally disturbed and developmentally disabled children. Gradually she began to see the children as suffering less from a medical problem than from an educational one.

As her views on exceptional children became known, she was offered a position as codirector of a small facility that housed a variety of problem children, some of them thought to be hopeless. Montessori, with colleagues, worked with the children through long days, trying to find the best ways to educate them. She traveled to London and Paris in hopes of discovering the latest educational methods. It wasn't that she denied the limitations in the children under her care—she knew they had limitations, but she wanted to maximize whatever talent they had.

She researched the work of important educators of the past, trying to understand their approaches. Much of Montessori's general belief about children could be traced back to Jean-Jacques Rousseau (1712–1778), the French philosopher. Rousseau had emphasized the need for children to follow their inborn tendencies and not be restricted by the demands of society. He saw development as a natural unfolding of an inner timetable. Montessori latched on to several of these themes as central principles of her method. Eventually, she discarded the role of the traditional teacher. Instead she envisioned a teacher to be that of an organizer who would establish a prepared environment in which children would teach themselves (Lillard, 2017).

Montessori was particularly taken by the work of Jean-Marc Gaspard Itard (1774–1838) and Édouard Séguin (1812–1880). Itard, best known for his work with Victor the Wild Boy of Aveyron, had focused on teaching Victor through sensory exercises that he created. (His story is told in Chapter 2.) Édouard Séguin, briefly a student of Itard near the end of his career, further developed the latter's methods and eventually became well known for his work with developmentally disabled children. Montessori was so impressed with their ideas that she copied out their books by hand, simultaneously translating them from French to Italian. Throughout her life, she acknowledged the debt that her system owed to earlier educators, particularly Séguin.

To her great satisfaction, Montessori had almost immediate educational success with the children in her school. Some of them were so successful in learning to read and write that they outshone the children in the regular schools. Her approach was apparently working. As pleased as she was, the results suggested an important question to her. If her children could do so well, despite their limitations, how effectively were the "normal" children being educated? She concluded that the traditional educational methods of her time needed an overhaul and that her methods might be applicable for all children.

Montessori's work was interrupted in an unanticipated way. She had become close to another physician at the institution, Giuseppe Montesano (1868–1961). Their relationship became intimate, and she became pregnant by him. His family objected to them marrying, and so the couple reached a personal compromise. They agreed to remain unmarried but committed to each other. However, the agreement was short lived. Montesano broke his promise and married another woman. Montessori had been betrayed.

Montessori gave birth to her son, Mario, secretly in 1898. For many years, he was raised by a family outside of Rome, with her visiting only occasionally. He was not told that she was his mother. Montessori kept knowledge of his birth from virtually all of her friends and colleagues. Some speculated that her deep love of children was partially nurtured by the early separation from her son. When Mario reached his teens, Montessori reunited with him. They became inseparable, and together they would spread the word of her method around the world.

Maria left the institution in 1901 to pursue further study at the University of Rome. Her focus this time was not on medicine but on psychology and education. During this period, she also occupied a chair at one of the two women's colleges in Italy and, in 1906, became a professor of anthropology at the University of Rome, in addition to her private practice. All this activity was a prelude to the next, most important, chapter in her life.

THE CASA DEI BAMBINI

The University of Rome, where Montessori had studied and worked, was located near a poor section of Rome called the San Lorenzo Quarter. It was described as one of the most crowded, unsanitary, and crime-ridden sections of Rome. As part of an early urban renewal project, a large apartment complex had been built in the area to accommodate the great number of impoverished locals. But the managers of the building had a problem—when the parents left the apartment complex during the day, they would leave behind a group of approximately 60 young children to fend for themselves.

The children, roughly ages 3 to 7—mostly too young for school—had formed little gangs and were going around the complex systematically defacing it. The sponsoring real estate association, in an attempt to save on the constant repair and repainting of their building, approached Montessori. They hoped she would be willing to supervise a day care center in their building to accommodate the young children. To their surprise, she said "yes." But she had more than a day care center in mind—she was planning to establish a school.

In many ways, Montessori had been preparing for this opportunity for most of her professional life. She would finally have the chance to apply her methods to "normal" children. The new school officially opened on January 6, 1907, in an apartment house at Via dei Marsi 58. Montessori dubbed it the *Casa dei Bambini*, or Children's House. She said it was her laboratory. And, indeed, it was through her observations of the children during this early period that she began to formulate her educational system. At the same time that she was developing her instructional techniques, she was also constructing a theory of early development. As a result, she was becoming not only an educator but a psychologist as well.

The school had a limited budget, and Montessori was forced to use small tables in the classroom instead of the traditional desks. Locked cabinets were installed to hold the instructional material. Slowly, Montessori began to change the physical environment for the children, making the cabinets lower and accessible. Friends of hers donated furniture such as armchairs, which Montessori cut down to make the items child sized.

She preferred tables and chairs that were light in color and weight. When children made marks on the furniture, sometimes with dirty hands, she wanted them to see the marks they left behind. Similarly, if the children bumped into a chair or desk, she wanted it to move so the children would be aware of their awkwardness. In both instances, she intended the material to lead to self-correction. Because of her other duties, she could not be present in the classroom at all times. Instead, a young woman she had trained was in charge of the one-room school. In retrospect, Montessori considered these supposed limitations to be advantages. A traditional teacher, for instance, would likely be stuck in the old ways of teaching and reluctant to use Montessori's new methods.

PRINCIPLES FOR THE CLASSROOM

Through her observations, Montessori began noting behaviors in her children that she felt had been unappreciated by other educators. Among the first ones were the children's capacity for deep concentration and their need for repetition, a conclusion that grew out of her observations of one child. Among the materials that Montessori had brought into her school was a wooden form board. It required nothing more of the child than to insert wooden pieces of various sizes and shapes into corresponding spaces on the board. Montessori noticed a particular child who seemed to take the task very seriously.

The 3-year-old girl took the wooden pieces out of their slots, mixed them up, and then replaced them in their proper slots over and over again. Montessori counted. The child repeated the complete exercise 42 times. When Montessori tried to disrupt the child by moving the armchair she was sitting in, the child ignored her. But when the child was done, she was completely done. She put the task aside and never went back to it. It was as if she had satisfied some unnamed, inner need. Once the need was satisfied, there was no reason to revisit the form board (Standing, 1962).

Montessori made other observations that would eventually find their way into her system, many of them based on spontaneous behaviors of the children. Contrary to typical expectations, she observed the children's need for order and completeness. The youngest children actually preferred to keep the classroom neat. As a result, her classroom was arranged so that children could retrieve the material they wanted to work with on their own and return it as well. Surprisingly, she saw little need for outside reinforcement, neither reward nor punishment, a staple of most educational approaches. The children were being reinforced by the activities themselves. She wrote that the children seemed to prefer work to play. She also observed a great sense of personal dignity in her children, which she was certain not to violate. Later, she would conclude that in a well-run Montessori classroom, the children engaged in spontaneous self-discipline (Standing, 1962).

Among her most important ideas was her belief in sensitive periods in the development of her students, an idea that would be a cornerstone of ethological developmental theory decades later. She believed there were periods in development when children were more likely to benefit from certain kinds of learning than at other times. Language was one of the most obvious examples. Children seemed to have a special ability to learn language in their first dozen years or so. After that, language learning becomes a much more difficult task. It is as if a window of opportunity opens but remains open only for a limited number of years. She would soon suggest the possibility of sensitive periods operating in a whole host of abilities and behaviors, from color differentiation to success as an altar boy. She argued that children learned differently at the youngest ages, something she called "the absorbent mind." However, the single item that propelled her system into one of great visibility was the so-called "explosion into writing."

LEARNING "EXPLOSIONS"

Montessori prepared the children for reading and writing by having them trace sandpaper letters with their fingers while giving them the sounds of the letters. (It probably helped that the children's language was Italian.) She made no specific attempt to teach them reading or writing. It was a method Itard had developed to teach Victor, the Wild Boy of Aveyron, to read—part of his so-called physiologic method.

In a dramatic passage in one of her books, Montessori later described the results of her method. She had taken the children to the roof of their building to get some air. She gave one of the children a piece of chalk and asked him to draw a picture on the roof. He complied but suddenly began shouting, "I can write. I know how to write." The boy knelt down on the roof and proceeded to write a series of words on the floor of the roof terrace, writing them completely for the first time, words he had never written before. Not understanding the preparation that had gone into his performance, he acted as if the words had come to him out of thin air.

As he continued with his task, the other children gathered about him. When they understood the source of his joy, they asked for chalk too and proceeded to write on the roof "with a species of frenzied joy." None of them had ever taken chalk in hand for the purpose of writing. Yet they wrote words spontaneously and completely. When the children were followed up with, it was found that they were writing everywhere, including the floors of their homes and even on the crust of their loaves of bread. Many of the parents, in order to save their homes from further destruction, were persuaded to give their children presents of paper and pencil (Standing, 1962, p. 48–49).

Curiously, although the children could write words, they didn't immediately understand the concept of reading. Montessori wrote notes on the blackboard in front of the room with messages to the children, such as, "If you can read this, come kiss me." At first there was no response. But after a few days, a child came to the front of the room and kissed her. Little by little, the other children caught on to the secret. Soon the entire class understood what was happening.

These "explosions," as Montessori termed them, became commonplace and were not confined to reading and writing. Mathematics was another common area in which the children would seem to have these sudden insights. A good part of the reason for these explosions lay in the materials that Montessori developed. The classroom material had been constructed to lead children systematically to specific learning opportunities. For all the flexibility in her system, Montessori insisted that the materials be used in the way they were intended to be used or else the entire point of the material would be lost.

MONTESSORI'S INFLUENCE SPREADS

Word began to spread about the remarkable things that were happening at the *Casa dei Bambini*—in part promoted through newspaper articles—and the school hosted some distinguished visitors. Within months, Montessori opened another school in the San Lorenzo Quarter. As more people learned of her success, Montessori was encouraged to develop schools in other parts of Italy and beyond. In 1909, Montessori held her first training course in her method to encourage others to pursue her approach. Most of her contemporaries agreed that she was a superb lecturer.

In only a few years, schools sprang up in many parts of the world, including India, Japan, Australia, and most of Europe. The Netherlands became a particularly active site for Montessori education. Samuel S. McClure, the founder and editor of *McClure's Magazine* in the United States, also became an enthusiastic supporter and promoted Montessori endlessly through articles in his magazine. The first Montessori school in the United States opened in 1911 in a section of a large, private home in Tarrytown, New York, owned by Edward Harden and was later moved to larger, more independent quarters a few miles north. Alexander Graham Bell, the inventor of the telephone, and his wife became ardent followers and opened a Montessori School in their home in Washington, DC.

▶ **Image 10.1**   The Harden Mansion, Tarrytown, New York. Site of the first U.S. Montessori School

Courtesy of Catherine Casella

MONTESSORI IN THE UNITED STATES

In early 1913, Samuel McClure, the Bells, and other dignitaries organized a Montessori Educational Association to help promote Montessori's methods. To their surprise, she was not entirely pleased with the association. Throughout her life, she insisted on being fully in charge of her work, fearing that others would dilute it. Nonetheless, the association was able to arrange a 3-week-long lecture tour for Montessori in the United States.

Montessori arrived by ship on December 3, 1913, in Brooklyn, New York. Newspapers were alerted to her arrival, and she was greeted by throngs of people on the dock, followed shortly after by a news conference at her hotel. She did not speak English but had the questions and answers translated by one of her former students. After New York, she traveled to Washington, DC, where she lectured and was greeted at a reception as if she were a visiting head of state. Then on to New York City where she lectured to an overflow crowd at Carnegie Hall. *The New York Times* reported that a thousand people had to be turned away (Gutek & Gutek, 2016). Her rigorous tour continued with one successful lecture after another. She finally returned to Europe on December 24.

At
**Carnegie
Hall**

Monday

**Dec.
8th**

at
8:15 P. M.

Dr. Montessori Giving a Lesson in Touching Geometrical Insets

Dr. Maria Montessori
The Greatest Woman Educator in History
ILLUSTRATED LECTURE
"The Montessori Method in Education"
Lecture Illustrated with Motion Pictures

Seats 50c. to $2.00   Boxes $15 and $18
Tickets on sale at Carnegie Hall Box Office
Auspices The Montessori Educational Association

▶ **Image 10.2**   Advertising Montessori's lecture at Carnegie Hall.

Seemingly, Montessori had won over the hearts of the United States. In 1915, she returned for another lecture tour, this time sponsored by the National Education Association. In addition to running a training session for prospective Montessori teachers, she created a glass-walled demonstration classroom at the Panama–Pacific International Exposition in San Francisco. Thousands of visitors had the opportunity to observe 21 students in what was advertised as a typical Montessori classroom.

Although her international influence continued to be strong, surprisingly her impact on American education turned out to be relatively short lived. Montessori had many critics in the United States as well as some competitors. One of her strongest critics was William Kilpatrick, an influential education professor at Columbia University and a strong believer in the new educational approach being proposed by John Dewey. Among other criticisms, U.S. educators argued that Montessori relied too much on sense training. Moreover, they believed that she underestimated the importance of play and social development. The Montessori classroom, her opponents argued, stifled creativity.

One of the greatest impediments to her continued U.S. success, however, came from one of her earliest supporters. Montessori and Samuel McClure, who had used his magazine to promote Montessori and her work, had a falling out. She had continued to be very protective of her material and methods, insisting that they be carried out in very specific ways. In her view, McClure had promoted her work too zealously and had betrayed her trust. In addition, she felt she had been deceived by her U.S. business partners who benefitted greatly from the sale of her educational materials while she received little compensation. Soon after her 1915 visit, her influence in the United States began to fade. It would not be restored until the 1950s (Gutek & Gutek, 2016)

POLITICAL UNREST

In the period between the World Wars, Montessori spent much of her time lecturing and writing. After returning from the United States, she established a base in Barcelona, Spain, where a special laboratory school had been created for her. Her son, Mario, and his wife joined her with their four children, who spent their formative years in Barcelona. Montessori had long given up her private practice to devote herself to education. Despite her success in Spain, political unrest continued to increase in the country. Finally, with the beginning of the Spanish Civil War in 1936, Montessori left Spain permanently. But her exposure to political unrest did not end there.

▶ **Image 10.3** Maria Montessori at one of her schools

As World War II approached, Montessori faced a threat from her home country. She had been on friendly terms with the Italian leader, Benito Mussolini, who supported her schools. However, when it became clear that he intended to use Montessori schools to promote his own vision for the country—one of fascism—Montessori was appalled. She immediately closed down all of the Montessori schools in Italy, and she and her son Mario left on an extended lecture tour around the world. She would return to Italy only rarely for the rest of her life.

Montessori and her son were in India when World War II broke out. Because they were Italian and Italy was an active participant in the war, they were placed under house arrest. They endured a short period of separation. Eventually, however, the arrest became more *pro forma* than real as they were given a great deal of personal freedom, even being allowed to travel out of the country toward the end of the war. After the war, Montessori, now in her 70s, moved to Amsterdam, where the offices of the International Montessori Society had been established. The society remains there to this day.

THE FINAL YEARS

Montessori continued to work until the end of her life, promoting the movement and writing books and other material describing her system. Among many honors, she was nominated for a Nobel Prize on three different occasions. One of her followers in Switzerland was Jean Piaget, one of the most influential developmental psychologists of his era.

While visiting friends in the small town of Noordwijk, not far from Amsterdam, Montessori became ill and died of a cerebral hemorrhage on May 6, 1952. She was 82. Her remains were interred in the Catholic cemetery in the town where she died. Her son Mario served as the director general of the International Montessori Association until his death in 1982 at age 83. His youngest daughter, Renilde, later became deputy secretary of the association and then its president.

EVALUATING MONTESSORI AND HER MOVEMENT

Virtually from the beginning, some well-meaning educators appropriated material from Montessori's method but without the proper training in the material. In addition, some schools used selected parts of the method but not others (Lillard, 2017). Montessori and her successors made it clear that the method worked best when it was used in its entirety. As suggested earlier, Montessori could be quite rigid about training requirements for potential Montessori teachers. Some of the criticism later directed at her involved her inflexibility (Kramer, 1988).

One of the fears often expressed about Montessori education is that children would flounder when they entered the "real world" after experiencing the artificially free world of the Montessori school. For many years, it was difficult to conduct research on Montessori-educated children. The reason usually stated was that Montessori devotees were so confident of their success, they didn't need any outside evaluation to verify their results. Montessori herself was a strong believer in the value of science and considered her approach to be based on sound scientific principles.

Recent estimates from the North American Montessori Teachers' Association indicate that there are 4,500 Montessori schools in the United States and approximately 20,000 schools worldwide. When contemporary research has been conducted on Montessori's method, the results have generally been positive (e.g., Lillard & Else-Quest, 2006). Children from Montessori schools appear to be more successful both academically and socially, at least up to age 12 or so, when matched with their non-Montessori school counterparts. Rather than being less creative, as frequently predicted, they seem to be more so. Both their attitude toward the general community and the ability to engage with the community appear stronger. Other parts of Montessori's system are not as strongly supported by modern science.

Perhaps the most important outcome of the Montessori method is a less obvious one. With her unique method, Montessori helped to move education away from the rigid form of instruction that was dominant in her day to one that has become more child focused. Rather than trying to instruct through constant repetition and rigid rules, as had been the norm, she encouraged the children to find their own paths and to make their own choices. Thousands of Montessori schools around the world attest to the appeal and success of that simple idea, an idea that is all the more surprising for having grown out of a single room in a slum section of Rome with a group of poor children.

REVIEW/DISCUSSION QUESTIONS

1. What sources did Montessori draw from in developing her method?

2. Describe a few of the basic principles of the Montessori method. Can you identify any of their historical antecedents?

3. What is the role of the teacher in a Montessori school?

4. The Montessori method seemed to flourish in the United States in early 1900s and then die out for a long period. What happened?

5. What is the current status of the Montessori method around the world?

6. Montessori was an educator. In what ways was she also a psychologist?

NOTE

The book by Gerald L. Gutek and Patricia A. Gutek referenced in this chapter (see References) is a wonderfully detailed account of Montessori's life and work, with particular emphasis on her visits to the United States. Unlike some other accounts, it presents her in a less adoring, more objective, fashion.

CHAPTER ELEVEN

SIGMUND FREUD'S ONLY VISIT TO AMERICA

The founder of psychoanalysis, Sigmund Freud (1856–1939), visited the United States in 1909, the only time he came to America. He had been invited by G. Stanley Hall (1844–1924), the president of Clark University in Worcester, Massachusetts, to give a series of lectures. The university was celebrating the 20th anniversary of its founding, and the Freud lectures were to be part of a larger number of presentations given by notables in psychology and education. Freud's visit was an opportunity to spread the word of psychoanalysis, which was not widely known at the time. But it was also an opportunity for U.S. psychologists to evaluate him.

Scholars debate the impact of the conference—many psychologists present were skeptical of Freud's approach. They were particularly suspicious of his belief in unconscious motivation. As it turned out, Freud was not overly fond of America and Americans either. However, it wouldn't be long after his visit that Freudian theory would become an important part of American culture. In effect, Freud would become the public face of psychology in the United States. Despite his impact on the public, he remained a controversial figure among psychologists, largely damned by experimental psychologists, but praised by psychoanalysts for his insights into the very nature of mankind.

THE INVITATION

In 1909, Freud was 53 years old and a resident of Vienna, Austria, his home since his family moved there when he was four. The father of six children, he and his wife Martha lived in a large apartment at Berggasse 19, only a few blocks from the University of Vienna. The apartment included his office as well as extensive family living quarters. His sister-in-law, Minna, also lived with them.

The invitation to speak at Clark University was undoubtedly an honor, but a mixed one—Clark was celebrating the 20th anniversary of its founding, not a sign of a lengthy intellectual history. Freud considered the university to be "small but serious," with a distinguished faculty, but he initially turned down the invitation. The conference was scheduled for July 1909, and attendance would require him to give up at least two weeks of his work schedule, something that he was reluctant to do. He had a large household to support. Freud wrote to Hall to thank him for the invitation and to explain that the date made it impossible for him to attend.

As plans for the conference developed further, however, Hall was forced to move the date to September, and so he wrote to Freud again. In addition to an increased honorarium, this time Hall offered Freud an honorary degree. The second invitation was more appealing, and Freud had some help coming to a decision. Carl G. Jung (1875–1961), a 34-year-old Swiss psychiatrist who had recently befriended Freud, advised him to accept the invitation. Jung immediately recognized the importance of the invitation. He saw it as an opportunity to spread the word of psychoanalysis outside of Vienna, in fact, outside of Europe. One of Freud's visions was that the psychoanalytic movement not be confined to Vienna or the Jewish community. He envisioned a worldwide movement. Freud accepted the invitation and began planning the journey that would eventually include as traveling companions not only Jung but also Sándor Ferenczi (1873–1933), a Hungarian psychoanalyst (Rosenzweig, 1994).

THE CLARK CONFERENCE

G. Stanley Hall, the president of Clark University, was himself a psychologist. In fact, he is usually recognized as the first person to receive a doctoral degree in psychology in the United States. It was his idea to devote Clark University to research and graduate studies. Jonas G. Clark (1815–1900), the university founder and benefactor, had wanted to create an undergraduate college first, resulting in a great deal of conflict among Hall, Clark, and the university trustees, and a rocky start for the fledgling institution (Koelsch, 1987).

Hall was regarded as something of a character among his fellow psychologists, known for his occasional grandiosity and high-handedness. But he was also a very effective organizer. In one prescient act, he had organized the American Psychological Association in 1892, the first national association of psychologists in the world, a group which remains a very powerful international force in psychology today.

Hall, whatever his faults, was also an omnivorous reader and one of the first to recognize the potential importance of Freudian ideas to U.S. psychology. As early as 1901, Hall was mentioning Freud in his lectures, and he cited some of Freud's writings in his massive book *Adolescence* (1904), a work that effectively created that period of life as a separate stage of development. Freud's work also fed into Hall's interest in human sexuality, one of the few psychologists of the period to tackle the topic.

Hall had organized a conference in 1899 to celebrate the tenth anniversary of the founding of Clark University, and his plans for the 20th anniversary were even more elaborate. He invited several important European psychologists to attend and receive honorary degrees, including Wilhelm Wundt, the "founder of experimental psychology." Wundt turned him down, citing his advanced age—he was then in his late 70s. Wundt was also planning to participate that fall in the celebration of the founding of the University of Leipzig. As Wundt was quick to point out to a friend, while Clark University was celebrating the 20th anniversary of its founding, Leipzig was celebrating its 500th anniversary (Evans & Koelsch, 1985).

Among the European dignitaries who accepted Hall's invitation was Hermann Ebbinghaus, well known for his strikingly original experiments on memory and one of the first to identify the topic as subject matter for psychology. Unfortunately, Ebbinghaus died a few weeks after his acceptance. Alfred Binet, the creator of the first successful intelligence test, also declined the invitation. Among the participants who did attend was German psychologist William Stern, best known for his work on individual differences.

Sometime after Freud's second invitation, Carl Jung was also invited. He was asked to present three lectures at the conference and to receive an honorary degree. Freud was delighted that Jung would be honored at the conference—he felt the invitation made the conference even more important. Jung's work on word association incorporated some ideas that were similar to Freud's but were also evidence that Jung was creating his own psychodynamic theory apart from Freud's. Despite the presence of many other notables from several different areas—in all 29 honorary degrees were bestowed—Freud's presence would become the central focus of the conference. Over the years, the meeting would almost always be referred to as the "Freud Conference" (Evans & Koelsch, 1985).

THE JOURNEY TO AMERICA

Freud, Jung, and Ferenczi traveled to Bremen, Germany, where they were to board the German steamer *George Washington* for the journey to America. While at dinner the night before they sailed, Freud fainted, an event that has been a source of continued interest to historians. Freud, Jung, and Ferenczi were psychoanalysts, after all, and in their world all behaviors had meaning, even a fainting episode.

For many years, Freud had suffered from a phobia associated with travel. Could his fainting be a reoccurrence of some long-forgotten fear? Jung offered to help Freud find the psychological source for his fainting, but Freud would have none of it. To do so would require him to be completely open about his personal life. He chose not to. In his words, he could not "surrender his authority" to Jung. Some historians see this interaction as the first visible sign that the relationship between Freud and Jung would not endure.

The sea journey was uneventful. The three reportedly kept away from most of the other passengers and spent much of their time analyzing one another's dreams.

The ship arrived on August 29 at its port in the United States—Hoboken, New Jersey. There they were met by A. A. Brill, an emigrant from Eastern Europe and a one-time student of Jung. Brill accompanied the group into Manhattan, where they were joined by analyst Ernest Jones, who had traveled from Toronto to see them. Years later, Jones would become the first important biographer of Freud.

The visitors spent several days as typical tourists, sampling the range of local delights the city offered. Their activities included a visit to the Cloisters, the famed medieval museum in upper Manhattan, as well as an evening at a rooftop entertainment "garden" in Times Square. According to one account, Jung and Freud traveled to Coney Island together, although the claim that they rode through the "tunnel of love" may be apocryphal. During a visit to Central Park, Jung attempted to interpret a dream that Freud had related to him. When Jung asked for further details, Freud declined. Jung later interpreted this as another sign that their relationship would not last.

CLARK UNIVERSITY AND THE LECTURES

After 6 days in New York City, the visitors took an overnight boat to Fall River, Massachusetts, where they boarded a train for Boston and then another train to Worcester, Massachusetts, the site of Clark University. They arrived a day earlier than expected. After spending a night at a local hotel, Freud and Jung were invited to be guests at Hall's campus home, the President's House. They accepted, but Freud may have regretted his decision. He found the ambience of the home too casual for his tastes. He seemed particularly bothered by the lack of privacy. One of his later criticisms about his visit to America was the informality of everyday life (Hale, 1971). Jung, on the other hand, appeared delighted with the arrangements and found Hall to be a "distinguished old gentleman." Hall was 65 at the time.

The psychology presentations were given in the art room of the university library, and Hall gave a brief introduction to open the conference. There were 175 people in attendance when the meeting began. The first speaker was William Stern, from the University of Breslau, who discussed his work on forensic psychology and individual differences. The psychoanalytic group apparently found his presentation to be dull and left to explore the area around the outskirts of town. Freud's lectures were scheduled for 11:00 a.m. for five consecutive days, Tuesday through Saturday, beginning on September 7. It was the prime speaking position. Freud had not composed his lectures in advance, but each day before his lecture, he would walk with Sándor Ferenczi, who helped him to organize his thoughts.

The lectures were given in German, and there was no concurrent interpreter present. Learned academics at the time were often familiar with the

▶ **Image 11.1** Sigmund Freud

German language but many in the audience were not, including a good number of the journalists present. Freud was concerned that his lectures would not be understood. But Jung pointed out that it didn't matter—the invitation was the important thing. In fact, Freud's lectures received very good reviews in the press. There was an extensive and very positive article written about him in *The Nation*. Many years after G. Stanley Hall's death, it was discovered that Hall had written a longer version of the article in advance of the lectures. Freud had once remarked that Hall had something of the "kingmaker" about him (Rosenzweig, 1992).

Freud began his lecture series by giving credit for the founding of psychoanalysis to Anna O. and Joseph Breuer. Freud would rarely be so generous with his comments in the future. Anna O. had been a patient of Breuer, and several of her insights became pivotal in the development of psychoanalysis. (The case of Anna O. is discussed more fully in Chapter 5.) Breuer had been a friend and mentor to Freud for many years, and it was his discussion of the case with Freud that led to further development of psychoanalysis. Freud and Breuer had a falling out after the publication of their book of case studies, *Studies on Hysteria* (1895), in which the case of Anna O. appears. They never spoke again.

Freud had a knack for using effective metaphors to illustrate his point, and that ability was put to good use in his lectures. In describing the unconscious, for instance, he spoke of an unwanted visitor knocking at the door of the lecture hall, trying to get in. It was a striking image. In other lectures, he described his views on hysteria, his use of dream interpretation, and the "psychopathology of everyday life." Perhaps the most controversial topics he presented were on the oedipal complex and sexuality in children. In years following the conference, he would introduce a few new ideas, but the major parts of psychoanalysis were in place by 1909.

William James (1842–1910), considered to be the founder of American psychology, traveled from his home in Cambridge near Harvard University in time to hear Freud's fourth lecture. James had been the first to introduce Freud's work to America when he abstracted material Freud had written on hysteria for the publication *Psychological Review* (1894). While at the conference, James is said to have remarked to analyst Ernest Jones that the future of psychology was in psychoanalysis. However, his comments to other psychologists were more critical. The evidence suggests that James was more drawn to the work of Jung and their common interests in religion and parapsychology.

In the afternoon following the Friday lecture, Freud and James walked together to the train station for James's journey back to Cambridge. On the way, James had an attack of *angina pectoris*, a sign of his failing heart, a condition from which he would die almost a year later. James told Freud to walk on ahead, he would catch up with him. Freud later wrote how impressed he was with the courage that James had exhibited in the face of his declining health. Both were trained as physicians and well understood the implications of the angina symptoms.

On Friday of the conference week, honorary doctoral degrees were bestowed on Freud, Carl Jung, and some of the other speakers at the celebration. At age 34, Jung was (and remains) the youngest person ever to receive an honorary degree from Clark University. Despite the fact that Freud would later achieve extraordinary worldwide recognition, his degree from Clark was the only honorary doctoral degree he received in his lifetime.

IMMEDIATELY AFTER THE CONFERENCE

There was another group in the United States that was interested in Freud's work, primarily for its impact on psychotherapy. For several years before Freud's visit, a group in Boston led by Morton Prince (1854–1929), a physician, and James Jackson Putnam (1846–1918), a Harvard neurologist and psychiatrist, had been meeting to discuss various approaches to psychotherapy. Putnam invited Freud and his party to visit a camp that Putnam owned in the Adirondacks. Freud was delighted with the opportunity, and they made plans to visit after first making a trip to Niagara Falls, virtually a requirement for Europeans traveling in the United States at the time. During their 4-day stay at the Putnam camp, Freud saw a porcupine, an animal unknown in Europe. He said, probably with tongue in cheek, that the sighting alone made the trip worthwhile. The travelers arrived back in New York City on September 19th and began their 8-day journey to Bremen, Germany, on the 21st, sailing on the steamer *Kaiser Wilhelm der Grosse* (Rosenzweig, 1992).

Despite all the honors associated with his U.S. trip, Freud was not particularly impressed with the United States. In fact, he called it a mistake. Almost three decades later, when he was forced to flee Austria because of the anti-Semitism of the Nazis, he is said to have considered only two possible destinations—England or the United States. Psychoanalysis had flourished in both countries, while it did not in many other locations. Freud chose England, where he lived his final year. It helped that several of his relatives had already settled there.

THE IMPACT OF THE "FREUD CONFERENCE"

In addition to the formal lectures, Hall held evening gatherings at the President's House where the guests could mingle and become acquainted with one another. Edwin B. Titchener (1867–1927), an experimental psychologist from Cornell University, was a speaker at the conference who used an evening meeting to discuss the future of psychology with Freud. Titchener was strongly committed to an experimental approach to psychology and suspicious of any application of psychology. The approaches of Freud and Titchener appeared completely at odds with one another. Despite their apparent personal respect for each other, Freud referred to Titchener as "the enemy," giving voice to the strong division between them.

American psychology was at a turning point at the time of Freud's visit. It had long strayed from its original experimental subject matter and approach and had branched out into many practical applications. It seemed to lack a central unifying core. Some thought it might die as an academic discipline. Freud's ideas added another potentially divisive element. His work would not become commonplace in academic psychology for many years, although it would be taught at a few universities. Hall's interest in Freud's work continued for the rest of his career, although with some reservations. He retired as president of Clark University in 1920. His last doctoral student was Francis C. Sumner (1895–1954), the first Black American to receive a doctoral degree in psychology. The topic of Sumner's dissertation was the psychoanalysis of Freud and Adler.

It may be a surprise for some to learn that psychotherapy was not universally recognized as an important part of psychology in its pioneer days. Psychotherapy was largely seen as the domain of medicine and remained so in many locales. Freud himself did not believe that training in medicine was necessary to function as an effective analyst and published a book on "lay analysis," that is, psychoanalysis conducted by nonphysicians. Other groups both within and outside of psychology continued to carry Freud's thoughts forward. By the 1930s, Freud's dynamic ideas of development were entering academic psychology to a significant degree, and there they have remained in the decades since.

THE RETURN TO VIENNA AND FREUD'S FINAL DAYS

Freud and his party arrived back in Bremen, Germany, on September 29, 1909. When Freud returned to Vienna following the conference, Hall requested that Freud write out the lectures he had given at Clark for publication. The lectures were later printed in the *American Journal of Psychology*, a publication founded by Hall in 1887 (Freud, 1910). Comments from some of those present at the conference attest to the fact that the published versions were accurate reproductions of the original lectures. While there was little new in the lectures—they were mostly a review of ideas that Freud had already published—they were nonetheless an excellent introduction to psychoanalysis. One of the curious things about the publication of the lectures is that they may have helped to introduce Freud to Europe. Although Freudian thought was not well accepted in Europe, the *American Journal of Psychology* was a popular publication among European psychologists.

For Freud, the next decade was filled with more writing and greater attention from the world community. But his life also became more difficult. He became estranged from many of his early followers who would not stick to the "party line." Several would advance their own form of psychodynamic theory and become very prominent. Alfred Adler, Karen Horney, and even Carl Jung and Sándor Ferenczi would break with Freud, along with many others. One of his most fervent followers, who would expand his theory but never violate it, was his daughter Anna.

Beyond the professional disappointments, Freud began to suffer in his personal life. One of his beloved grandchildren died, and not long after, the child's mother, his daughter Sophie, died of Spanish influenza. His own health showed some ominous signs. He had been diagnosed with precancerous spots in his mouth in the early 1920s, attributed to his habit of smoking 20 or more cigars a day. He continued to smoke, and during the 1920s and 1930s had dozens of operations on his mouth and jaw. Motion pictures of him taken during his final days depict him constantly moving his mouth, undoubtedly due to the discomfort he felt with his prosthetic jaw. In addition, the Nazis had overtaken Austria and, as a Jew, he was at great personal risk. Freud was reluctant to leave Vienna, intending to die there, but the threat to his family was great, and he finally agreed to move to England, where he spent the final year and a half of his life.

Freud had a long-standing agreement with his physician, Max Shurr, that if his pain grew too great, Shurr would assist in his death. On September 21, 1939, Freud said that "it didn't make any sense" to go on living. After consulting with Freud's family, especially Freud's daughter Anna, Shurr administered a dose of morphine that put Freud into a coma. Other doses followed. Freud died on September 23. His ashes reside in a crematorium in greater London, not far from his final home, along with those of five of his six children. His daughter Sophie, who died in her twenties, was buried in Baden-Baden, Germany, where she lived at the time with her husband and children. The ashes of Freud and his wife Martha are interred in an Etruscan *krator* (vase) that was a gift from one of his patients.

CLARK UNIVERSITY TODAY

There are virtually no vestiges remaining of the Freud visit to Clark University. The room where all the psychology presentations were given, the "Art Room of the Library," has since been converted into a modern, sloped classroom. The President's House, a large Victorian mansion where Freud and Jung stayed, was demolished in the 1960s. Even the site of the famous group picture taken on the fourth day of Freud's talks has vanished. The entrance was remodeled to accommodate the erection of another adjoining building.

In 1957, a bronze statue of Freud was presented to the university by the American Psychoanalytic Association to commemorate the 1909 lectures. There is another statue of Freud in front of the main building that was erected more recently. It is not very imposing, with a seated Freud looking uncomfortable, and with one of his feet dangling off the ground.

In 1950, the university hosted a visit from Anna Freud, Sigmund's daughter. More than simply being the daughter of Sigmund Freud, Anna had developed her own specialty within psychoanalysis. Many of the "ego defense mechanisms" attributed to Sigmund Freud are actually the creation of his daughter. Like her father, she too would receive an honorary doctorate from Clark University. In fact, in her lifetime she would receive a dozen honorary degrees, far outpacing her father. She remarked that Clark University was the site of the first international recognition of her father's work. The university has continued to honor the event in more recent years, at least partially making up for the relative indifference that it displayed toward it for so many years.

REVIEW/DISCUSSION QUESTIONS

1. How did G. Stanley Hall first learn about Freud? Why was he so interested in having him lecture at the conference?

2. Who were some of the other notable psychologists at the 1909 conference?

3. Freud's five lectures were later printed in a U.S. journal. How are they evaluated today?

4. What was Freud's impression of America?

5. Why were so many American psychologists reluctant to accept the work of Freud? What is the current status of Freudian thought?

NOTE

Saul Rosenzweig (1907–2004), whose book is cited in this chapter (see References), is a "must read" for anyone wishing to probe more deeply into the Freud visit. Rosenzweig developed an early interest in the visit when he was a faculty member at Clark University and spent more than fifty years collecting relevant information on it, including a great deal of primary information.

CHAPTER TWELVE

HUGO MÜNSTERBERG

Pioneer Applied Psychologist, Torn Between Two Worlds

Hugo Münsterberg (1863–1916) was a German-born American psychologist who helped to move U.S. psychology away from its focus as an academic discipline to one that was more applied. Among the areas in applied psychology to which he contributed were forensic psychology, industrial–organizational psychology, clinical psychology, and media psychology. As a distinguished professor at Harvard University, he developed relationships with many world leaders, including U.S. President Theodore Roosevelt. His willingness to express an opinion on practically every subject made him popular with the press, although less so with his academic colleagues. At one point, he was characterized as the best-known psychologist in America.

Münsterberg has also been described as vain, autocratic, and a constant self-promoter. To the chagrin of many of his colleagues, he was fond of praising Germany and German culture to the detriment of U.S. culture and values. With the approach of World War I, his continued support of Germany became highly controversial, and he became a professional and public outcast. Harvard was encouraged to fire him.

Münsterberg died suddenly at age 53, a premature death that is often linked to the stress he suffered from being vilified by his community. For many years, his contributions were ignored or minimized, and his appearance in textbooks on the history of psychology were few. But recent generations have come to realize the importance of his work, particularly his contributions to applied psychology.

BEGINNINGS

Hugo Münsterberg was born in the Prussian city of Danzig (now Gdansk, Poland) on June 1, 1863. His father, Moritz, was a lumber merchant and his family was moderately well off. He had two older half-brothers from his father's first marriage and another younger brother from his father's second marriage. The family was Jewish, and the home atmosphere has been described as intellectual, artistic, and somewhat idealistic.

Hugo's mother died after a long illness as he was approaching 12 years of age. When he was 17, his father died. Shortly after, three of the sons, including Hugo, converted to Christianity and were baptized. Their conversion was not unusual at the time. As a practical matter, many more opportunities would be open to them as Christians.

From his early school years, young Hugo showed evidence of being gifted, and he worked hard to fulfill that promise. He began his study of medicine at the University of Leipzig, a typical choice for a student interested in science. However, after hearing a lecture by Wilhelm Wundt and working in his laboratory, he decided to study psychology. Only a few years before, Wundt had created

▶ **Image 12.1** Hugo Münsterberg

what is considered the first experimental laboratory for psychology in the world. After completing his doctoral degree in psychology under Wundt in 1885, Münsterberg enrolled at the University of Heidelberg for a medical degree, which he completed in 1887 at age 24.

Beginning as an unpaid instructor at the University of Freiburg, Münsterberg created an experimental laboratory in two rooms in his home using his own money. Ambitious and controversial from the beginning, his work was both criticized and praised. The laboratory had not been the only major change in those early years. Shortly before beginning at Freiburg, he had married a distant cousin, Selma Oppler.

In 1889, Münsterberg had attended the first International Congress of Psychology held in Paris, a meeting that would change his life. While there, he met William James, who had introduced the new psychology to America at Harvard University. James had read some of Münsterberg's publications, was impressed with them, and they began corresponding. In 1892, Münsterberg was offered a paid position at Freiburg, the equivalent of an associate professorship. Also in 1892, Münsterberg received a job offer from Harvard arranged by William James.

▶ **Image 12.2**   Münsterberg's laboratory at Freiburg

James had grown tired of his laboratory work and was turning increasingly to philosophy. But in order to vacate the position, he needed someone to take his place. He saw Münsterberg—young, bright, industrious, and ambitious—as the perfect choice. Münsterberg was offered a 3-year position, one that James hoped would eventually become permanent. But Münsterberg had different long-range plans. When he accepted the offer, he considered the position to be temporary. He was more interested in obtaining a permanent position in Germany. In his view, Harvard may have been an important university in America, but it could not compare to the best German universities.

MÜNSTERBERG AT HARVARD

When Münsterberg arrived at Harvard in 1892 with his wife and two young daughters, he spoke no English. During his first year and a half of residence, he completed a book on psychology (in German) and devoted himself to the laboratory, attempting to invigorate an enterprise that had gone stale. His efforts were successful. Before long, the Harvard laboratory became known as the most successful psychology laboratory in the country (Spillman & Spillman, 1993).

Despite his success (he was now delivering lectures in English and his classes had strong enrollment), Münsterberg returned to Germany in 1895, still hoping to secure an academic position in his homeland. Why he did not is somewhat of a mystery. Münsterberg alluded to possible anti-Semitism as a factor, despite his conversion to Protestantism. His arrogance may have also played a role. In any case, he was unsuccessful and returned to Harvard and the United States in 1897.

His reappearance at Harvard signaled the beginning of a change in his approach to psychology. Earlier in his career, he had spoken out against the application of psychology—he insisted, for instance, that teachers had no use for scientific psychology. But for the remaining two decades of his life, Münsterberg's most important contributions consisted of application. This change in direction was more than a little unexpected. After all, he had been hired as a research psychologist, specifically to oversee the Harvard laboratory. But even his laboratory work took on a more practical direction.

Applied psychology had many detractors in the pioneer years of the discipline. And the tension between research and application remained for many years. Wundt considered experimental psychology to be a discipline much like philosophy, with little or no application. But others saw it differently, including some of Wundt's former students.

Two of Wundt's students, Walter Dill Scott (1869–1955) and Lightner Witmer (1867–1956) were particularly active in blazing new applied trails for psychology. Scott promoted the psychology of advertising, writing one of the early books on the subject (Scott, 1903). Later, he formed his own business consulting company. Witmer is credited with opening the first psychological clinic in 1896. G. Stanley Hall (1844–1924), not a formal student of Wundt, promised that psychology could offer great benefits to education and child development, and he lectured widely on both topics. Clearly, Münsterberg was not the first to argue for the benefits of an applied psychology, but he became one of its strongest promoters.

FORENSIC PSYCHOLOGY

Münsterberg's interest in forensic psychology came about because of a 1906 court case involving a mentally disabled man accused of murdering a young housewife (Benjamin, 2000). Both Münsterberg and William James were asked to comment on the case. James suggested the case should be reopened for a reappraisal of the man's mental status; Münsterberg insisted the man was innocent. His statement was made public to some hostile public reaction. (The accused was eventually convicted and hanged.)

Münsterberg took the execution as a personal rebuke. In the months following, he wrote a series of articles for popular magazines in which he tried to demonstrate how much psychology could contribute to the legal system. Included were articles on such judicial-related topics as eye witness testimony and jury selection. The application of psychology to law had been growing in Europe, but Münsterberg was the first to introduce it to America in a forceful way (Hale, 1980).

Although Münsterberg had allowed women in his classes in Freiburg, an uncommon practice at the time, he thought that they should not be allowed on juries—he believed women were "mentally stubborn" and therefore unfit. Not surprisingly, his comments were strongly criticized by women's groups. Eventually, his law-related articles were brought together in a book *On the Witness Stand* (1908), a volume that is generally seen as Münsterberg's most important contribution to forensic psychology.

Münsterberg's involvement in a murder case in 1907 was also effective in promoting the connection between psychology and the law. William Haywood, a prominent, radical labor leader, was accused of ordering the murder of the former governor of Idaho, Frank Steunenberg, who had a history of being antilabor. Harry Orchard, the gun for hire, was scheduled to testify against Haywood. The defense attorney for Haywood was the famed Clarence Darrow. The accusations, as well as the visibility of the participants, held the promise of a dramatic trial and an event of national interest.

Münsterberg was hired by *McClure's Magazine* to travel to Idaho and report on the trial. His immediate observations suggested that Haywood was innocent and that Orchard was lying. But he went beyond simple observation and arranged to evaluate Orchard using dozens of tests, including physiological measures and a word association test. In the end, he was convinced that Orchard was telling the truth and that Haywood was lying. As usual, Münsterberg had no problem sharing his views with the public. His conclusion seems not to have affected the outcome of the trial; Haywood was acquitted. But in the process Münsterberg became a public sensation. Part of his celebrity was based on something that he only hinted at in his report on the trial—the suggestion that psychologists had developed a method for detecting lies (Benjamin, 2000).

Although Münsterberg was cautious when he discussed the possibility of a lie detector, he held strong ideas on the subject. Based on the work of other researchers, he originally proposed that reaction time to certain word associations could be used as an indicator of lying. Later, he refined his method to focus more on physiological responses such as blood pressure and galvanic skin response. He did not develop this work further, but one of his students did—or at least tried to.

William Moulton Marston (1893–1947) had come under the influence of Münsterberg while an undergraduate student at Harvard. Although Münsterberg died before Marston was able to complete his Harvard doctorate, his ideas continued to influence Marston's work. In the early 1920s, Marston created an early form of a lie detector test based on systolic blood pressure, a measure that continues to be part of the modern polygraph. Marston has another distinction in the history of U.S. culture. He was the creator of the comic book heroine Wonder Woman. Curiously, among her many attributes, Wonder Woman wields a lasso with magical powers. Anyone caught in its grip is required to tell the truth.

INDUSTRIAL-ORGANIZATIONAL PSYCHOLOGY

As previously noted, Münsterberg was not the first to connect modern psychology with the world of work, although he gave little credit to those who came before him, often acting as if he had discovered the topic. In his book, *Psychology and Industrial Efficiency* (1913), he outlined several of the ways in which business and psychology could work together. Of particular interest to him was matching the worker and the job. Using tests that he developed, he evaluated employees from many walks of life, including telephone operators, trolley car drivers, and ship captains (Benjamin, 2000; Spillman & Spillman, 1993).

Münsterberg's interest in industrial psychology coincided with a period of dramatic change in America's businesses. Jobs were becoming more specialized, and efficiency had become the watchword. For one of his projects, Münsterberg sent out questionnaires to a thousand managers asking them what mental skills were necessary for various jobs. He followed up on the responses by visiting many of the job sites. His task, as he saw it, was to determine the essential elements of a particular job and devise a test instrument to measure them.

Münsterberg's reputation grew, and he was called in as a consultant and problem solver by several companies. After developing selection tests for various jobs, he turned to the workers themselves, focusing on working conditions and job satisfaction. Many of his ideas seem quaint to contemporary eyes, but his belief that psychology was an important tool for industrial efficiency never wavered. He met with some resistance from both the psychology and business communities. Even the workers themselves had suspicions about his questionnaires. On the other hand, a number of his ideas were adopted by businesses, and industrial–organizational psychology would soon become a thriving subspecialty (Hale, 1980).

OTHER CONTRIBUTIONS

Münsterberg was one of the early psychologists to conduct psychotherapy. As noted earlier, he held both a doctoral degree in psychology and a medical degree and considered them to be the best background for a psychotherapist. His approach was direct, often using hypnosis, suggestion, and persuasion. He charged no fee for his counseling. As for the subconscious, he said simply, "There is none." In his view, there was a physiological basis for all mental illness, a typical belief among professionals at the time. In 1909, he published a book titled *Psychotherapy* outlining his major ideas on the subject.

His involvement in psychotherapy resulted in a frightening incident. According to one account, a female patient developed paranoid delusions about Münsterberg and threatened him with a gun outside of his lecture hall. No injury was involved, but as a result of the publicity and legal implications, Harvard's president, Charles Eliot, recommended that Münsterberg stop using hypnotic techniques with women and exclude them as subjects in his laboratory. Münsterberg readily agreed (Moskowitz, 1977).

Münsterberg also became a devotee of an increasingly popular entertainment— movies or "silent photoplays." This was somewhat surprising in view of his earlier stance. He had maintained that it was undignified for a Harvard professor to attend a movie. His book on the subject, *The Photoplay: A Psychological Study* (1916) addressed several features of this new phenomenon. He explained the science behind motion pictures, that is, the illusion of movement that comes from viewing a series of still pictures. Movies held particular interest for the psychologist, he believed, since the movement in film is created by the mind.

Münsterberg compared movies to theater and argued that movies had their own place as an art form. His writings were among the very first examples of serious film criticism. As a result, he earned the gratitude of many in the fledgling film industry as he helped to make film legitimate when critics often characterized it as a frivolous and low-level form of entertainment.

GERMANY, WORLD WAR I, AND GROWING PROBLEMS

Despite the years he spent in the United States, Münsterberg never became a citizen. Throughout, he retained his German accent and style, right down to his waxed moustache. And he placed such a high value on Germany and German culture, he could be described as a strident nationalist. Although his home was in Cambridge, Massachusetts, he traveled to Germany on a regular basis, usually every two years.

Münsterberg wrote that Americans had some good qualities—he considered them hard working and productive, among other positive traits. But he had no qualms about criticizing American culture, which he considered inferior to German culture. Over the years, he began to see his role as that of a liaison between the two countries, interpreting German culture for the Americans and American culture for the Germans. Consistent with his role, Harvard appointed him an exchange professor at the University of Berlin, where he helped develop their American Institute. His appointment would become a source of later criticism.

At first, Münsterberg's nationalistic opinions were acceptable, or at least tolerated, by his friends and colleagues. His views seemed to have little impact on his professional life. In 1898, at age 35, he was elected president of the American Psychological Association. (He remains the youngest president in its history, although just weeks younger than James McKeen Cattell, also 35.) However, over time his excursions outside of academia began to take on a more political tone. When he supported the idea of a Germanic Museum at Harvard, he received a stern rebuke from Charles Eliot, the Harvard president. Eliot recommended that Münsterberg retreat from discussing political issues and confine himself to academic matters. Münsterberg was obviously hurt by the rebuke but agreed to Eliot's demands. However, his acquiescence was short lived.

As World War I approached, Münsterberg became even more active in his support for Germany, which included writing articles urging the United States not to enter the war. The public and professional attitude toward him began to change. Germany was generally seen as the aggressor in the war, and Münsterberg's position was becoming intolerable. His life was threatened, and some even called him a German spy. Several colleagues and students turned against him. In September 1914, the *London Times* published an article accusing Münsterberg of colluding with Germany and identified Harvard as a center for pro-German activity. A newspaper reported that a former Harvard student planned to remove a $10 million bequest to Harvard in his will unless Münsterberg was fired. Although the offer was considered insincere and made by someone without the necessary funds, the public notice of it cranked up the controversy even further (Hale, 1980).

Whatever pro-German sentiment was left in the United States mostly vanished with the sinking of the *RMS Lusitania*, a British ocean liner, on May 7, 1915, by a German U-boat. More than a thousand passengers and crew were killed, including 128 Americans. The sinking of the ship was a major reason the United States entered the war on Germany in 1917. In reaction to the sinking, one of Münsterberg's closest friends on the Harvard faculty, Josiah Royce, abandoned him. Even the president of Harvard appeared to be looking for an excuse to fire him. Increasingly Münsterberg was becoming an outcast at his own university.

The effect on Münsterberg was noticeable. He dropped out of most campus activities and social clubs, maintaining only his teaching schedule. As a trained physician, he recognized that his ostracism was having an impact on his health. On December 16, 1916, a cold Saturday morning, he was scheduled to teach a class at Radcliffe College. He began his lecture, but after only a short time into it, he collapsed. Harold Burtt, a recent doctoral student, was called from another classroom and tried to revive him but was unsuccessful. Münsterberg was dead at 53. One of his colleagues requested the university have his salary continued to support his wife and children, but Harvard would not agree. His remains were cremated and sent to Germany. His wife and daughters remained in the United States.

MÜNSTERBERG'S PLACE IN HISTORY

At the time of his death, Münsterberg was likely the best-known psychologist in America. But his public fame worked against his academic stature. For many years after his death, his contributions were minimized. E. G. Boring, who wrote one of the first important histories of psychology, placed Münsterberg in a section of his book titled "The Periphery of the 'New' Psychology." He described Münsterberg as beginning at the core of psychology but "lured to other interests in America" (Boring, 1929, p. 418). Boring was not fond of applied psychology.

Münsterberg remained largely peripheral in history texts that followed. The fact that he had a contentious personality and frequently promoted unpopular views did not endear him to his contemporaries and may have contributed to his relative obscurity. However, he has been rediscovered in recent decades and his role, particularly in the promotion of applied psychology, has been recognized.

REVIEW/DISCUSSION QUESTIONS

1. If Münsterberg was so fond of German culture, why did he come to the United States, and why did he stay for so many years?

2. Is it fair to say that Münsterberg was the founder of applied psychology? Forensic psychology? What other areas of applied psychology did he contribute to?

3. Münsterberg's personal qualities are often said to have played a role in his ostracism. Explain.

4. How did Münsterberg's love of Germany and German culture contribute to his decline?

5. What were Münsterberg's enduring contributions to psychology?

CHAPTER THIRTEEN

MARY WHITON CALKINS

An Academic Pioneer in Search of a Doctoral Degree

When psychology began to develop as a science-based field in the late 19th century, there were few opportunities available in it for women. The social climate of the time effectively barred women from many activities. Motherhood was typically viewed as a higher calling than work outside the home. But the study of psychology posed an additional, though related, barrier. Psychology required advanced academic training, and most institutions of higher learning were not hospitable to women either as faculty members or as students. It was the lack of advanced academic credentials that posed one of the biggest difficulties for women attempting to enter the field.

Mary Whiton Calkins (1863–1930) challenged the existing academic standards for women in higher education. Determined to learn more about the emerging field of psychology, she petitioned to study alongside men in classes at Harvard University, an audacious request at the time. To some extent she prevailed and was able to train with several of the most important psychologists in the country. Ultimately, she would become one of the leading psychologists of her era, adding an important new technique to the study of learning and challenging the subject matter of psychology itself. Despite her accomplishments, her journey was neither smooth nor without hardship.

EARLY EDUCATION

Mary Calkins was born on March 30, 1863, in Hartford, Connecticut, the daughter of a Congregationalist minister and the oldest of five children. After living in upstate New York for many years, the family moved to Newton, Massachusetts, when Calkins was 17. She would live in Newton for the rest of her life. Her family placed a high value on education and for part of her early years she was home schooled.

Because of her strong educational background, she was able to enter Smith College as a sophomore. Smith College, founded in 1871 in Northampton, Massachusetts, was one of the few colleges available to women at the time. It remains a women's college to this day. Calkins studied Greek, Latin, and philosophy at Smith and thought that one day she might tutor students in those subjects. She had no plans to become a university professor.

Calkins's studies at Smith were interrupted when her sister became seriously ill. She returned home to be with her sister and help her ailing mother run the household. Her sister's eventual death would leave an indelible mark on her. Calkins eventually returned to Smith to resume her studies and graduated in 1885. After graduation, she accompanied her parents and younger brothers on a 16-month trip to Europe. Within a week of her return, she received a surprising invitation. Wellesley College, an institution for women, located in Wellesley, Massachusetts, a short distance from the Calkins home, had a sudden opening in the Greek Department. Calkins was offered the position. Wellesley was a relatively new college, admitting its first students in 1875, with a president, faculty, and student body composed entirely of women. After some hesitation, Calkins accepted the appointment, beginning in the fall of 1887 (Furumoto, 1980, 1990).

CALKINS MOVES INTO PSYCHOLOGY

Calkins had not anticipated the job offer and she was initially concerned about her ability to teach. However, it did not take long before she was comfortable in her new role. She had been teaching for about a year when she received another surprise. The administration at Wellesley was committed to a curriculum that incorporated science. They had become aware of the newly emerging scientific approach to psychology and decided that it should be part of the Wellesley curriculum. But who would teach it?

The likelihood of finding a woman scholar who was competent enough to teach the subject seemed remote. Instead, the administration attempted to find someone in their current faculty who would be willing to pursue training and teach the subject at Wellesley. In her brief time at the college, Calkins had already established herself as an excellent teacher. Additionally, during her undergraduate studies at Smith she had taken some courses in psychology, although they tended to be of the older, philosophical kind, not the newer experimental approach.

The administration saw Calkins as a prime candidate for this new position, and they offered it to her. Interested but uncertain, Calkins sought the advice of a former professor at Smith who encouraged her to accept the position. After much soul searching, she agreed. The college had one stipulation: She must engage in the study of psychology for one year before returning to teach the subject. But where would she study? (Scarborough & Furumoto, 1987).

In 1890, there were limited opportunities to study psychology on an advanced level regardless of gender, but there were virtually no opportunities for women. The premier destination at the time for anyone wanting to be a psychologist was the University of Leipzig in Germany where Wilhelm Wundt, a German professor with a medical degree and a philosophy background, had established the first doctoral research laboratory for psychology in 1879. Students came to Leipzig from around the globe, including many who would become prominent American psychologists. Calkins spoke fluent German, a legacy from her parents who were fond of German culture. Although not German themselves, her parents spoke German at home, and it became her first language.

It was possible for Calkins to apply to Leipzig, but as in many other countries, higher education in Germany was relatively inaccessible to women. In fact, up to that time Wundt had never had a woman work in his laboratory. In addition, Calkins was very close to her parents, and as the oldest child and only surviving daughter, she was expected to take care of them. This has been referred to as "the family claim" and had an impact on the plans of many women at the time. She decided it was unrealistic to consider universities that were too distant from her home in Massachusetts. Besides, weren't there enough colleges and universities in the United States? She was convinced that she would be able to find a suitable university to fit her needs.

One possibility was Yale University, which had recently admitted a woman to doctoral study. However, Yale didn't have a psychology research laboratory. The laboratory was the hallmark of the new science, and Calkins saw it as essential for her training. The University of Wisconsin was unsuitable for the same reason. What other possibilities were there? As it turned out, Calkins needed only to look within her own backyard to find two of the most important emerging institutions for psychology (Scarborough & Furumoto, 1987).

Forty miles to her west, in Worcester, Massachusetts, was Clark University, only recently established as a graduate institution but already becoming eminent. The president of Clark was G. Stanley Hall, arguably the first person to receive a doctoral degree in psychology and one of the pioneers of American psychology. Psychology was one of the five graduate programs available at Clark, seemingly a good fit for Calkins. The sticking point? Hall made it very clear that Clark did not accept women into its doctoral program, his primary justification being that the original charter of the university did not permit it.

Instead, Calkins set her sights on a university a little to the northeast of her—Harvard University. William James, considered the founder of American psychology, was on the Harvard faculty. James had introduced the new experimental psychology to America, teaching the first course in it at Harvard beginning in 1875. He had just published a two-volume work titled *The Principles of Psychology* (1890), a textbook that would become a classic of early American psychology. In it, he essentially redefined much of the field, taking it in a distinctly American direction. Unfortunately, Harvard didn't accept women either, but Calkins thought that she still might have a chance.

Calkins had not been the only woman seeking to take courses at Harvard—though she was one of a handful requesting advanced-level courses. Due to mounting requests from would-be students, and under pressure from faculty and alumni who had female relatives eager to take Harvard courses, the university had established a program of instruction for women beginning in 1879 that was labeled the "Harvard Annex." This program typically consisted of Saturday classes using the same faculty and facilities as Harvard but under a different title. It had no formal connection to Harvard.

Calkins wrote to Josiah Royce, a faculty member who taught psychology at the Annex, asking if she would be able to take a course under him. Shortly after, William James, who did not teach at the Annex, was alerted to Calkins's request. Although it is not certain who made the suggestion, Calkins was persuaded to ask permission to attend the regular seminars of James and Royce. Her father met personally with Charles William Eliot, the president of Harvard, and was encouraged to write a letter on his daughter's behalf. The president of Wellesley wrote a letter as well. It was assumed that their prominence would help her case. In addition, Calkins was no ordinary student; she was a faculty member at another institution (Furumoto, 1980, 1990).

CALKINS AT HARVARD

Calkins was accepted to Harvard, but not precisely in the way she had hoped. Charles Eliot, the president of Harvard, was primarily responsible for turning Harvard into the world-class university that it later became, but his openness to change did not extend to matriculating women into the university. To be fair, he needed the permission of the Harvard Corporation and Overseers to make such a change, and their disposition was strongly against coeducation.

As Eliot explained to Calkins in a letter, she would be allowed to attend classes at Harvard—he specifically mentioned her status as a faculty member at Wellesley and her father's reputation as a minister as contributing to his decision. However, it was to be understood that she was not a matriculated student, that is, she would pay no fee and she should not consider herself enrolled for a degree. She would be allowed to attend classes as a hearer, what is usually referred to today as an auditor. Since Wellesley did not require Calkins to obtain a degree, but only required her to study psychology for a year, she accepted these conditions. She prepared to begin classes in the fall of 1890.

Years later, in an autobiographical chapter, Calkins wrote about her first educational experience at Harvard (Calkins, 1930). Her initial class was to be with William James. There were four other students enrolled in her class with James, all men, but they "fell away" in the early weeks of the course. She doesn't tell the reader why they dropped out, but there is a strong possibility they were protesting the intrusion of women into their male-only classes and institution. Harvard students at the time had expressed such concerns. However, Calkins assured her readers that the class worked out well in the end. Calkins met with James at his home near the campus. (This would not have been unusual for the time.) They sat at each end of the fireplace in his library and discussed his newly published book. She considered her experience to be a particularly welcome introduction to psychology.

There was no department of psychology at Harvard during this period, and there wouldn't be for many years. All of the faculty members with whom Calkins studied, including William James, were members of the Department of Philosophy. The dividing line between the two subjects had not yet been clearly drawn, and Calkins, like James, would ultimately be equally conversant in the philosophy and psychology of their day. And, it turned out, she was able to receive some assistance from Clark University after all. Although G. Stanley Hall would not permit Calkins to enroll at Clark, he did ultimately offer her support in setting up a psychology laboratory. One of Hall's recent doctoral students, Edmund Sanford (1859–1924), then on the faculty at Clark, was considered an expert on psychology laboratories, and Calkins was able to work with him on a private basis. With his help, Calkins opened one of the early psychology laboratories in the country at Wellesley in 1891.

Sanford was not only of enormous help to Calkins in establishing the laboratory, but together they also conducted a piece of research based on their dreams, which they had monitored for 7 weeks. Sanford presented their research at the first meeting of the American Psychological Association (APA) in 1892, and it was later published. (Calkins joined APA the following year, one of the first two women to become members.) An Austrian physician by the name of Sigmund Freud would later take favorable notice of their research and cite it in his monumental *Interpretation of Dreams* (1900).

WELLESLEY AND HARVARD REDUX

Calkins returned to Wellesley in the fall of 1891 after her year of study. However, it wasn't long before she felt the need for further instruction in psychology. Most of her fellow psychologists had received the doctoral degree, and she felt the need for it as well. Several people, including Sanford, encouraged her to go to Europe. He pointed out that Hugo Münsterberg, a student of Wundt, now teaching at the University of Freiburg, had allowed a woman to attend his classes. Calkins planned to write to Münsterberg, but James convinced her to delay her decision. The reason soon became obvious. Harvard had hired Münsterberg with a 3-year contract beginning in the fall of 1892. Calkins did not have to go to Europe to study with him, he was coming to her. (The life and work of Hugo Münsterberg is discussed in Chapter 12.)

Calkins again wrote to President Eliot of Harvard asking if she could be admitted as a regular student. She specifically requested to work in the laboratory of

Professor Münsterberg. (On Münsterberg's arrival in the United States, James had turned over the Harvard laboratory to him.) Predictably, she received the same reply as earlier—she would be admitted to the university but not as a regular student.

She began working with Münsterberg in the laboratory in 1893 while still teaching at Wellesley. Later, she took a leave from Wellesley to work full time in the laboratory. Her abilities impressed Münsterberg, and her fluency in German helped the two to form a bond. Münsterberg became her strong supporter, even requesting that she be admitted as a regular doctoral student—though the request was again denied.

One of the outcomes of her laboratory research was an experiment in learning, using something that was later called the *paired-associate method*, a technique that she invented. Participants in her study learned a series of paired colors and numbers. They were then presented with the color and tested on their ability to remember the number associated with it. The technique was a clever and concrete way of measuring learning and the various conditions under which it could flourish. Many other researchers would later adopt the technique in varying forms. It went on to become a popular method to study the learning process.

In 1895, Münsterberg's contract with Harvard was coming to an end (though he would later return to Harvard). Calkins asked if she could be given an unofficial doctoral examination, and the members of the philosophy department agreed to do so, one that would be comparable in all respects to an official doctoral examination. The committee, consisting of William James, Hugo Münsterberg, and other

members of the Philosophy Department, met and questioned Calkins as they would for any doctoral candidate. Their decision was unanimous. She had not only passed, but she had done so at an exceptionally high level. In fact, James declared it to be the best doctoral oral exam he had ever witnessed. A report of the exam was sent to President Eliot, noting the details of the examination and recommending that Harvard confer a doctoral degree on Calkins. Eliot acknowledged the examination but took no further action (Scarborough & Furumoto, 1987).

▸ **Image 13.1** Mary Whiton Calkins.

Calkins, though disappointed, returned to Wellesley in the fall of 1895, where she continued to teach, write, and conduct research in her laboratory. She was promoted to full professor in 1898. She became increasingly interested in promoting a form of self-psychology. Disappointed with atomistic approaches to psychology, she conceived psychology to be the study of the conscious self in relation to other selves and the outside world (Calkins, 1909, 1915). She would continue to defend her definition of psychology for the rest of her life.

Although she made no further attempts at gaining a doctoral degree after her examination, her saga was not quite over. By 1894, the Harvard Annex program had grown substantially and was supported to such a degree that, in its place, Harvard established a "sister college" known as Radcliffe College. Radcliffe had its own location, separate from Harvard, and classes were not coeducational, although the faculty and courses were the same as at Harvard. Women attending classes received degrees from Radcliffe—not from Harvard. It has been suggested that the sole reason for Radcliffe's existence was to allow Harvard's administration to avoid coeducational classes.

Several years after Radcliffe's founding, the issue of granting advanced degrees to women who had fulfilled all the necessary requirements from Harvard was revisited. In fact, Radcliffe had never offered graduate courses or laboratory courses. The advanced courses taken were Harvard courses. Münsterberg, who had now returned to Harvard permanently, told Calkins of the possibility of her being offered a Radcliffe degree and urged her to accept it. In 1902, while traveling in Europe on a sabbatical leave, Calkins received a letter from a dean representing Radcliffe. Calkins was told that in view of their work at the university, the university was prepared to confer doctoral degrees on her and three other women—as expected, not Harvard degrees, but degrees from Radcliffe College.

Calkins's response to the letter has become something of a classic in psychology. She thanked the dean for the offer and acknowledged that she would be pleased to hold the doctoral degree since she occasionally found the lack of it to be an "inconvenience." However, she felt now that the Radcliffe degree was being offered to women, the Harvard degree never would be. She wrote that in her view it would better serve the ideals of education if the Radcliffe degree were not offered. As a result, she felt that she could not take the easier course of accepting a degree from Radcliffe. And so she refused the offer—a bold and telling decision (Benjamin, 2006). Harvard did not grant doctoral degrees to women until 1963—thirty-three years after Calkins's death.

In 1909, Columbia University conferred an honorary Doctor of Letters degree on Calkins; in 1910, Smith College, her alma mater, presented her with an honorary Doctor of Law degree. Near the end of her career, in 1927, a group of Harvard alumni petitioned Harvard to grant her the doctoral degree, but they were unsuccessful. The effort was revived again, long after Calkins death, this time with the goal of granting her a posthumous degree. But Harvard held firm and Calkins never received a Harvard degree. Even now a petition still circulates from time to time, asking Harvard to confer the degree.

Despite the "inconvenience" of lacking the doctoral degree, Calkins continued with her research and writing. In a survey of American psychologists conducted in 1903, Calkins was ranked 12th in a list of the most important psychologists in America. Her high ranking was particularly noteworthy since it was conducted among her fellow psychologists. In 1905, she became the first woman president of the American Psychological Association (APA), a distinct honor, and one of only a handful of APA presidents to lack the doctoral degree. In 1918, after shifting her interests somewhat, she was elected president of the American Philosophical Association, a position that several other past APA presidents had also held. She was the first woman to hold that position.

In 1929, Calkins retired from Wellesley at age 65. Her mother had been diagnosed with cancer, and Calkins felt she needed to care for her. Calkins never married. If she had done so, she probably would have had to give up her position at Wellesley. She lived with her parents for her entire life. In the early 1900s, she had been offered a position at Columbia University but turned it down. In her refusal, she said that she did not feel comfortable relocating her aging parents to New York City, and she could not leave them at their advanced age. Calkins herself died of cancer on February 26, 1930, a few months before her mother's death. She was 66 years old. Her memorial service was held at Wellesley (Furumoto, 1980, 1990).

THE LEGACY OF MARY WHITON CALKINS

Two of Calkins's most important contributions to psychology can be found in the paired associate method and the form of self-psychology she promoted. But her struggle to obtain a degree may be her greatest legacy. The burden of being the first at anything is often unappreciated, and Calkins surely carried a burden. The denial of a degree for her, particularly after she had proven herself so worthy, earning support from such luminaries as William James and Hugo Münsterberg, must have been particularly painful. At a time when pursuing a scholarly life at all was difficult for woman—married or unmarried—she not only did so but rose to the forefront of her field and broke down longstanding barriers.

Other women would challenge the "rules" about women in higher education, in some cases with more success. The first woman to receive a doctoral degree in psychology was Margaret Floy Washburn in 1894, only a few years after Calkins began her journey. Washburn had originally enrolled at Columbia University as a hearer, in the same limited role as Calkins had been. But after a year at Columbia,

James McKeen Cattell, the head of the psychology department there, advised her to apply to Cornell University instead. He held out little hope that Columbia would ever let Washburn matriculate for a degree. E. B. Titchener, a new Wundt doctorate, had just arrived at Cornell. Cattell thought he might make for an interesting mentor. And indeed he did. Washburn was accepted at Cornell on a full-time basis. Titchener, who she said "didn't know what to do with me," was nonetheless helpful and accepting of her (Scarborough & Furumoto, 1987).

To some degree, Calkins was the victim of unfortunate timing. If she had been born a few years later, and if she hadn't been so close to her parents, even if she had applied to a different university, perhaps her story would have turned out differently. But none of those things were true for her. Like most of us, she was a captive of her time and circumstances. In the end, she prospered despite the limiting regulations that were imposed on her. And with that, she earned her place in history as a courageous and principled pioneer.

REVIEW/DISCUSSION QUESTIONS

1. Why were women generally denied admission to graduate programs in the late 1800s?

2. Did psychology as a discipline discriminate against women?

3. How did Calkins get along with her professors, particularly William James and Hugo Münsterberg?

4. What were Calkins's most important accomplishments?

5. When did the attitude toward women in graduate education begin to change?

6. What is the status of women in psychology today?

NOTE

The volume referenced in this chapter, *Untold Lives: The First Generation of American Women Psychologists* by Elizabeth Scarborough and Laurel Furumoto, has lengthy portraits of five women pioneers in psychology and cameos of seven more, an excellent source for the topic. The volume by Ludy Benjamin Jr. (2006) contains fragments of original correspondence relevant to Calkins's life and contributions.

CHAPTER FOURTEEN

HENRY GODDARD, DEBORAH KALLIKAK, AND THAT TERRIBLE FAMILY OF HERS

In November 1897, an 8-year-old girl was admitted to the Training School for Feeble-minded Boys and Girls in Vineland, New Jersey. She had not been performing well in school, and it's possible she was suffering from mild intellectual disability. (At the time, she was described as "probably feebleminded.") Although she had no clear signs of disability, she did have problems with authority figures. The thinking of the time was that it was best for her to be admitted to the facility where she would be taken care of. Young women with her kind of intellectual deficit and attitude were likely to be preyed upon by some members of society—she would be safer in an institution. As it turns out, she would remain institutionalized for the next 81 years, until her death at 89.

The specific circumstances surrounding the girl's admission to the facility were somewhat unusual. Her mother was being pressured to marry the man with whom she had been living, but the prospective groom refused to marry as long as her children from previous relationships were still in the household. His insistence was the driving force for approaching the institution about admitting the girl. The emotional toll on the child was never determined, but being separated from her mother and family at such a young age must have been difficult, at the very least. Moreover, did this 8-year-old really belong in the training school? Would she have fared so poorly in society if allowed the opportunity to try to fit in? In fact, how valid was the conclusion regarding her "feeblemindedness"? These kinds of questions are still being raised long after her death.

THE KALLIKAK FAMILY

The young girl is known as Deborah Kallikak, although that was not her real name, and most writers have been reluctant to reveal her true identity. She became well known primarily because she was the focus of a study by a much-maligned psychologist of her era, Henry H. Goddard (1866–1957). In 1912, Goddard published a book, *The Kallikak Family: A Study in the Heredity of Feeble-Mindedness*, which was based on her genealogy. Deborah later referred to it as the book that made her famous. The book purported to offer a description of the power of heredity in determining human behavior. Specifically, it used Deborah's genealogy to illustrate how "defective" genes can lead to generations of negative family characteristics.

Goddard made up the name Kallikak—a combination of the Greek words for beauty (*kallos*) and bad (*kakos*). He believed, consistent with the thinking of many people of his time, that Deborah had inherited genes that were responsible for her limited abilities. The work of the Austrian monk Gregor Mendel (1822–1884) on the genetic transmission of traits had been rediscovered about a dozen years before, and it had a powerful effect on many leaders in society. It offered a simple explanation for an array of human behaviors, including problem behavior. If plant characteristics could be inherited according to the few simple rules that Mendel described, perhaps more complicated behaviors such as criminality, alcoholism, and prostitution could be explained in the same way. In addition, a common view at the time was that mental retardation, often associated with many of society's ills, was due to a single recessive gene.

The so-called nature–nurture debate was a topic of much interest during this period, and Deborah's genealogy would be used as proof for the inheritance of certain psychological traits. Although there were those who argued for the power of the environment even then, the general consensus of the time fell heavily on the side of biological inheritance. The impact of Goddard's research went far beyond his description of a single family, commenting on the society at large. It has even been argued that it was used as the basis for a number of social and legal reforms, though that discussion is beyond the scope of this chapter.

HENRY H. GODDARD

Although he has often been demonized, Henry H. Goddard was usually described as a good-hearted, religious individual by those who knew him. Raised a Quaker, he cared deeply about his fellow man and felt an obligation to use his abilities in the service of mankind (Zenderland, 1998). After a period as a high school teacher and principal, he enrolled at Clark University, where he received his doctoral degree under the tutelage of G. Stanley Hall, one of America's pioneer psychologists. When he accepted the position at Vineland, Goddard became one of the first psychologists to work full time outside of an academic institution. Most psychologists in his era were experimental psychologists who worked at colleges and universities, with limited interest in applied aspects of the field.

Goddard was hired to direct the research laboratory at Vineland to try to discover the causes of "feeblemindedness," a catchall term that was used at the time to describe people with a variety of intellectual deficits and learning disabilities. But

Goddard was also interested in the very practical aspects of prevention and management. Almost from the start, he saw heredity as the major culprit. He had little expectation that feeblemindedness could be significantly changed through education and training, but he thought it might be prevented.

A few years before the publication of his book, Goddard had spent time traveling in Europe, trying to determine if the explanations for the cause of feeblemindedness offered by psychologists there were any better than those being used in the United States. During his travels, he obtained a copy of a newly minted intelligence test, the first successful one of its time. Although Goddard did not meet the French authors of the test, Alfred Binet and Theodore Simon, he brought a copy of the Binet-Simon Scale back with him to the United States. Soon after, he had it translated and began administering it to the children at Vineland.

The test results corresponded very well with his expectations for the children. Since he had worked with them for several years, he believed he understood their capabilities, and the test appeared to mirror his own perceptions. Encouraged by his findings, he distributed copies of the scale to teachers in the area and asked them to administer it to children whose abilities they were familiar with. Again, the test appeared to be successful in characterizing the children. Goddard concluded that the test was both reliable and valid, with substantial potential for classifying levels of retardation. Subsequently, he became a promoter of the test, distributing copies of it throughout the country. Unlike Binet, who felt that intelligence was a flexible construct that could be enhanced by education and training, Goddard concluded that intelligence was largely fixed by biology.

Goddard was particularly interested in individuals judged to be *morons*, a word that he created. (Many words from the early descriptions of mental disability, such as *moron, imbecile,* and *idiot,* had specific meanings attached to them. However, they became terms of such derision that they are not used in professional contexts today.) For Goddard, morons constituted one of the most perilous forms of retardation. Children

▶ **Image 14.1** Henry H. Goddard

with more severe disability were likely to be identified and prevented from marrying and passing on their limitations to future generations. Morons, on the other hand, could easily be mistaken for "normal" individuals and allowed to enter society and marry. Though their deficits were less obvious, their impact on society could be more profound. Goddard perceived them as a great danger.

Soon after Goddard arrived at Vineland in 1906, he decided that to understand the causes of feeblemindedness, he would need to send trained workers to the homes of the children to gather additional information about them. He later wrote that he was surprised at the degree of feeblemindedness found in the families of the children and concluded that a large percentage of the children had been touched by the "hereditary taint." By the time the study was concluded, he and his assistants had been able to document the relationships, living conditions, and personal qualities of 300 families. He later published an account of this work in his book *Feeblemindedness: Its Causes and Consequences* (Goddard, 1914). But there was a curious side story that developed when he and his assistants were conducting the study—and it would end up eclipsing the larger story.

In the course of investigating the families of the institutionalized children, Elizabeth Kite, a field assistant of Goddard, came across a curiosity. Deborah Kallikak's family had the same last name as another family living in the area. But this second family was very different from the first in practically every way, including educational level, occupations, and lifestyle. Was it possible that these two families were related? They seemed so different. Kite was assigned the task of investigating the genealogy of the families. While interviewing a woman she had met with several times before, a relative of Deborah Kallikak, Kite was given information that linked the two families. Later, she was able to verify the connection from another interview (Smith, 1985). These families would become the centerpiece of the 1912 book titled *The Kallikak Family*.

MARTIN KALLIKAK AND HIS ANCESTORS

According to Elizabeth Kite, Deborah's line could be traced back to a man referred to as Martin Kallikak Sr., Deborah's great-great-great-grandfather. As a young soldier in the American Revolution, Kallikak Sr. had become involved with a barmaid at a tavern frequented by soldiers. The barmaid later gave birth to his son, referred to as Martin Kallikak Jr. By the time of Kite's research, she concluded that Martin Jr. had produced 480 descendants, only 46 of whom were found to be of normal intelligence. Additionally, Goddard concluded that 143 of the descendants were feebleminded, mostly based on descriptions of their lives. The remaining descendants were of unknown or inconclusive intelligence (Goddard, 1912). Most of these conclusions had little hard data to back them up, only judgments, and would be considered highly controversial by contemporary standards.

But Martin Sr. was to produce another line of descendants. Around the time of the birth of his son with the barmaid, Martin Sr. married a woman of his own social station, producing a separate line of 496 descendants. The contrast between the two lines could not have been greater. While the line with the barmaid produced an unusually high number of alcoholics, criminals, and prostitutes, the line with his wife had an entirely different quality. Not only were the latter much more likely to be landowners, but they married into the most prominent families in the state—from signers of the Declaration of Independence to founders of universities to prominent politicians. Their members were involved in prestigious occupations, including many doctors, lawyers, and teachers. The difference between the two groups was almost too perfect to be true. They were two families, living within the same county, yet separated by enormous gaps in their intellectual skills and social standing (Goddard, 1912).

These differences struck Goddard as virtually irrefutable proof of the power of heredity. Goddard recognized the possibility that different environments might have played a role in the outcomes of the two families. But since he was already inclined to believe in heredity as the stronger determinant, he viewed the huge gulf between the families as further evidence for the role of inheritance. The book electrified many readers, giving them strong warnings about the danger of defective genes.

CRITICISMS OF THE STUDY

Although not everyone agreed with the conclusions of the book, the climate of the times was strongly in favor of Goddard's views and many psychologists found themselves in his camp. Still, as time went on, the number of dissenters grew. Questions were asked about the methodology involved in the Kallikak data collection; even the manner in which subjects were classified as mentally defective came under renewed scrutiny. And there was much to criticize. There were not many documents available to trace the poorer Kallikaks beyond some birth records and death notices. Elizabeth Kite often had to rely on memories of relatives and others in the community for her data. It was difficult for her to be objective about many of the families who were poor and living at the lower end of society, sometimes in squalor. How bright could such people be?

Since so few objective or scientific measures of the subject's mental status were available, the designations "feebleminded" and "defective" were often applied subjectively. It was clear that intellectual level was frequently inferred from status in society, confounding the two variables. Goddard spoke of testing some individuals in the study, but he was also known to downplay results that were not consistent with his hypothesis. Moreover, intelligence tests were in their infancy. It was not until Goddard's friend and former classmate at Clark University, Lewis Terman, published the Stanford Revision of the Binet-Simon Scales in 1916 (generally referred to as the Stanford-Binet) that intelligence testing gained the rigor that many critics would require.

The biggest problem of all, however, was the old nature–nurture one. How does one separate the two? Isn't it likely that, given a better environment, the children of the poorer Kallikaks would have turned out differently? How difficult it must have been for a single mother who supported herself as a barmaid to raise Martin Jr. and provide a stimulating environment for him. Researchers into the genetic basis of behavior today have a very different understanding of the impact of the environment. They consider all behavior to result from the complex interaction of inherited traits and environment. Indeed, the power of the environment has been shown to be so strong it can even shut down the effects of some genes. By any modern standard, Goddard's views of the nature–nurture issue were too simplistic. But he was not alone; remnants of these older ways of viewing nature and nurture can be seen even today.

THE REAL NAME OF THE KALLIKAK FAMILY

Goddard and his associates were careful not to reveal the real names of the members of the Kallikak family. Even decades after the story was published, the officials involved at the institution would not release any of the records that would verify the family name. But for various reasons, including the fact that the family had lived for so long in the same general location and that Deborah became somewhat of a celebrity, the real name of the family began to leak out. Professional genealogists also became involved and were able to trace the Kallikak family. The revelation of the family name meant that public and private records of the family could be compared to the printed record as presented in Goddard's studies. The comparison was telling.

A careful reading of the data suggests that Goddard and his associates relied too much on assumptions, rather than objective reality, to classify their subjects. Scores of close relatives of Deborah Kallikak, including her half siblings, had been classified as feebleminded when the public record suggests otherwise. Later interviews showed that many of the subjects whom Goddard classified as feebleminded were educated, although at a relatively low level. Still, they could read and write. The family did have its share of alcoholics, prostitutes, and others judged to be unsavory, but there was no basis to conclude that they were feebleminded.

As for Deborah herself, the chronicle of her life, even as Goddard presented it, led many to believe that she was not developmentally disabled at all. While at the institution, she engaged in a whole host of activities, including sewing and ministering to the sick. It was reported that visitors sometimes confused her with staff.

She may have suffered from learning disabilities, which would account for her academic difficulties, but her general level of functioning did not suggest she was disabled.

There was one final nail in the coffin of the "natural" experiment concerning the two Kallikak families. Many years later, it was discovered that the original premise of the experiment was in error. The man identified as Martin Kallikak Jr. was not the son of Martin Kallikak Sr. after all. They were cousins. The error may have come from the faulty memory of one of the subjects of the interviews, compounded by the fact that there were many similar names in the two families. In any case, the model that was adopted for the study, which led to many of its most important conclusions, was simply wrong (Smith & Wehmeyer, 2012).

▶ **Image 14.2** Deborah Kallikak at her sewing machine

Public domain

AFTERWARD

Henry Goddard's involvement with the Kallikaks was not his only controversial foray into the public eye. In 1913, he was invited by immigration officials to evaluate new arrivals at Ellis Island in New York. His conclusion about the limited mental status of many of the new immigrants has frequently been reported. He seemed to take little account of their educational backgrounds, the effects of their long journey, language barriers, or even the strangeness of the questions they were being asked. For him, the only variable of interest was their intrinsic level of mental ability as measured by his intelligence scales—which, as we now understand, were not culturally sensitive assessment tools. Sadly, these measures of intelligence were used to send a share of these new hopeful immigrants back to their former countries.

Goddard stayed at the Training School for Feebleminded Boys and Girls until 1918, at which point he accepted a position in the Ohio Bureau of Juvenile Research for a significantly greater salary. In 1922, he became a professor of psychology at Ohio State University in Columbus, Ohio, a position he held until his retirement in 1938. Although he defended the Kallikak study long after its publication (Goddard,

1942), his heart no longer seemed to be in working with the developmentally disabled. The main focus of his work after leaving the institution was on the opposite end of the intellectual spectrum, with the gifted. Goddard died in 1957, in Santa Barbara, California, at the age of 90.

Deborah Kallikak remained in an institution for her entire life. When she was old enough, she was transferred from the training school to another facility just across the street, and there she stayed. Many of her activities during her years there are well documented. As she grew older, she developed arthritis and was given the opportunity to leave the institution. She declined. She seemed to understand the difficulty she would face in the outside world. Deborah died at the age of 89 and is buried in the cemetery associated with the institution.

IMPACT OF THE KALLIKAK FAMILY

The intense interest in the publication about the Kallikak family spoke to larger societal issues in the United States. The high rate of immigration raised many concerns about introducing defective genes into the general population. Various sectors of the society began to talk more openly about eugenics—adopting particular methods to actively manage the growth of society with particular concern for the defective. Many states passed laws that allowed involuntary sterilization of those who were judged to be of low-level intelligence. In some cases, the victims did not know the nature of the operation they were about to undergo. Others were lied to and told they were having an appendectomy.

Some observers have seen a direct line between the publication of Goddard's book on the Kallikaks and the adoption of the restrictive immigration act of 1924. Others take it even further, suggesting a link from the Kallikaks to the Nazi genocide of World War II. Indeed, the Nazis were directly influenced by the eugenics movement in the United States. Goddard himself was primarily interested in segregating the feebleminded from the rest of society, and he even changed his mind about that later in his career.

However controversial those links may be, there can be little doubt that eugenics was a powerful influence on society during a crucial period in U.S. history and that many prominent psychologists supported it. It was only after the horrors of World War II were fully realized that most American psychologists did an about-face and became avid environmentalists. Still, some of these early arguments linger. One has only to note the controversies surrounding the publication of *The Bell Curve* (Herrnstein & Murray, 1994) or the arguments against the effectiveness of early intervention for minority populations. For all of that, the Kallikak study remains one of the best examples of how we are all captives of the period in which we live. If we were alive in 1912, how likely is it that we would have been in agreement with Goddard?

A FINAL NOTE

The real name of Deborah Kallikak was Emma Woolverton. Professional genealogists have conducted studies and verified her identity. As it turns out, the Woolverton family (sometimes spelled Wolverton) has produced any number of solid citizens over the last century, business owners and teachers included, a surprising ending for a family that has been severely maligned for so many decades.

REVIEW/DISCUSSION QUESTIONS

1. What did the word *feebleminded* mean in Goddard's time? On what basis was Deborah considered feebleminded?

2. Why was Deborah's family so willing to give her up?

3. How did Deborah react to her institutionalization? Would she have been better off outside of the institution?

4. Why was Goddard so concerned about identifying "morons"?

5. What was the impact on the Kallikak study on other psychologists? How is the Kallikak study interpreted today?

CHAPTER FIFTEEN

LITTLE ALBERT
Teaching a Child to Be Afraid

Almost every psychology major has heard about Little Albert, the subject of a 1920 publication by John B. Watson and Rosalie Rayner. The article has been among the most cited papers in the psychology literature. A case study, it attempts to demonstrate how relatively simple psychological principles can be used to explain a variety of more complex behaviors. The fact that the research involved an infant less than 1-year-old only adds to the appeal. The study is also used to illustrate behaviorism, a school of psychology and an approach to conducting research that dominated American academic psychology for decades.

Despite its popularity, however, researchers and historians have pointed out the flaws in the study. In fact, some suggest that it is virtually worthless as a piece of research. Though it has been cited less in recent years, it has not disappeared entirely as a topic of interest. Most recently, researchers have tried to find out what happened to Albert. Specifically, they ask if the experiment had any long-term impact on his behavior and well-being. But the new attempts to determine the identity of Albert have only provoked more controversy.

JOHN B. WATSON AND BEHAVIORISM

The story of Little Albert (in the original article he is called Albert B.) begins with John B. Watson (1878–1958), the founder of behaviorism. In the early part of the 20th century, psychology was sprawling and unfocused, with little agreement on methodology or even subject matter. It was mostly an academic discipline that had yet to prove itself. Many psychologists of the time were faculty members in departments of philosophy. Some academic psychologists even had doubts that the field would survive.

To add to the problem, there was a proliferation of applied psychology, sometimes by legitimate members of the discipline but often by charlatans, offering solutions to every kind of problem imaginable. But psychological research at the time offered limited support for practical applications. Behaviorism would come to the rescue, offering a clear methodology and unifying much of U.S. academic psychology. In retrospect, not everyone agrees that was a good thing.

Several individuals had been promoting a form of behaviorism before Watson, most notably Ivan Pavlov, the Russian physiologist, and Edward L. Thorndike, an American educational psychologist. But neither of them was explicit about starting a school of behavioral psychology. Pavlov, in particular, didn't even want to be identified as a psychologist for most of his life. For him, psychologists were too invested in the study of consciousness and internal states, an approach that he considered unscientific. He required something more objective. Thorndike, operating independently of Pavlov, arrived at his own form of objective psychology, also encased in a theory of learning. As different as the works of Pavlov and Thorndike were, they each devised a system that would have long-reaching effects on behaviorism.

Watson's great breakthrough was to recognize the difficulties facing psychology and to offer a concrete solution that, he believed, would ensure its survival. In an address delivered at Columbia University in 1912, and published in an article in 1913, he presented "a behaviorist manifesto." In it, he proposed a new direction for psychology, one that would make a clean break from the older approaches and establish it as a genuine science. The new approach would focus on behavior as the subject of study. He argued that such an approach was the only way for psychology to be scientific. Attempts to investigate inner states or consciousness, as much of the old psychology had done, were a hopeless enterprise. How could inner states be evaluated in any objective way? (Some critics made the observation that this was the time when psychology lost consciousness.)

Watson's behaviorist manifesto went on to decree that the new approach recognized no border line between humans and lower animals, the implication being that humans are simply complex animals and that the study of lower animals would be useful in generating information about human behavior. Watson also declared that the focus of psychological research should be the study of learning. In effect, Watson argued that all behavior could be understood in terms of the laws of learning (Watson, 1913). Some years later, another early behaviorist, Edward C. Tolman (1886–1959)

George Rinhart/Corbis via Getty Images

▸ **Image 15.1** John B. Watson

would take it a step further. He wrote that everything we need to know about learning can be discovered by examining rats in a maze.

The Little Albert study was to be an example of the way in which emotions can be learned and then generalized. In this particular case, Albert was going to be taught to fear a white rat. For the study, Watson planned to use a model derived from the work of Ivan Pavlov, the Russian physiologist. (Pavlov and his research are discussed in Chapter 8 of this volume.)

THE STUDY

Watson had argued in an earlier publication that there were three basic emotional reaction patterns in infancy: fear, rage, and love. He further argued, without any solid evidence, that a child's home life provided many opportunities to develop additional emotions through a process of conditioning or learning. He planned to demonstrate how these emotional responses could be learned. Watson chose to focus on the fear response. Since one of the ways to elicit a fear response was to subject the infant to a loud noise, he would capitalize on that connection in his experiment.

The child Albert was chosen, the authors wrote, because of his stolid temperament. He didn't show fear easily and he practically never cried. His mother was a wet nurse at the Harriet Lane Home for Invalid Children in Baltimore, where the research was conducted. (A wet nurse was hired to breast-feed other infants in the hospital.) The very first phase of the experiment was to subject 9-month-old Albert to a variety of stimuli, such as a burning newspaper, a dog, a rabbit, and a white rat, to show that Albert had no intrinsic fear of any of these things. And indeed, when the items were presented to him, he exhibited curiosity but not fear.

Albert was also tested with a loud noise to determine if he would show a fear response. The experimenters suspended a 4-foot steel bar behind Albert, and while he looked in another direction, one of the experimenters struck the bar with a hammer. Albert was startled and the experimenters noticed a sudden change in his breathing, but Albert didn't cry. When the bar was struck again, Albert repeated his response, but this time his lips began to tremble as well. When the bar was struck a third time, Albert began to cry. The experimenters were satisfied that a loud noise would produce fear in Albert, and so they were able to proceed to the next part of their research (Watson & Rayner, 1920).

After waiting 2 months, Albert who was now 11 months old, was again presented with the white rat. But this time when the rat was presented to him and he reached for it, the bar behind him was struck with the hammer. These presentations continued over 2 days, a week apart, for a total of seven pairings. Toward the end of the trials, Albert began to whimper, cry, and fall to his side in reaction to the rat and the noise. After the seven joint presentations, Albert was presented with the rat alone, without the accompanying noise. Even without the bar being struck, Albert began to cry and fell to his side, trying to crawl away as soon as he saw the rat.

The experimenters had demonstrated to their satisfaction that a neutral stimulus (the rat) could be taught to be an object of fear. But could this fear also generalize to other objects? Watson and Rayner now presented Albert with a range of white and furry objects, including a dog, a rabbit, a fur coat, and Watson himself in a Santa Claus mask with a white beard. The researchers concluded that Albert's fears did generalize to other objects. For instance, when the rabbit was presented to Albert, he leaned as far away from the animal as he could and then burst into tears. Albert had learned to be afraid of not only a white rat, but he had also learned to be afraid of objects that had some of the same characteristics, like white or furry. When the experimenters presented several wooden blocks to Albert, he played with them contentedly. Clearly, Albert's fears did not generalize to other objects that were dissimilar to those on which he had been trained (Watson & Rayner, 1920).

In the final phase of the research, Watson and Rayner waited a month to test Albert again. They wanted to determine if the fear response would last. They concluded that it did. A month after first conditioning Albert, they could still see vestiges of his fear responses in subsequent tests. But, as many critics would later note, Watson and Rayner made no attempt to remove the fear response from Albert. The researchers knew that Albert's mother was planning to take him away from the hospital, and presumably they would have had enough time to institute such procedures if they wished. Instead, in the final part of their article, they discuss what they could have done to reduce his fear, methods that would later be employed in behavior therapy, but they didn't actually employ them.

ETHICS AND LITTLE ALBERT

Did Watson and Rayner act in an unethical way? Shouldn't they have been more concerned about the welfare of Albert? In the beginning of their article, Watson and Rayner make it clear that they are concerned about the well-being of the child they selected. They write that they chose Albert specifically because of his stolid temperament, and they felt that by carrying out the experiment they "could do him relatively little harm."

By the end of the article, however, they appear to be callous in their assessment of Albert's postexperiment life. They write that if Albert ends up on a psychoanalyst's couch years later, the analyst will probably trace Albert's fears to a dream containing his mother and some sexual elements. Instead, Watson and Rayner suggest, the psychoanalyst should have looked at the simple conditioning of a few basic emotions.

The Little Albert study could not be conducted now. Ethical concerns would not permit it. Colleges and universities have review boards that evaluate research in order to protect humans and animals, and they would run a high risk of losing government funding if they violated these standards. No such boards existed when Watson and Rayner conducted the study. In fact, no formal code of ethics for psychologists even existed at the time. Still, should they have known better? Most researchers would say yes.

FURTHER CRITICISMS OF THE LITTLE ALBERT STUDY

In 1979, Ben Harris, a historian of psychology, published a devastating critique of the Little Albert study. He pointed out that the depiction of the study in many textbooks was simply inaccurate. Sometimes the errors were small, such as the number of trials employed or the spelling of Rayner's name. But sometimes the mistakes were much larger and with important implications, such as stating that Albert had been deconditioned. Moreover, he asserted, the study was not a very good one. He used primarily two items to make his point: the written report of the study itself and a motion picture record that had been made of some parts of the study.

Based on the evidence available, Harris concluded that there was no firm evidence that conditioning even took place. For instance, no criteria for a fear response had been established or employed in the study. Albert's behaviors were not that clear cut. Furthermore, there was contamination in the experiment. On one occasion, a dog used in the study frightened everyone with his barking. Additionally, the authors wrote of "freshening up" Albert's responses. In the end, Harris wrote that the results were "interesting, but uninterpretable" (Harris, 1979).

One of the lessons of this research, he proposed, was the critical need to read original sources. He argued that if other researchers and textbook authors had read the original article, they would have been reluctant to report the study as they did. Surely, the study would not have attained its almost mythic status if the original paper were known in detail. Perhaps, most importantly, he noted, when researchers attempted to replicate the study, they were unsuccessful.

However, a few years after the original study, a related study was conducted. The author referred to it as a sequel to Watson and Rayner, with supplementary material on the development of emotions. Later it would be recognized as an early example of behavior therapy.

THE CASE OF PETER

When the Little Albert study was conducted, Rosalie Rayner was 19 years old, a recent graduate of Vassar College, pursuing graduate studies at Johns Hopkins. One of her acquaintances, Mary Cover Jones (1897–1987), a former schoolmate from

Vassar, heard Watson speak about the Little Albert study and became fascinated with it. In her work at Columbia University, Jones had come across a young boy who, she wrote, was like Albert grown up a bit. She called him Peter. When he was first observed, he was almost 3 years old, of average intelligence, and generally well adjusted. However, he was afraid of a white rat and would cry when presented with other items such as a wool coat (Jones, 1924).

Since Watson and Rayner were able to demonstrate that fears could be produced in a laboratory, Jones thought she might be able to demonstrate how they could be removed. She also hoped to make the research on Peter the subject of her doctoral dissertation, and she approached Watson to help her. By this time, Watson had become somewhat of a pariah in academic psychology for reasons not connected directly to the study, and he was reluctant to take a visible role in her research. He thought it would not do her any good to have him associated with her project, but he agreed to serve as an informal adviser nonetheless. She ended up conducting her study of Peter with Watson's help.

In the initial phase, Peter sat in a crib while a white rat was introduced from behind. As soon as Peter saw the animal he recoiled and screamed in fear. The next day he was observed whimpering or crying when in the presence of a fur rug, a fur coat, cotton, and a hat with feathers. He did not respond in the same way to other toys and dolls. Later it was determined that Peter showed the most fear to a rabbit, and so that animal became the focus of removing his fears.

Peter was brought into the playroom with three other children, and the rabbit was brought in later. This play period generally took place once or twice a day but was somewhat irregular. The other children were specifically chosen because they had shown no fear of the rabbit. Initially, Peter showed a fear response just by being in the same room as the rabbit. Eventually, however, he was able to tolerate the situation when the rabbit was 12 feet away in a closed cage. Little by little, the cage was moved closer. Then the rabbit was allowed to run free. Through a series of increasing "degrees of toleration," or desensitization, Peter found himself fear-free. Eventually, he was able to fondle the rabbit and even let the rabbit nibble on his fingers.

Unfortunately, there was a setback. Peter was hospitalized with scarlet fever and did not return to the playroom for 2 months. On his return, he and the adult accompanying him were frightened by a large dog. After that incident, Peter's fear of the rabbit immediately returned to its original level. This time, another approach was used to decondition him. Peter was placed in a high chair and fed foods that he liked. The rabbit was brought into the room in a cage while Peter was eating. However, the rabbit was not initially brought close enough to Peter to arouse any fear. Over time, Peter was brought into closer contact with the rabbit, always in the presence of satisfying food or the presence of other children who were not afraid of the rabbit. Eventually, Peter's fear completely subsided. Toward the end of the experiment, Peter was even able to verbalize, "I like the rabbit." Follow-up indicated he had developed a genuine fondness for the rabbit and was not afraid of the rat, feathers, cotton, or related items (Jones, 1924).

The work of Mary Cover Jones is considered an early example of a behavioral intervention. Although she later made important contributions to other areas of psychology, particularly her longitudinal work in the Oakland Growth Study, her role in behavior therapy was largely ignored. To be fair, she had not engaged in any systematic follow-up to her original study. Toward the end of her life, however, her work was finally acknowledged for the innovative contribution that it was. Joseph Wolpe (1915–1997), one of the founders of behavior therapy called her "the mother of behavior therapy."

WATSON AND RAYNER AFTER THE EXPERIMENT

The Little Albert experiment was one of the last pieces of research that John Watson conducted. He had become romantically involved with Rosalie Rayner, his assistant on the research, a student more than 20 years his junior. He eventually divorced his wife and married Rosalie, but because of the scandal related to his affair, he was forced to resign from Johns Hopkins University. He never held a permanent academic position again.

However, Watson did not separate himself from psychology completely, or at least not right away. Although he became a very successful advertising executive, during the 1920s he wrote several books on behaviorism and child development. He and Rosalie had two children and they attempted to raise them in a "behavioral way." Unfortunately, Rosalie died in her mid-30s and Watson never seemed to recover from her death. He ceased his contributions to psychology and eventually retired from advertising. In 1957, one year before he died, the American Psychological Association presented him with a gold medal in recognition of the significant contributions he had made to psychology. He had planned to attend the ceremony, but at the last minute he sent one of his sons to receive the award in his place. He later confessed that he was afraid he might become too emotional if he went himself.

WHATEVER BECAME OF LITTLE ALBERT?

Many psychologists have been curious about Albert's ultimate fate, and there have been several attempts to track him down. Most have met with failure since the records related to his time at the Harriet Lane Home have been lost. But Hall Beck, a professor at Appalachia State College, employed a different approach to find him. Using census records from 1920, he and his team were able to identify a child who seemed to fit the bill. All of the information about the child closely resembled the descriptive data in the original experiment. Their efforts to verify his identity read like a detective story.

They concluded that Albert's real name was Douglas Merritte, the son of Arvilla Merritte, an employee of the Harriet Lane Home during the appropriate period. Sadly, the object of their search, the child Beck considered the "real" Albert, died before reaching his sixth birthday (Beck, Levinson, Sharman & Irons, 2009). A more recent evaluation of a filmed record from part of the Little Albert experiment added even more fuel to the fire. These writers concluded that Douglas Merritte had likely been a neurologically impaired child from birth and that Watson must have known he was (Fridlund, Beck, Goldie, & Irons, 2012), a conclusion that many considered to be highly speculative.

And the story didn't end there. Still another group of researchers, building on some of the earlier research of Beck et al., discovered another child who fit the description of Little Albert even better. His mother had also been a wet nurse at the Harriet Lane Home at the time of the experiment, one of only three. The name of their candidate is William Albert Barger, who was known as Albert for most of his long life. He lived to be 87 (Powell, Digdon, Harris, & Smithson, 2014).

LOOKING BACK AT ALBERT B.

What can be learned from the case of Little Albert? Harris's comment about the use of original sources is certainly worth noting. Historical information can be so easily distorted when passed from source to source. Also, Watson and Rayner lived in a time when safeguards for subject protection were less evident. Ethical standards for research have grown considerably since the Albert study was conducted.

Another message from the study is the overemphasis that the experimenters placed on the power of the environment to mold a child's personality. It has been an enduring theme of much historical research in child development, almost to the exclusion of biological influences. Finally, it should be noted that the behavioristic approach has undergone extensive modification since the time when the Little Albert study was conducted though many of Watson's basic principles continue to have a significant impact on psychology today.

REVIEW/DISCUSSION QUESTIONS

1. What is behaviorism? What model of learning did Watson and Rayner use for their study?

2. Is there any indication that the researchers were concerned for the welfare of the child before they began the experiment?

3. What is the evidence that Albert's fear generalized? How strong is the evidence that Albert developed a fear in the first place?

4. Why didn't Watson and Rayner decondition Albert? Were they committing an ethical violation by not doing so?

5. Why has there been so much interest in what happened to Albert? Have the searches for Albert's true identity been successful? What is the evidence?

CHAPTER SIXTEEN

WHEN GENIUSES GROW UP
The Terman Study of the Gifted

In 1921, Lewis M. Terman (1877–1956), a psychology professor at Stanford University, began a study that would turn out to be one of the longest and most comprehensive studies in the history of the social sciences. His initial goal was relatively modest. Terman wanted to know if contemporary beliefs about intellectual "geniuses" were true. Specifically, he hoped to determine if people with high IQs were socially odd and physically clumsy people who "burnt out" early—common beliefs of his time.

His initial plan was to identify a sample of 1,000 young people with IQs of 140 or higher whom he would track for approximately ten years. As it turned out, he ended up increasing his sample size to 1,528 participants, and they continued to be followed even after Terman's death. In the end, the study yielded an enormous amount of data that remains a source for insights on development and intelligence today. Some of the results have been surprising, others more obvious.

Over the years, approximately thirty of the participants have been identified by name. The individual lives of many of them have become a fascinating addendum to the larger study. They include a handful of important contributors to our culture, one of whom—according to a distinguished historian of psychology—would later become the president of the United States.

TERMAN'S BACKGROUND

Lewis Madison Terman was born in Indiana to a family of farmers. One of 14 children, there was little in his early life that would foreshadow his eventual success. However, when he was young, a salesman and phrenologist "read the bumps on his head" and predicted great things for his future. Despite the limited educational opportunities in the area where he grew up, Terman was able to acquire several academic degrees. Eventually he was accepted into the doctoral program in psychology at Clark University in Worcester, Massachusetts.

The president of Clark University at the time was G. Stanley Hall, a pioneer American psychologist. Hall had built Clark into a formidable institution, with psychology as one of its greatest strengths. Terman greatly admired Hall and delighted in the intellectual atmosphere that the university provided. Before long, Terman had settled on a dissertation topic—a comparison between seven "bright" and seven "dull" boys. His interest in intelligence had begun early.

By the time Terman graduated with his doctoral degree in 1905, he had been diagnosed with pulmonary tuberculosis, a serious condition that had affected other members of his family. As a result, he limited his initial job search to geographic climates that would be beneficial for his health. He accepted a position as a high school principal in San Bernardino, California, but it was not his first choice. He had hoped to land a university position and continue with his research. Fortunately, within five years, he was offered a position at Stanford University, where he remained for the rest of his professional life.

THE BINET-SIMON SCALES

Shortly after his arrival at Stanford, Terman became aware of the work of French psychologist Alfred Binet, who had been developing a measure of intelligence. Terman's friend, Henry H. Goddard, an American psychologist who had also been a doctoral student of Stanley Hall at Clark, was traveling in Europe and learned of the scales. Although Goddard didn't meet Binet, he managed to secure a copy of Binet's measure and bring it back to the United States. Goddard was the director of research at a school for the "feebleminded" in Vineland, New Jersey, so intellectual assessment was highly relevant to his work. (The phrase *feebleminded*, a catchall term, would soon give way to other terminology, including the more contemporary *developmentally disabled*.)

Goddard became convinced of the worth of the scales and became their great supporter, popularizing them throughout the United States. However, it was Lewis Terman who would make the greatest impact with the test. Although Terman was also impressed with the scales, he found that they had limitations. Among other things, American children did not respond in exactly the same way as French children. The scales needed to be restandardized and renormed for use in the United States. Secondly, some items were not appropriate for American children and needed to be changed.

Terman immediately began revising the scales. In 1916, he published the Stanford Revision of the Binet-Simon Scales, which almost immediately became known simply as the Stanford-Binet. Terman's revision became the most important intelligence assessment of its time and the standard against which most intelligence tests would be measured for decades.

THE LONGITUDINAL STUDY

Terman believed that the future of America depended on nurturing its intellectually gifted younger generation since they would become the innovators and leaders of the next generation. He felt the more that psychologists learned about them, the better off the nation would be. The original title of his longitudinal study was "Genetic Studies of Genius." In those days, *genetic* simply referred to development, not to a direct examination of genes. For Terman, being a genius meant having a high IQ. Today such a person would probably be called "gifted." The colloquial term *genius* is generally reserved for people who have achieved noteworthy accomplishments. Terman would eventually change his terminology and make it more in line with the contemporary meaning.

Terman was able to secure a grant from the Commonwealth Fund, as well as additional money from Stanford University, to conduct the study. Along with several assistants, he began to search the public schools in California, hoping to secure a sample of 1,000 participants. His subjects were required to have an IQ of 140 or greater, a score that would place them roughly in the top 1% of the population in intelligence. (He later accepted some participants with IQs as low as 135. They were typically siblings of other participants.)

The sample selection usually began with classroom teachers who nominated the brightest children in their classes. The children were then tested, in some cases several times, to ensure that they belonged to the select group. It is estimated that Terman and his team surveyed more than 250,000 children before they obtained his initial sample of 1,470. Later he added gifted siblings of his original sample, bringing his final sample to 1,528, consisting of 857 boys and 671 girls. Terman was bothered by the greater number of boys in the sample and tried to account for it, investigating the possibility of a biased selection process. He was never able to arrive at a satisfactory explanation for the difference.

The typical subject in his sample was born in 1911, but

▶ **Image 16.1** Lewis M. Terman

there was a good deal of variability in his group. The oldest was born in 1900, the youngest in 1925. The sample was not representative of the general population in a number of ways, from its ethnicity to its socioeconomic level. For instance, there were comparatively few participants with an Asian or Latino background, and there was an overrepresentation of Jews in his sample. Terman's method of selection had not been systematic; his budget would not allow it. For economic reasons, he tended to conduct his surveys in the large population centers. As a result, it would be difficult for him to make comparisons to a similar sample with a lower average IQ later on. Though the issue of sampling was a matter of concern, Terman had succeeded in his main objective: identifying a large sample of children with very high IQs (Terman, 1926).

INITIAL RESULTS

Terman's review of his initial data corroborated his earlier suspicions. Rather than confirming the stereotypes of oddness and frailty among the gifted, the results suggested just the opposite. His sample of gifted children was physically stronger and healthier than average children of their age, with equally strong social skills. They participated in school activities and had many friends. They were hardly the oddball nerds that the stereotype held them to be. The lone "negative" characteristic he found was that members of his sample were more likely to wear glasses.

Many of the gifted had skipped grades in school and were frequently in the same classroom with older children. This age disparity, along with inevitable comparisons between classmates, may account for some of the folklore about the gifted, particularly when it came to physical comparisons. An age difference of just a year or two in children could result in significant physical differences. Not surprisingly, the gifted children were unusually successful in school-related tasks—they received better grades, moved more quickly through the school system, successfully applied to college, more often graduated from professional schools, and so forth. But surprisingly, for their ages, they were also taller and heavier, and had fewer health problems. It would be easy to conclude from these early data that good things go together. In fact, that is exactly what Terman wrote. Later, he would determine that the issue was more complicated than that.

Follow-up studies of the children began just a few years after the initial survey and continued in the decades that followed. In the early years, family members and teachers were interviewed, in addition to the subjects. All were asked to fill out questionnaires. Later, spouses of the gifted were asked to do the same. The participants developed a common bond and referred to themselves as "Termites." Terman was pleased to find that the intellectual superiority of the participants continued to exist beyond the original assessment, verifying his belief in the "fixity" of intelligence.

However, he also found that some participants had significant drops in their IQ scores, particularly among the females. With the addition of more grants, and the royalties from his own tests, he was able to carry the study further than he had ever anticipated as his participants entered adult life. Later, the study would be supported by donations from some of the Termites themselves.

THE GIFTED AT MIDLIFE AND BEYOND

Perhaps the greatest advantage of the gifted in his sample was found in their advanced education and professional achievement. They tended to cluster in occupations in which their verbal and abstract skills were the most needed and rewarded. Compared with the general population, they had a much higher percentage of individuals who became physicians, college professors, lawyers, scientists, and successful business people. Their incomes were considerably higher than average for their age cohorts, not surprising in view of their high occupational levels. The women in the study reflected their times. Compared with the men, fewer of them went on to advanced education or to professional jobs. Close to half spent their lives as housewives, without outside employment. Nonetheless, as a group, they were higher achieving in educational and professional pursuits than their counterparts of average IQ (Terman & Oden, 1959).

As members of the sample aged, some of their early advantages seemed to diminish. As a group, they always remained superior in areas that were directly related to their advanced verbal and abstract skills. Their higher income and, presumably, their intelligence were even correlated with health benefits. But their intellectual strengths did not shield them from life problems such as divorce, alcoholism, or even suicide. In terms of mental health, they were no more or less stable than the general population. From a personal and occupational perspective, some of the participants would have to be judged unsuccessful. Their lifetime occupations simply did not match the high level that their measured intelligence would have predicted.

When comparisons were made between the most successful and the least successful men in the sample, with occupational status as the major criterion, it was found that the two groups had virtually no difference in their IQs. The difference in their level of achievement could be attributed to personality characteristics such as ambition and drive—variables that could be seen early in their lifetimes. As important as elevated intelligence was, it was far from the only variable in determining occupational success.

A later comparison was made between 26 participants with unusually high IQs (180 or above) and 26 randomly selected participants in the study (average IQ in the 150s.) Although there were some differences in level of occupation and life satisfaction in favor of the higher IQ group, the differences were modest. The author concluded that even among those with extremely high IQs, there was nothing to suggest true genius, in the usual meaning of the word (Feldman, 1984).

A FEW OF THE NOTABLE PARTICIPANTS

The identities of most of the participants in the study remain confidential to this day. For some, their participation became known through their obituaries; others have self-identified. The participants who are known tend to be among the more culturally visible and therefore present a biased depiction of the sample. Nonetheless, they offer a fascinating picture of the range of contributions of the gifted.

Ancel Keys (1904–2004) may not be known to most readers, but his scientific contributions have touched a large segment of the population. Although he was born in Colorado, his family moved to San Francisco when he was young, just before the great San Francisco earthquake of 1906. His superior intellectual abilities were recognized early. Later he earned doctoral degrees from two different universities. His most important contributions came in the areas of diet and health. While trying to develop a balanced diet for combat soldiers in World War II, he created K rations, a much maligned but well-intentioned contribution to the war effort.

Later, using volunteer conscientious objectors during World War II, Keys investigated the effects of a "starvation diet" on mental and physical health. His results had practical implications for prisoners of war, internment camps, and even the general population following the war. (See Chapter 17 for further discussion of the Minnesota Starvation Study.) His most important contributions, however, may have been his efforts to determine the relationship between cardiovascular disease and cholesterol. It is a relationship that the medical community is still addressing today (Shurkin, 1992).

Since the selection for the study took place in California, it is not surprising that several participants had connections to the film industry. Edward Dmytryk (1908–1999) had one of the more dramatic stories of the study participants. Dmytryk grew up with an abusive father, ran away from home, and got in trouble with the law. Even though Terman and Dmytryk never met in person, Terman served in some ways as a substitute father, writing a letter on Dmytryk's behalf that resulted in his being placed with a nurturing foster family. Eventually, Dmytryk worked his way up through the film industry, becoming a film editor and director. When the "Red Scare" of the 1950s erupted, he became one of the Hollywood Ten, a group that was blacklisted by the industry. He would eventually spend several months in prison after being held in contempt of Congress. On his release, he was able to resume his film career. He is best known for directing such film classics as *The Caine Mutiny* and *The Young Lions*. He directed 23 films in all.

Jess Oppenheimer (1913–1988) was also a product of Hollywood, but he made his mark in television, not movies. After studying at Stanford University, he held a variety of jobs in television, mostly writing comedy material for performers such as Fred Astaire, Jack Benny, Edgar Bergen, and Charlie McCarthy, among many others. Later he would be the brains behind the development of the groundbreaking television show, *I Love Lucy*. It was the most successful television show of its time and would become Oppenheimer's crowning achievement. Lucille Ball, the star of the show and a highly regarded actress and comedienne, said that the show owed its basic structure and content to Oppenheimer (Shurkin, 1992).

A third member of the sample who went into show business was the actor Dennis O'Keefe (1908–1968). Born Edward Vance Flanagan, he wrote vaudeville skits and contributed scripts to the *Our Gang* comedies as early as age 16. He appeared in dozens of small movie roles under the name Bud Flanagan. On the recommendation of actor Clark Gable, the movie studio MGM renamed him and put him into bigger roles, although mostly in small budget films. He was particularly active in movies in the 1940s. He later appeared in several television shows.

There were several instances of "scholarly incest" in the sample. One of the participants in the study was Frederick Terman (1900–1982), Lewis Terman's son. Fred Terman demonstrated that his selection was no accident. After receiving his doctorate in engineering from the Massachusetts Institute of Technology (MIT), he returned to Stanford University as a faculty member, eventually becoming the dean of engineering and then provost of the university. He decided to turn some unused Stanford-owned property into an industrial park and encouraged two of his graduate student advisees, William Hewlett and David Packard, to begin a company there. The development of their company is generally considered to be the beginning of Silicon Valley. As a result of his contributions, the engineering center at Stanford is named for Frederick Terman (Shurkin, 1992).

Frederick Terman later invited William Shockley, coinventor of the transistor and 1956 Nobel Prize winner in physics, to set up shop on the Stanford-owned property. Shockley is also seen as a major force in developing Silicon Valley. Shockley had been tested as a child for inclusion in the gifted study but was not chosen for the final sample.

Robert R. Sears (1908–1989), a well-known psychologist as well as a professor at Stanford, was also intimately connected to the study. He took over the study in 1956 after the death of Lewis Terman. At that time, he revealed that he was one of the subjects in the study. His friend and collaborator, educational psychologist Lee J. Cronbach (1916–2001), was a subject in the study as well. Both of them had distinguished careers in psychology, and each had been elected president of the American Psychological Association, a rare honor.

For years there had been speculation about Richard M. Nixon (1913–1994) and his possible participation in the study. Nixon, the 37th president of the United States, was born in Yorba Linda, California, and would have been eligible for the study by reason of his age and location. Several early reports denied that he was a participant. However, Henry Minton, a distinguished historian of psychology, has revealed that, in fact, Nixon was a member of the sample.

LIMITATIONS OF THE STUDY

One of the limitations of a longitudinal study—a study of the same people conducted over a period of time—is the dropout rate. It is difficult to know why dropouts take place. The reasons may have a selective bias and are therefore capable of distorting the data. Because of the cohesion that developed among the participants of the Terman study, very few of the subjects were lost, thus leading to a more accurate result.

On the negative side, there was a certain amount of contamination in the study since the subjects were aware of the nature of the research. Indeed, some of the less successful subjects reported later that they felt a level of guilt for not living up to the standards expected of them because of their intellectual endowment. To add to the experimental contamination, Terman kept in touch with many of the participants, frequently writing letters of recommendation for them for college and other opportunities. He was also in touch with many of their parents, advising them on the development of their children. The impact of his involvement on the personal lives of the participants and, hence, on the results is unknown.

Longitudinal studies present still another problem. How accurately do they represent individuals raised in a different historical period? The Terman study participants grew up in a particular time in the United States, experiencing both the Great Depression and World War II. They did not have television as children, or for that matter home computers or handheld devices. Women at that time had a very different set of vocational opportunities available to them. In short, the Terman subjects lived in a different world from the children and younger adults of today. How useful are their data in describing people born at a different time?

In addition, there were limitations on the sampling itself. As previously mentioned, the selection process relied heavily on the availability of participants at the cost of identifying a more representative sample. The inclusion of family members as study participants would probably be frowned upon today as well. Terman was also criticized because he had missed selecting some individuals for his sample who, later evidence revealed, should have been selected.

Terman recognized that there were practical barriers to perfect participation. Among other issues, some parents simply found it inconvenient to travel relatively long distances to have their children tested and retested. Other parents—and sometimes school officials—refused to have children tested. Given these barriers, Terman was more than satisfied with the sample he was able to select.

As previously noted, the Terman study, through its initial information gathering and follow-ups, collected an enormous amount of data, practically spanning the 20th century. Since then, many additional studies have been completed using those archival data. As one example, in 1989, health scientists Howard Friedman and Leslie Martin began mining the Terman data for insights about health. In their book, *The Longevity Project* (2011), they challenge several contemporary ideas about health and longevity, discussing such factors as social connections and marriage, and personality traits such as dependability and persistence. Their book is one example demonstrating that so many decades after the initial sample was selected, Terman's study continues to provide insights on ways to live a successful life.

THE GIFTED TODAY

Several other longitudinal studies of the gifted have since been conducted, mostly inspired by the work of Terman. In fact, Terman is considered the father of gifted studies (Warne, 2019). One of the goals the studies have in common is the early identification of those with exceptional abilities. Consistent with Terman, these studies hope to identify and nurture young and gifted individuals since they hold the promise of being the future researchers and leaders of society. Rather than focus on the broad spectrum of cognitive abilities, however, the newer studies typically emphasize fewer abilities, for instance, those related to skills necessary to thrive in the so-called STEM disciplines (i.e., science, technology, engineering, and mathematics; Clynes, 2016).

One noted example is the work begun in 1971 by Julian Stanley, a psychologist at Johns Hopkins University. His Study of Mathematically Precocious Youth (SMPY) was modeled after the Terman study and included talent searches to identify gifted youth, particularly in mathematics. Once identified, Stanley monitored their development and proposed various educational acceleration programs for their benefit. The study continues today under the leadership of Camilla Benbow and David Lubinski at Vanderbilt University, a husband and wife team of researchers who have been codirecting the project since 1991. (The project had been transferred to Benbow in 1985.) SMPY's database has since grown to include over 5,000 intellectually talented participants and five cohorts (Lubinski, 2016).

While the benefits of nurturing the gifted have been generally accepted, it is worth noting that they also exhibit wide individual differences, with strengths, weaknesses, and different levels of passion and drive. It would be wrong to view the gifted solely on their intellectual dimensions. Any long-term prediction about their educational, occupational, or creative outcomes must take into account their multifaceted natures (Lubinski, 2016).

REVIEW/DISCUSSION QUESTIONS

1. How were the subjects selected for the Terman study? Did the selection present any future problems of interpretation?

2. How did Terman's subjects develop educationally, socially and emotionally?

3. Did all of Terman's subjects turn out to be psychologically healthy adults? How did the women fare?

4. Gifted individuals have often suffered from the stereotype of being odd and socially inappropriate. How do such beliefs originate?

5. What are the advantages of a longitudinal study as compared to a cross-sectional study? The disadvantages?

6. Why is the nurturance of gifted children so important—can't they take care of themselves?

PART THREE

ENTERING THE MODERN ERA

CHAPTER SEVENTEEN

THE MINNESOTA STARVATION STUDY

In a discipline with many curious—even odd—studies, the Minnesota Starvation Study ranks among the most unusual. Begun in 1944, toward the end of World War II, the study had very practical goals. As the war was nearing a close, it was known that many individuals in war-torn countries, as well as prisoners of war, had lived for long periods under conditions approaching starvation. What was the impact of food deprivation on these people, both physically and psychologically? What kind of behavior could be expected from them after the war ended? And, most important, what would be the best treatment to bring these nutritionally deprived individuals back to some level of normality?

It was hoped that the proposed research might even provide answers for more general and far-reaching questions. The history of the world has been marked with famines. An uneven food supply is ever present. And yet there had never been a systematic study of the effects of food deprivation. The study had the potential to yield vital information about a phenomenon tied to one of the most basic features of human existence.

Rather than trying to answer their questions theoretically, the researchers proposed to answer their questions empirically. Thirty-six male volunteers agreed to be put on a diet of very limited calories—about half a normal diet—and be closely monitored. All of them had been conscientious objectors to the war, and although they had been against the war itself, most were not only willing to participate in the experiment, but they were also eager to do so. Some of them felt guilty for not being involved directly in the war. Most of them considered their participation in the experiment as a way to demonstrate their loyalty to their country despite their refusal to join directly in the war. Also, many of the volunteers were genuinely altruistic and were more than willing to participate in an experiment that might provide a larger benefit for mankind (Tucker, 2006).

Some possible effects of severe food deprivation were already known. One of the most dramatic instances in the United States involved the famous Donner Party wagon train expedition in the winter of 1846 to 1847. After being stranded in the Sierra Nevada mountain range near the California border during a particularly harsh winter, some members of the group resorted to cannibalism to survive, an outcome that many find shocking even today. But similar degrees of food deprivation had developed in several European countries during the war, notably in Leningrad during the famous siege beginning in 1941. Millions of people were believed to have starved to death in Leningrad in this period, with many horror stories emerging in its aftermath.

The Minnesota study was carefully planned, with virtually every aspect of the volunteers' behavior monitored for a year. It was a unique study and one that would likely never be replicated for several reasons. The combined circumstances of the war and the pacifist inclinations of a segment of the citizenry provided the subject pool, a committed group that would be difficult to duplicate. There would also be ethical considerations to take into account.

At the time the study was conducted, human experimentation was common and ethical standards for research with human subjects were vague. Some of the increased sensitivity to human experimentation would grow out of the war when accounts surfaced of horrific experiments by both the Germans and Japanese. Modern interpretations of research ethics would likely not permit the kind of subject manipulation employed in the study.

Nonetheless, the climate of the times permitted the study to take place, yielding results that were both helpful and surprising. Several of the results pertained to phenomena that had not been originally proposed for study, such as eating disorders.

BACKGROUND OF THE STUDY

The chief investigator for the study, and the person who conceived of it originally, was Ancel Keys (1904–2004), a bright, energetic health researcher with an impressive background and series of accomplishments. (Keys was a participant in the Terman "gifted study" discussed in Chapter 16.) Although he had held a variety of appointments, at the time of the study he was the director of the Laboratory of Physiological Hygiene at the University of Minnesota, a position he would retain for the remainder of his professional life. Not only did Keys hold two doctorate degrees, he was the primary inventor of K rations, the staple food of many soldiers during the war. Despite the jokes about them, K rations were devised to be compact, portable, attractive, and nutritionally sound sources of food. By most objective standards, they succeeded on all counts.

Among the other researchers in Keys's laboratory who played a crucial role in the research was Josef Brožek (1914–2004), a Czechoslovakian-born psychologist who obtained a doctorate degree from Charles University in Prague in 1937. Brožek, who had only been in the United States a few years when the study began, was the chief psychologist for the study.

Due largely to his success with developing K rations, Keys was approached by the U. S. Army to solve other problems it faced regarding issues of health and nutrition. He conducted several studies for them including research on vitamin deficiency and the effects of temperature variations. When the idea for the starvation study occurred to Keys, he realized immediately that one of the most important elements was securing an appropriate subject pool. The Civilian Public Service (CPS) camps, overseen by the military, seemed a particularly good source, and it was not hard to convince the military of the need for the new study. The CPS camps were composed mostly of pacifists with both religious and personal objections to war. The funding for the study would come from a variety of sources, including church groups, commercial companies, and the University of Minnesota.

THE PROPOSED STUDY

Keys envisioned the study as divided into three parts. For the first 3 months, the volunteers would be on a regular diet. Their specific caloric needs would be evaluated, and their normal weight determined. These data would provide a baseline for the remainder of the study. In the second phase, lasting 6 months, the participants would be fed an individualized diet consisting of roughly half their normal caloric intake. The goal was to reduce their weight by approximately 25% during the 6-month period. Keys estimated that such a loss of weight would provide the kind of information required for the study, would not endanger the health of the volunteers, and was realistic. The third phase of the study, lasting 3 months, was the recovery phase. The volunteers would be divided into groups and fed according to several tracks, consisting of different levels of calories and food elements, such as protein and carbohydrates. The goal in the recovery phase was to determine which of the recovery methods produced the best results.

THE VOLUNTEERS

Keys prepared an elaborate brochure for the recruitment of subjects. In it, he wrote of the benefits to mankind in general that might flow from the research, accurately predicting that such an appeal would be popular among the CPS members, many of whom were highly idealistic. Large groups of CPS members had been working in forestry camps or mental hospitals, with varying degrees of satisfaction. Many felt they were involved in "busy work." More than two hundred responded to the call from Keys. He was careful making the final selection, recognizing that the selection of volunteers was crucial to the success of the experiment.

Several researchers from the laboratory were sent to CPS camps to evaluate the volunteers. Keys insisted that the participants in his study be in good physical and mental health. The latter was measured by a new psychological instrument, an inventory called the Minnesota Multiphasic Personality Inventory, or MMPI for short. It had been created only a year or so before, but it would eventually become one of the most important and popular of all the objective personality tests. The inventory consisted of more than 500 items, many of them seemingly benign. It was structured so that the individual completing it would be compared to others with known mental health issues. The final scoring would provide a chart depicting ten different mental health categories with a score on each for the subject.

Keys also insisted that all the subjects chosen should be single and able to get along with others. He felt that married subjects might have too many conflicts as the study progressed. Finally, he wanted subjects who were committed to the goals of the experiment and were likely to see it through to the end. Keys correctly anticipated that the latter stages of the second stage would prove very difficult.

Thirty-six volunteers were eventually selected, all male, between the ages of 20 and 33. In addition to meeting the initial criteria, it turned out they were well educated and considerably more intelligent than the general population as determined by several objective measures. Keys knew that he had not chosen a random sample of participants, but there were other considerations that overrode the need for such a sample. He recognized that he was experimenting with human beings, a sensitive issue for him. There were dangers associated with the experiment, both physical and psychological. He was careful to explain the dangers to his subjects as best he could. At the same time, he realized that despite his planning, he was entering unknown territory.

THE STUDY BEGINS

The volunteers assembled for the beginning of the experiment at the University of Minnesota in mid-November 1944. Their primary venue was the large warren of rooms underneath the stands of the university stadium. It was also the site of the Laboratory of Physiological Hygiene run by Ancel Keys. Here they would sleep and participate in many of their tests. Their food, very carefully monitored, would be provided in a cafeteria especially set aside for them in another part of the large campus.

Wallace Kirkland/The LIFE Picture Collection/Getty Images

▶ **Image 17.1**   Minnesota Starvation Study participants

In the initial days of the research they were subjected to a variety of tests, with a particular focus on body weight and fat content but also on their sense acuity and stamina. Their food, which most of them found appetizing and more than adequate, was calculated to find the precise level for each individual at which body weight would be maintained. They were instructed to engage in walking several miles each day for a total of 22 miles a week. Daily activities were organized for all of them, based on individual talents and interests. A few volunteers with scientific backgrounds worked with the researchers to analyze data from the study. Other volunteers attended regular classes at the university. Some with special talents or abilities offered classes to the other volunteers. All things considered, it was an easy 3 months. But they knew it would not last.

SIX MONTHS OF STARVATION

The second phase of the experiment began on February 12, 1945, approximately three months after the initial evaluations. Available caloric intake was reduced to slightly more than 1,500 calories a day, roughly half the calories available during the first phase. The diet was constructed to resemble the food available to citizens of several war-torn countries, consisting of large portions of potatoes and cabbage and minimal amounts of meat. Macaroni and cheese was one of the most popular meals, but its calories were limited and portions strictly controlled. Whereas three full meals were available in the initial phase, now the participants had only two meals—breakfast and an evening meal. The volunteers were allowed unlimited access to black coffee and water and were supplied with a daily quota of cigarettes.

During the initial weeks, there didn't seem to be any great difference in the behavior of most of the volunteers. They marveled at their weight loss, particularly noting the way their clothes no longer seemed to fit. There was some loss of strength, but their mood was generally good. However, there were wide individual differences. A book on the study by Tucker (2006) contains many case studies which illustrate the variety of responses. Tucker points to one subject, for instance, who began cheating on his food intake only a few weeks into the second phase of the study and soon gave evidence of psychotic behavior. After he was hospitalized and returned to a regular diet, his mental symptoms disappeared. Not surprisingly, he was dropped from the study. However, as a result of his behavior, the remaining volunteers were closely scrutinized for possible cheating.

Keys laid down new rules that prohibited the participants from attending any activities on their own. They were required to find another volunteer who would accompany them, whether it was to a university class or even on a date. Despite much grumbling, the volunteers complied. But larger issues began to present themselves.

▶ **Image 17.2** A volunteer in the second phase of the study

The food deprivation was beginning to show up in other, often unexpected, ways besides loose-fitting clothes. Food became the central focus of the lives of the participants. Whether they were reading a magazine or looking at a movie, any reference to food became a source of immediate interest.

The volunteers began to have food related dreams. They developed odd eating patterns. Plate licking was common. Other parts of their lives began to change as well. Several of the men had been dating, but their interest in dating—and any potential sexual activity—was one of the first things to disappear. Among the subjects who had pursued classes and other cultural activities, their interests in such activities were significantly diminished. Classes run by the volunteers came to a halt. The subjects were easily irritated and seemed to care less what their fellow volunteers thought of them. As the second half of the starvation phase began, other physical symptoms appeared. Participants were constantly cold, and their body temperature and pulse rate dropped. Keys concluded that their bodies were trying to conserve as much energy as possible.

Sitting became uncomfortable. They no longer had the padding afforded by normal weight. Fighting off food-related urges was a constant battle. The MMPI recorded significant increases in depression, hysteria, and hypochondriasis. Some participants thought they were on the brink of madness. Their odd and antisocial behaviors became even more pronounced. Another volunteer admitted to cheating, and before a final decision was made, he developed a physical condition that required him to be dropped from the study. The subject pool was down to 34. Two more subjects were dropped because of known or suspected cheating. They simply had not lost the weight they should have if they had been observing their diets. When the final day of the starvation phase arrived near the end of July, there were 32 subjects left in the pool. As a group, they had lost 24% of their initial weight, very close to the value Keys had sought.

THE FINAL PHASE BEGINS

The last phase of the study was labeled the "rehabilitation phase," but it was not the food-filled extravaganza that some participants had hoped for. Instead, it consisted of the remaining subjects being divided into four groups, with each group receiving the same kind of foods they had received earlier but with an increase in calories. The lowest group received a 200-calorie-per-day increase; the highest group received an 800-calorie increase. The changes were meager by any standard and the recovery reflected that. Weight gains were very small and slow in coming. The men became more antagonistic and troubled than at any time during the experiment. One man chopped off three of his fingers while cutting wood, and there was a strong suspicion that he had done it purposely. Even he was not certain if he had done it on purpose. Whether it was an accident or not, Keys was prepared to drop him from the study. However, the subject made an impassioned request to be retained and Keys allowed him to remain (Tucker, 2006).

After consulting with his fellow researchers, Keys decided to deviate from the initial plan and increase the calories substantially. The men went back to three meals a day, at a level resembling a more normal diet. The requirement that all participants have a buddy with them whenever they were away from the experimental site was dropped. The mood of the men immediately brightened. In the meantime, the war had officially ended, and Keys hurried to write an interim report that would be of some help to relief workers. Unfortunately, the experiment was not yet completed, and Keys felt it would take months—if not years—to sift through all of the data that had been collected. Reluctantly, he published a provisional report in October 1945, describing the study, but it contained little of practical value. His scientific mind would not let him draw conclusions from incomplete data. He did not publish a complete report until several years later (Keys, Brožek, Henschel, Mickelsen, & Taylor, 1950).

Fortunately, one of the psychologists who had helped him devise the study, Harold Guetzkow, was less constrained. In January 1946, he published a decidedly nonscientific manual, filled with cartoons and practical suggestions, which would be of great value to relief workers (Guetzkow & Bowman, 1946). One thing that everyone agreed on—the human body was a remarkable thing. Its evolution had prepared it for all kinds of assaults, including the possibility of starvation. In the end, its evolutionary history produced a highly resilient organism.

MASLOW'S THEORY OF NEEDS

Abraham Maslow (1908–1970) was a little-known psychologist teaching at Brooklyn College in the 1940s. But while there, he wrote a paper that would form the foundation for his later fame and would also, unintentionally, comment on—or perhaps explain—many of the phenomena observed in the Minnesota study (Maslow, 1943). His paper described a hierarchy of human needs that build on one another. He envisioned them as a pyramid. At the bottom of the pyramid are the most basic needs, physiological requirements such as oxygen and food. At the next higher level are safety needs, followed by the need for love and belonging, which are in turn followed by needs for esteem. At the very top of the hierarchy is the need for self-actualization, that is, a desire to live up to one's potential. For Maslow, self-actualization included a sense of being fully alive and finding meaning in life.

Maslow was flexible about the way in which needs dominated behavior, but one of his strong beliefs was their hierarchical nature. In his model, it was important for lower needs to be satisfied in order for higher needs to be explored and fulfilled completely. For instance, an individual lacking fulfillment in basic physiological needs, such as hunger, would have a more difficult time pursuing higher needs such as love or friendship. Needs at the very top of the hierarchy, including cultural interests and further education, would be at the greatest risk. Any deficiency in need fulfillment at the lower levels would jeopardize fulfillment at all of the higher levels.

Applying Maslow's model to the Minnesota Study provides a useful outline for the subject's behavior in the second phase. As their food supply was increasingly compromised, their inclination to pursue higher order needs was diminished. The items at the very top of the hierarchy, such as learning and creative expression, were the first to go unaddressed, followed by the next highest level—esteem needs. As the assault at the lowest level continued, other levels were compromised. While Maslow's model should not be followed too strictly—for instance, it does not address cultural variations—the hierarchy represents a compact set of guidelines to describe and summarize much of the aftermath of the starvation section of the experiment. It also provided insight into the treatment of disorders such as anorexia nervosa and bulimia. The implication from both the Minnesota study and Maslow's model is to treat the physical symptoms of starvation before attempting to treat the psychological issues involved.

FOOD AND THE WAR

Keys and his experimenters had accurately predicted the impact of the war on food supplies around the world. The United States had rationed certain foods such as sugar and coffee virtually from the beginning of the war, and citizens were encouraged to grow "victory gardens," which many of them did. Psychologist Kurt Lewin and others conducted studies on the best ways to encourage people to eat organ meats—such as kidney and liver—as a way to add options to the food supply, which were nutritious but not popular. However, few people were prepared for the images that would emerge from the German concentration camps. Survivors were walking skeletons. The war in Europe ended about halfway through the second phase of the experiment, so the study was not as helpful to wartime survivors as originally intended. Still, it is referenced today as one of the most important pieces of research on food and psychological issues.

AFTER THE STUDY

When the study ended, Ancel Keys did not drift into obscurity. In fact, he became even more famous with his research on the causes of heart disease. He became particularly well known for linking cholesterol and heart disease, a connection that has become commonplace in contemporary health care. Josef Brožek became a university professor and a noted historian of psychology. The subjects drifted back to a more normal life. Consistent with their levels of intelligence and education, they entered a variety of professions, with teaching and social work being among the most common. Six of them received doctorate degrees. Long after the study was completed, they continued to value their time in the study. They were unanimous in saying that they would do it all over again (Kalm & Semba, 2005).

The study continues to remind us of the relationship between food and a host of items, including mood, ambition, and body image. Dieters who have difficulty sticking to their regimen need to be reminded that it's not all about willpower. There is a built-in biological need to maintain body weight, a preservation mechanism. When that balance is challenged, the result is likely to be felt in other aspects of our lives, including the psychological.

REVIEW/DISCUSSION QUESTIONS

1. How were the subjects in the study selected? Is there a problem generalizing from the study because of its selective sample?

2. Would the results be different for women? Would age matter?

3. Are there ethical questions about the way the study was conducted? If so, what are the issues?

4. Describe Maslow's hierarchy of needs. Can you summarize the results of the study using Maslow's hierarchy as a guide?

5. What benefits were derived from the study? Does the study offer any suggestions for the modern treatment of eating disorders?

NOTE

The book by Todd Tucker cited in this chapter (see References) is a highly readable overview of the study, with many compelling case studies included. It is strongly recommended for anyone wishing to learn more about the study.

CHAPTER EIGHTEEN

THE BURT AFFAIR
Fraud or Political Ideology?

Science has relied on the honesty of its researchers for much of its progress. Data are expected to be collected, analyzed, and reported in an objective and dispassionate manner, independent of personal circumstances and institutional biases. Such an approach goes to the very heart of the scientific method. But expectations don't always match reality. Infrequently, though with some regularity, scientists have violated the standards of their profession. Some may lie about their results to ensure continued funding of their research. Others may distort the data to support a particular point of view. Whatever the aim, forged science has damaging outcomes, sometimes to the general public and almost always to the researchers involved.

The case of Cyril Burt (1883–1971) has been one of the more controversial in the history of scientific fraud. One psychologist called it "probably the most bizarre episode in the entire history of academic psychology" (Jensen, 1991). Burt, a British psychologist generally respected throughout the world of psychology, held a strong view regarding the nature of intelligence—he thought it was mostly inherited. His position rested on a body of evidence based on twin and family studies from which he believed he was able to tease out the relative contributions of heredity and environment. He had critics—the source of differences in intelligence has been one of the most hotly debated issues in all of psychology—but it was difficult to argue with his data. Still, some opponents did just that.

An American psychologist argued that the data Burt published later in his career seemed improbable and too good to be true. Others began to point to additional questionable behavior on Burt's part. The debate continued to grow and became even more heated. Scientific and newspaper articles appeared, as well as two books. The debate about Burt's results grew into a public affair. By the time the dust settled, there seemed to be general agreement that Burt had lied. His fraudulent data called into question the validity of his earlier conclusions. His name and data—which were frequently cited, even appearing in introductory textbooks—were now discussed only in connection with the scandal.

However, the story did not end there. After the initial controversy had begun to calm down, a curious reversal began developing. Articles appeared not only supporting many of Burt's claims but also questioning the motives and the behavior of the individuals who had raised issues about him in the first place. Was the vilification of Burt simply a way to discredit the hereditarian position? Evidence was presented in two books that appeared to nullify at least some of the criticisms. Burt's advocates also noted that his critics had been highly selective in the material they presented. Finally, there was the question of the role that the media played in promoting the controversy.

There the debate has remained, somewhat of a standoff between the two positions. But the central question was still unanswered: Did Burt really lie, or was he the victim of political ideology?

BURT'S BACKGROUND

Cyril Lodovic Burt was born in London, England, on March 3, 1883. The son of a physician, he sometimes accompanied his father on his patient visits. It was through these visits that he came in contact with Sir Francis Galton, a renowned explorer and inventor who in the latter half of his life had become fascinated with the subject of intelligence and its inheritance. (A discussion of Galton's life and work appears in Chapter 7.) After one of his father's visits to the Galton family, the young Burt remarked that when he grew up, he would want to be someone like Francis Galton. In some respects, through his interest in individual differences and statistics, he did.

Keystone Pictures USA/Alamy Stock Photo

▶ **Image 18.1** Cyril Burt

Burt attended Oxford, where he studied philosophy and psychology under William McDougal, the noted Scottish psychologist. McDougal, knowing of Burt's interest in psychological testing, encouraged him to write his senior thesis on the topic. From the pioneer days of scientific psychology, England had placed more emphasis on quantitative aspects of psychology than other pioneer countries, and Burt continued in that tradition. His work was also in the tradition of Galton, who had invented many statistics, including the correlation coefficient. These quantitative measures were found to be particularly valuable in the advancement of educational and psychological testing, which at the time focused mostly on intelligence.

Early in his career, Burt participated in a national survey of the physical and mental characteristics of the British people that further strengthened his interest in psychometrics. After a brief appointment at Liverpool University, in 1913 he became a consultant to the London County Council and would effectively operate as a school psychologist for the next 20 years. For all practical purposes, he became the first school psychologist in England (Fancher, 1985).

Later, Burt was a consultant to the committee responsible for implementing the English system of "eleven plus" examinations, a system that established educational tracks for students early in their educational experience. In 1946, he was knighted, the first British psychologist to be so honored. (Francis Galton had also been knighted at the very end of his career, but most do not consider him to have been a psychologist in a formal sense.)

BURT'S TWIN STUDIES

In 1931, Burt became a professor at University College, London, and chairman of the Psychology Department. It was from that exalted position that he extended the research and conducted the writing that would lead to his international reputation. His research on twins came about almost serendipitously when he learned of a set of identical twins who had been reared apart. This research would become the most persuasive, as well as the most controversial, part of his research program. He found that identical, or monozygotic, twins (who share 100% of their genes) were remarkably similar in intelligence whether they were raised together or not. Their separate environments seemed to matter very little as far as intelligence was concerned. They were certainly much more similar than nonidentical twins.

Nonidentical, or dizygotic, twins (twins born from two eggs and who have a genetic endowment equal to that of siblings) were, in fact, no more similar than siblings in intelligence. To Burt, the implications of these kinship comparisons were obvious. Genetic endowment was the primary determiner of intelligence, accounting for between 77% and 88% of the variation within a group. In Burt's view, the environment accounted for a much smaller piece of the variation in intelligence, perhaps 10% to 12%. The remainder was due to chance and other variables not yet fully understood (Burt, 1958).

Burt's conclusions were controversial among psychologists and others committed to a more egalitarian interpretation of intelligence. The prevailing view at the time was that the effects of genes were fixed—essentially a form of biological determinism. If variations in intelligence were due mostly to genes, then a child's level of intellectual functioning was largely determined at birth. What hope was there that superior parenting or a child's educational experience would have any impact on the child's eventual intellectual level? Equally important, would early enrichment programs have any effect on later intellectual development?

Burt's conclusions didn't seem to offer much hope. But, in fact, his beliefs were somewhat different from the way they were usually presented. While Burt believed in the heredity-based nature of intelligence, it did not follow that he believed in biological determinism. Heredity may set limits, but it does not determine the outcome completely. His earlier writings are demonstrations of this belief, though they were largely ignored by his critics. Instead, they seemed to interpret his work from a strict eugenicist point of view.

Many leaders of American psychology in the first half of the 20th century also held a strong position regarding the importance of inheritance to intelligence. After World War II, however, the attitude toward the importance of genetic endowment, at least insofar as determining psychological characteristics, began to change. Some of this shift arose out of the continuing influence of the behavioral school of psychology and its emphasis on the impact of the environment. But it also grew out of the realization that the horrors of the Holocaust were based on attempts to engineer a genetically "pure" race. As a result, there was some hesitation to attribute behavior to any genetic influences. With this shift in attitude, Burt's data came under increasing attack, particularly in the United States, though there were criticisms in England as well.

Burt, now somewhat elderly and suffering from Ménière's disease, tried to marshal more evidence to support his position, but his medical condition led to dizzy spells and made it difficult for him to collect more data himself. Instead, he used assistants to collect it for him—or so it appeared. Eventually, he published new reports that included additional cases of twins. They strongly supported his previous position. But therein lay a problem. They seemed to support it too well.

THE CONTROVERSY BEGINS

One of the statistics that Burt reported in his newer data was a correlation in intelligence between identical twins reared apart of .778, indicating a very strong degree of correspondence between the two. (A perfect positive correlation would be a 1.00.) However, psychologist Leon Kamin, from Princeton University, noticed something curious about Burt's new figures. They were identical to figures reported in two earlier papers, to the third decimal point. This struck him as improbable to the point of incredulity. While correlations may demonstrate a certain amount of stability among different samples, Burt's data were simply too similar to be true.

In 1974, Kamin published a book, *The Science and Politics of IQ*, that attacked the entire IQ "industry" but saved particular scorn for Burt. He contended that Burt had been vague and imprecise in describing his collection of data. Not only were his sample sizes frequently unclear, but the IQs themselves were based on estimates rather than sound psychometric principles. In short, Kamin concluded that Burt's data were useless for any serious scholarly discussion. This was no small item. Although other researchers had also investigated the IQs of twins reared together and apart, Burt had the largest sample by far—53 pairs in the final count. To describe his data as useless was to discard an important contributor to the nature–nurture debate.

Others joined the fray. In 1976, a science writer for the *London Sunday Times*, Oliver Gillie, wrote an article attacking Burt's scientific methods, questioning his results, and accusing him of outright fraud. With that, the controversy exploded. Burt had died 5 years earlier, and it appeared that no one was left to defend him. Burt had married somewhat late in life, had no children, and was estranged from his wife at the time of his death. However, his sister, Marion Burt, a physician, was his executor and had made arrangements shortly after he died for a biography to be written.

The prospective author of the biography was Leslie Hearnshaw, a noted British psychologist and a respected historian of British psychology. After the controversy began to emerge, Hearnshaw was concerned that Marion Burt might not be as cooperative as she had been, particularly regarding access to her brother's files and papers. As it turned out, she continued her support and encouraged Hearnshaw to make the biography as complete as necessary. She died in April 1978, a year before the biography was published (Hearnshaw, 1979).

While the controversy raged on, Burt's fate, in the eyes of many, rested on the outcome of the biography. Hearnshaw was known to be an accomplished historian, with no apparent ax to grind. His conclusions would be taken seriously. Moreover, it was known that he had access to many of Burt's papers and other personal documents. When the book was finally published, almost eight years after Burt's death, it did not reflect favorably on Burt. Hearnshaw concluded that, indeed, Burt had engaged in malfeasance.

Hearnshaw painted a picture of Burt's work that went back long before the controversy. He noted the different standards for testing that existed earlier in Burt's career and how World War II and the London bombings had likely resulted in the loss of a substantial amount of Burt's data. When Burt was called upon to defend his research, he was no longer able to do so effectively. As a result, Hearnshaw concluded, Burt had simply made up new data. In order to make the collection of new data plausible, Burt also made up two research assistants, a Miss Howard and a Miss Conway. Later, when others were trying to establish the validity of Burt's claims, attempts were made to locate both researchers. Ads were placed in newspapers in English-speaking countries around the world. No evidence could be found that either of them had ever existed.

Hearnshaw was able to point to other inappropriate behavior on Burt's part. For instance, as the editor of a leading journal in biometrics, Burt would publish letters to the editor, some of them with personal attacks on Burt himself. Burt would then write a rebuttal, defending his position. Hearnshaw determined that Burt had not only written the rebuttal but that frequently, under a pseudonym, he had written the original letter as well (Hearnshaw, 1979). The biography was a damning conclusion for Burt's supporters and one that carried a great deal of weight. Even one of his strongest enthusiasts, Arthur Jensen, a noted American psychologist, came to believe that Burt had lied—although he would later change his mind.

Burt's name could no longer be used in any argument to support the nature side of the nature–nurture argument. And still, this was not the end of the allegations. The husband and wife team of Alan and Anne Clarke claimed that Burt had written articles in their names, and modified other articles, all to benefit his name and position. Finally, a film was broadcast by the BBC in 1984, *The Intelligence Man*, which was highly critical of Burt. (Later, some of Burt's supporters would consider the movie to be a severe distortion of the truth, amounting to character assassination.)

THE TIDE CHANGES

It seemed likely that Burt's name and contributions were destined to be permanently removed from the history of psychology. But then a surprising thing happened. Burt's supporters became more aggressive in defending his name and position. Articles and books appeared questioning the conclusions of Hearnshaw and others. Most everyone agreed that Burt was somewhat eccentric and had become a curmudgeon in his later years, if not earlier. They also agreed that he engaged in a variety of tactics that were unseemly at best. But the conclusion that he had consciously fabricated data was another thing. There was simply no concrete evidence that he had done so. Moreover, data collected by behavioral geneticists completely independent of Burt, had arrived at almost precisely the same conclusions as he had.

One of the arguments that had been used against Burt was his diary. Oliver Gillie, the aforementioned newspaper reporter and one of Burt's early critics, had noted that several entries were suggestive of fraudulent behavior, though not enough of Burt's papers could be found to strongly support his position. Whatever papers and correspondence Burt saved had been given by his secretary, Gretl Archer, to his biographer. Hearnshaw, for his part, argued that the absence of certain information in Burt's diary and papers was evidence of his guilt. For instance, there was no mention of his assistants or the collection of new data. But there was another side to the story.

Soon after Burt's death, Liam Hudson, a professor of educational psychology at Edinburgh University, visited Burt's flat in London and looked over the crates of data that Burt had stored there. Hudson told Burt's secretary that he considered the data worthless without information that only Burt could supply. The secretary, apparently rattled by Burt's death and unsure of her options, agreed to destroy the data. She subsequently regretted her actions (Jensen, 1991).

It was only later recognized that the answers to Burt's accusers may have been found in those papers. Additionally, several individuals came forward to argue that Burt's assistants were not fictitious at all. Although both were now presumed dead, several psychologists claimed to remember them from meetings of various scientific societies. They had assisted Burt in the period before the war, and he was giving them credit years later as he reclaimed data that had been lost during the war.

It is also noteworthy that Burt's accusers held ideological positions that were at odds with his. Jack Tizard, a psychologist at the University of London who was strongly and vocally anti-Burtian, had assisted Gillie in preparing his case against Burt. Leon Kamin, Burt's original accuser, had long held a view on individual differences that conflicted with Burt's views.

FRAUD OR POLITICAL IDEOLOGY?

The debate over the importance of Burt's data is now largely moot. Additional studies of identical twins reared together and apart have been completed using more sophisticated methods and with much larger samples, such as the Minnesota Twin Study. Certainly, much of Burt's methodology and conclusions about the nature of intelligence are no longer acceptable. But the question remains: Did he knowingly forge his data?

There has never been any direct evidence that Burt committed fraud. As noted earlier, his results are in line with several other studies that have been completed since his death. In that sense, the research record has not been distorted, whether he committed fraud or not. But what about the personal impact of the charges? Burt's name has never recovered from the accusations that were made about him. If he was indeed innocent, an injustice his been done to him and to his memory.

In his edited volume, Mackintosh (1995) enlisted a group of contributors to debate the issue of Burt's guilt. He concluded that the arguments from both sides were flawed and that the case against Burt was "not proven." Still, he believed it was probable that Burt fabricated data. On the other hand, Jensen concluded that the books by Joynson (1989) and Fletcher (1991) clearly disproved at least some of the accusations against Burt.

There the matter has remained, with neither group offering a clear resolution. Fletcher pointed to a related issue that goes beyond the Burt controversy itself—that is, the power of the media to influence an argument that was largely a scientific one. And Fletcher expressed this concern at a time when many forms of modern media were still in their infancy.

REVIEW/DISCUSSION QUESTIONS

1. On what basis did Cyril Burt first arrive at his ideas about the genetic basis of intelligence?

2. Why were Burt's data originally questioned? Do you agree with his critics?

3. Why would Burt's critics engage in such an attack? Are their arguments based more on personal opinion than science?

4. How is the research of Burt currently viewed? What is the contemporary position on the genetic basis for intelligence?

5. Can you think of any other examples where the media have had a strong impact on scientific findings?

CHAPTER NINETEEN

TALKING TO ANIMALS
The Story of Nim Chimpsky

Several ancient philosophers, Aristotle among them, commented on the nature of the animal mind. Most saw a sharp dividing line between an animal's narrow experience of consciousness—involving sensations, images, and limited memory—and that of a human being. They believed that humans had a capacity for reason and language that was qualitatively different from anything that an animal could experience.

Charles Darwin (1809–1883) challenged that belief. Chief among his arguments was the belief in the continuity of humans and lower animals. And if continuity exists, doesn't it follow that animals can be studied in order to provide insights on the human condition? Psychologists have used this assumption to investigate a variety of areas. For instance, they have a long history of studying animals in an attempt to understand human learning. The use of the white rat in this type of research has become a cliché.

Another area of research has been an attempt to understand the cognitive processes of animals, particularly their capacity for communication. A string of studies has emerged from this research line, many of them involving the family of great apes. One of them involved the study of a mischievous but highly likeable chimpanzee named Nim Chimpsky.

NIM CHIMPSKY

The story of Nim Chimpsky began even before he was born. Herbert S. Terrace (b. 1936), a professor of psychology at Columbia University in New York City, was interested in testing the theory of Noam Chomsky (b. 1928) of the Massachusetts Institute of Technology on the nature of language. Chomsky famously argued that language is a uniquely human ability not found in lower animals. In his view, humans evolved in such a way as to possess a language acquisition device (LAD), a special kind of "hard-wiring" that allowed them to process language and rules of grammar in ways that no animal could. Chomsky's proposal had implications beyond an understanding of language. His theory helped to usher in a new school of cognitive psychology that was beginning to replace the older, dominate school of behaviorism.

Terrace proposed a research program with relatively simple questions at its base. Can a chimpanzee form a sentence? Can a chimpanzee learn basic rules of grammar? Because other researchers had previously demonstrated the verbal limitations of chimps, he planned to use sign language to test his hypotheses. His goal was to raise a chimpanzee in such a way as to provide as many human social experiences as possible, thereby increasing the potential for language development. He believed that while chimpanzees may not learn language as easily as human infants, there was no qualitative difference in their *capacity* for language. A chimpanzee, given the proper environment and language stimulation, he maintained, should be able to learn language. There was no need to posit a special LAD.

His proposal was a direct challenge to Chomsky and, by extension, to the cognitive movement emerging in psychology. Terrace had another goal in mind as well. He hoped that the chimp would learn sign language so effectively that he would be motivated to sign spontaneously. And with that signing, the chimp would be able to communicate his own feelings as well as his observations about people and objects in the environment (Terrace, 1979).

Several researchers had worked with chimpanzees earlier trying to promote language development. Among the earliest were Winthrop and Luella Kellogg, a husband and wife team of psychologists, who raised a chimpanzee, Gua, along with their son Donald for 9 months beginning in June 1931. When Donald began to imitate Gua's behavior, Donald's parents were afraid their son's development might be compromised, and they discontinued the experiment. In the 1950s, psychologist Keith Hayes and his wife Catherine took in a newborn chimpanzee they named Viki. Before the experiment ended, Viki could speak four words but not always clearly and only after enormous effort on the part of her caretakers.

The study that probably had the most impact on Terrace, however, was that conducted by researchers Allen and Beatrix Gardner who, in 1966, taught American Sign Language (ASL) to Washoe, a chimpanzee they had purchased from a government firm in New Mexico. By most accounts, Washoe learned to sign more than 350 words appropriately and created new sign combinations for novel items and situations (Candland, 1993).

But in all of these studies, a question remained: Did the chimps actually learn language or were they simply imitating the behavior of their caretakers? Herbert Terrace was convinced that he could teach a chimpanzee to learn genuine language.

Terrace had no experience with chimps and no funding for his research when a young chimp named Abe became available to him. He decided to work with Abe, but only as a preliminary to his main experiment. It was important for him to find out if his projected research was practical. After all, he was proposing to raise a chimp in a New York City apartment, not the usual environment for chimpanzees. A former student of Terrace, Stephanie Lee, agreed to take in Abe, at least temporarily, and raise him along with her other children. Terrace paid for a nanny to assist.

Terrace flew to Oklahoma to pick up 6-week-old Abe, who was quickly renamed Bruno, and dropped him off with the Lee family directly from the airport. The Lee children, particularly the youngest, Josh, age 5, were delighted with their new companion. But the arrangement didn't last long. Ralph Lee, Stephanie's husband, accepted a position with a theater group planning a summer tour in Europe. Bruno was left behind with graduate students as babysitters. Eventually Bruno was sent back to Oklahoma (Hess, 2008).

Little had been accomplished with Bruno, except perhaps to learn some basics about chimpanzee care. Several years would pass before Terrace again became involved with his language research. But once more, his former graduate student, now remarried as Stephanie LaFarge, would play a major role.

GETTING ORGANIZED

Nim Chimpsky was born in Norman, Oklahoma, on November 19, 1973, at a research station affiliated with the University of Oklahoma. Nim's mother, Carolyn, had given birth to six chimpanzees before, all of them taken from her within weeks of birth for research purposes. Nim would be no different. Ten days after birth, Stephanie LaFarge arrived in Oklahoma, Carolyn was sedated, and Nim was taken and flown to New York City, where his experiment would begin. The depiction of Nim being separated from his mother is heartbreaking to read (Hess, 2008).

Nim's name was an obvious riff on the name of Noam Chomsky, the MIT researcher whose theory Terrace hoped to repudiate. Nim's new home was in a brownstone on the Upper West Side of Manhattan. In addition to Stephanie, his caretakers consisted of her large family—three children from her first marriage and four of her new husband's children. In particular, Stephanie's daughter, Jenny, seemed to bond instantly with Nim. The role of all the caretakers was to provide Nim with the same kind of environment that a human infant might experience.

Terrace had not yet secured any funding for his project, but Stephanie's husband agreed to pay the bills to support Nim. He had come from a wealthy family and had many financial resources at his disposal. Although Stephanie had only limited experience with chimps, and her husband had none, they seemed to be under the impression that Nim could be treated as just another member of their already large family. The family's involvement with Nim included everything from toilet training and dining to social experiences. They even allowed him to smoke a joint with them, which he seemed to enjoy. Later, when Nim learned ASL, he would specifically request a joint. As it turned out, Nim was such an appealing creature, in so many ways like a human child, that his new caretakers went out of their way to provide a nurturing environment for him. He responded in turn (Hess, 2008).

Nim was playful, even mischievous, traits that contributed to his becoming a media celebrity. He even appeared on *Sesame Street*. Wherever he went, he was always the center of attention. However, he was also biologically a dominant male chimpanzee, and that became evident very soon. The entire LaFarge house had been rearranged to suit Nim. Before long, Stephanie's husband felt like he was being sidelined—which he was—and Nim seemed to take particular pleasure in tormenting him. Terrace visited the brownstone irregularly, particularly when it became clear that neither Nim nor the LaFarge children were particularly welcoming to him. But eventually, the experiment would have to start in earnest.

THE EXPERIMENT BEGINS

The first sign Nim was taught represented the word *drink*. His hand and fingers were molded into the appropriate sign, much as the Gardners had done with Washoe. Nim resisted, but within two weeks, he was using the sign spontaneously. In order to be certain Nim had actually learned a sign, strict criteria were established. The sign had to be observed by at least three different people over five successive days before it was accepted. In short order, more signs were added to Nim's vocabulary (Terrace, 1979). But as Nim's vocabulary increased, a problem arose.

Stephanie and Terrace had different ideas about the direction and speed of the experiment. Stephanie, who had been trained in the Montessori method, believed it was important to focus on the social needs of Nim, confident that learning would follow. Terrace, on the other hand, was eager to show progress to support his application for funding and insisted on a more rigorous training schedule. As a result, Stephanie eventually decided to step aside as Nim's teacher, although she would remain as his substitute mother.

Susan Kuklin/Science Source

▶ **Image 19.1** Nim learning sign language

As Nim grew older, it became difficult to discipline him, and discipline was frequently necessary as he seemed to enjoy biting people. Unfortunately, Nim enjoyed being physically disciplined—for him it appeared to be just another part of his roughhousing. However, Stephanie discovered that if she withdrew from him, ignored him or walked away, he would become upset. He hated to be left alone. He even learned to use the sign for *sorry* after he upset his caretakers.

It was also clear that Nim had a distinct personality. Besides his insistence on being the center of attention, his memory for faces was excellent, and he used it to ignore some people and accept others. People remarked that once you met Nim, it was difficult to forget him.

Terrace was able to secure a room and technical support from Columbia University so that he could observe Nim away from the free-for-all at the 78th Street home during the day. For him, it was a more scientific approach to studying Nim. He even hired an ASL teacher. But the conflict between Nim's handlers continued. In particular, LaFarge and the teacher clashed, and eventually the teacher was fired. Stephanie herself decided that she would have to give up her work with Nim—her marriage was suffering, and her role in the project had become little more than babysitting.

NIM AT DELAFIELD

When Stephanie left the project, so did the financial support that came from her husband. Terrace had applied for two government grants and had been rejected for both of them. But Columbia University stepped in to help. The University had been left a 17-acre estate named Delafield in Riverdale, a community just north of Manhattan. When Terrace became aware of it, he decided it would be the perfect place to raise Nim now that the 78th Street brownstone was no longer available. A new family was provided for Nim with Laura-Ann Pettito, who had been a student volunteer, as the mother and teacher. Eventually, she was named project director with a salary. (Pettito would later earn a doctorate and become a distinguished cognitive neuroscientist.)

Nim was 22 months old when the transition began. A month after the move to Delafield, Terrace received his first grant money. It was modest, but it was a beginning. A year later he would receive a much more substantial grant. Under the rigorous schedule established by Pettito, the rate at which Nim learned signs increased substantially, usually one or two signs a week. A large group of volunteers joined the project, all interviewed and approved by Pettito. Nim continued to be mischievous, taking great pride in opening windows and doors for a momentary escape, or terrorizing volunteers who were new to the project. But, all things considered, the experiment seemed to be going very well. Still more change was in order.

ANOTHER TRANSITION FOR NIM

Laura-Ann Pettito had put off graduate school to work with Nim. But she felt that she could not give up another year to work with him, and she resigned the project.

Several other workers left at around the same time. Terrace considered giving up the project, but it would mean the end to his additional plans for Nim. For instance, he had considered bringing another chimp to Delafield and have Nim participate in teaching the new chimp ASL. There was still another reason for not giving up at this point—the project had only recently become financially solvent.

Terrace replaced Pettito with Joyce Butler, who had been a part-time worker with Nim. Joyce and Nim seemed to have a special affinity for one another and would often work together for hours on end. Butler and her staff monitored every aspect of Nim's day, from the way he brushed his teeth to how he fell asleep at night. Nim developed an affinity for particular foods, with a special attraction to vegetarian lasagna. Hess (2008) wrote that if Nim heard Butler order pizza on the phone, he would go to the door and wait for it to be delivered.

The car trips to the Columbia University laboratory from Delafield were often difficult and required at least two people—one to drive, the other to keep Nim under control. Nim would get restless and squirm around, sometimes deciding he wanted to do the driving. His attendants had no choice but to hold him down. The trips were not without humor. Occasionally, Nim would be allowed to pay the toll, putting the money into the hand of the toll collector. The shrieks that followed delighted everyone in the car, including Nim.

In time, it became apparent that Nim was learning faster at Delafield and the trips to Columbia were discontinued, much to the displeasure of Herbert Terrace. Nim continued his celebrity with appearances on *Sesame Street* and other television shows, but the experiment was coming to an end. As he grew older, Nim was becoming increasingly aggressive, biting people, sometimes causing serious injury. Taking care of him became more and more difficult. On top of that, Terrace was not getting the additional funds he had hoped for. Terrace decided that he had had enough. Even putting aside the money issues and the problems with Nim, he felt that there was little more of scientific value to be learned from the project. Despite objections, Terrace called Nim's caretakers together and announced that the project had ended. Many of the caretakers were heartbroken. Still another problem arose. What would happen to Nim? Who would want him?

BACK TO OKLAHOMA

During the project, Nim had developed a daily routine and was in constant contact with his attendants. He was no longer a normal chimpanzee, at least in a cultural sense. And he wouldn't be of much use in additional behavioral research projects. His background was too unusual for that.

His caretakers made an unsuccessful attempt to adopt him themselves, but eventually arrangements were made to send Nim back to the Institute for Primate Studies in Oklahoma. Early one morning he was injected with a heavy tranquilizer and put aboard a private plane for the journey, accompanied by Terrace. From the beginning of the project, Nim had been uncomfortable with change, whether it was location or caretakers. Now he was about to undergo the biggest change of all.

Some of the changes awaiting Nim had the potential to be positive. The institute was the home of many other chimpanzees, including Nim's mother and several of his other biological relatives. He would be able to socialize with other chimps for the first time. But his daily life would be quite different. Among other things, he would be living in a cage. The introduction of a home-based chimp to a cage-dwelling future was typically traumatic for the chimps.

To the credit of Terrace, he stayed with Nim that first night in Oklahoma, hoping to make the transition as smooth as possible. The cages of other chimps were nearby, but when Nim awoke, he seemed more curious than frightened. Two of Nim's caretakers had also come to Oklahoma to help with the transition. Their emotional attachment to Nim had developed into a strong bond, and they wanted to help make his transition easier.

Plans were made to introduce Nim formally to another chimp, one who was thought to be more accepting of new chimps than most of the others at the institute. Indeed, when the other chimp was introduced to Nim, he seemed ready to play. But Nim would have no part of him. A day later, their interaction was friendlier, and they began to tumble together, a sure sign of mutual acceptance. Terrace seemed satisfied that Nim would have a good home and left after a day. His other caretakers stayed a little longer, less satisfied with the conditions in Oklahoma and still feeling very attached to Nim, but eventually succumbing to the reality of Nim's situation.

Once his former caretakers left, Nim sank into a depression and spent most of his day alone in the back of his cage. His experience with other chimps had been so limited, he didn't know how to respond to them. Over the course of 2 months, however, he eventually began to come around. He bonded with another chimp, Onan, who was in fact his biological brother. And the caretakers at the institute began to notice that there was something different about Nim. His signing was not only better; it was also spontaneous. Nim signed when he wanted something, even if that something was only to call attention to himself. He was also mischievous, a quality that had long been observed in him.

As different as Nim's life had become, even more changes were taking place in the background. Two of the principals involved in the institute, including its founder, William Lemmon, were having a major personality conflict. Roger Fouts, the individual most involved with language learning in chimps, left for another university. With him, hopes for additional funding evaporated. The University of Oklahoma made it clear to Lemmon that it intended to terminate financial support of his institute, arguing that it no longer met national standards and that the university could not afford the upgrade. Lemmon had little choice but to find another home for the majority of his animals.

Although Lemmon had avoided any type of biomedical research with his animals in the past, he was now forced to consider it. Eventually, and reluctantly, he sold off most of his animals to a laboratory affiliated with New York University. Nim was included in the sale. His new home would be a windowless, isolated prison in the suburbs of New York City; his only reason for being was to participate in a series of medical experiments on hepatitis.

Nim had become too famous for his relocation to go unnoticed. Several of his past caretakers went to the press and argued vehemently that Nim and all the chimps who had been raised in human homes for much of their lives deserved more than being isolated in cramped quarters, subjects of medical research. Even Terrace, who had now distanced himself from his earlier research, was aroused enough to argue on Nim's behalf.

The public outrage was successful. Many people volunteered their services to support Nim and his fellow chimps, including a lawyer. With legal representation, the pressure on NYU became much greater and it eventually relented. After less than a month at the research facility and before he could be used in any experiments, Nim was returned to Oklahoma and to Lemmon, his presumptive owner. The university removed itself from the controversy, arguing that it had no control over what happened to Nim.

However, Lemmon still had no financial support for his institute and needed to reduce his census. Eventually, he sold Nim to Cleveland Amory, a high-profile animal activist who was also well-off financially. Amory had taken a special interest in Nim and installed him in his rescue ranch in Texas, with its variety of species. What Cleveland did not seem to understand was that Nim was different from the other animals at his ranch who, in many ways, were self-sufficient, at least socially. Nim, on the other hand, needed social interaction and other chimps. In isolation, he grew increasingly depressed. Eventually, his caretakers found a solution. A chimp named Sally, 10 years older than Nim and also bought from Lemmon, was brought to the Texas ranch.

Nim and Sally took an almost immediate liking to one another, frequently spending hours a day grooming one another. When Nim escaped his cage, as he did frequently, he always took Sally along for the adventure. Their bond was strong, and they seemed content. But in 1997, after Nim and Sally had been together for 10 years, Sally suffered a fatal stroke. Nim was devastated. He became listless and withdrawn. It was evident that Nim needed companionship. And this time, three additional chimps were brought to Texas, two females—Lulu and Kitty—and Midge, a male. Very quickly they settled in, resembling a family.

Nim continued to sign, even teaching the members of his new family a few signs. When visitors came, he would sign for them and become frustrated if they did not sign back. None of his caretakers in Texas ever learned to sign. He took an interest in the other animals and the activities at the ranch. In a word, he seemed content. Then one morning, very suddenly, he fell dead of a heart attack. He was 26 years old, still reasonably young for a chimp. A documentary film titled *Project Nim*, by James Marsh, contains footage of both Nim and many of his caretakers.

CRITICISMS OF THE RESEARCH

The goal of the Nim Chimpsky project was certainly a grand one, as were the other attempts to break through the barrier between species to develop a form of communication. But the research with Nim did not end well for several reasons. The scientific ramifications of the research were questioned, and Terrace himself became dubious about the original point he had tried to make. In retrospect, in an article in *Science* (Terrace, Pettito, Sanders, & Bever, 1979), he concluded that, in fact, Nim never did learn any grammar, and his responses could not accurately be called language. They were merely imitation and did not possess the complex combinations that are ultimately seen in human language. Videotape analyses showed that most of Nim's utterances were in response to prompts by his teachers. Furthermore, Terrace blasted the entire attempt to teach language to chimps, not just his own efforts. He concluded that Chomsky had been right after all. Language is an inherently human capacity.

Attitudes toward animal studies have shifted since the research with Nim. Researchers have become much more sensitive to animal rights. They have rethought what we owe animals (Linden, 1986). There are even those who believe our approach to understanding animals is all wrong, arguing that we have been asking the wrong questions from the beginning.

Researchers have typically used human beings as the standard to measure animals. When we want to know how intelligent an animal is, we use tests that are made for humans. Authors such as Frans De Waal (2016) have argued against such a simplistic notion. Humans and other animals have evolved along different evolutionary lines, and the skills we need for survival have become quite different. If humans tried to compete with animals in any number of skills, they would fail miserably. Animals, like humans, are best evaluated in their own context.

REVIEW/DISCUSSION QUESTIONS

1. What is the position on Noam Chomsky regarding language development? Why was Terrace so interested in teaching Nim to communicate?

2. How had previous attempts to teach language to apes fared?

3. Why did Terrace conclude that Nim failed to learn language?

4. Are there lessons to be learned from the research that go beyond language communication?

NOTE

The book by Elizabeth Hess cited in this chapter (see References) presents a detailed account of the entire project, as well as the complex social and scientific environment in which Nim and his caretakers found themselves. Hess was also the author of the film documentary *Project Nim*.

CHAPTER TWENTY

FROM DOLL PLAY TO THE SUPREME COURT AND BEYOND

The Legacy of Kenneth B. Clark

In 1954, the U.S. Supreme Court issued a decision that some have called its most important pronouncement of the last 100 years. The case before the court was a challenge to the 1896 ruling *Plessy v. Ferguson*, which held that racial segregation in schools was acceptable as long as the quality of education was equal. More than half a century later, it had become clear that "separate but equal" was not working. Not only was the education offered rarely equal but the premise itself—the acceptance of segregation—was flawed and harmful.

Research results from the social sciences were used in the case, the first time such evidence had ever been accepted by the Supreme Court. Two of the people who helped to provide that evidence were Kenneth B. and Mamie Phipps Clark, a husband and wife team of psychologists. Their research began with Mamie's master's thesis in which she used dolls of different skin color to evaluate the self-concept of Black children, a topic that would later be pursued by both of them. Kenneth also played a pivotal role by organizing and coauthoring a paper summarizing the impact of segregation on the development of Black children.

Through his participation in the Supreme Court decision, Kenneth emerged as a figure of national importance. As the country entered a period of unrest and questions about its handling of racial issues became ever more prominent, politicians and educators looked to Black intellectuals such as Clark for answers. His characterization of the plight of Black children and the debilitating impact of social inequalities on their development spurred the creation of several programs to assist them (Philips, 2004).

By the 1960s, Clark was the most important social scientist addressing the public on issues of race. He eventually took on several significant roles in education and organizational psychology, including that of president of the American Psychological Association (APA), the first Black person to be elected to that office. (Two Black women have since been elected to the APA presidency, serving in 2018 and 2019 respectively.) As the years passed, however, Clark became increasingly disappointed in the limited success in the fight for racial equality. Moreover, he was concerned about the direction it was taking (Jackson, 2006).

PANAMA TO NEW YORK

Kenneth B. Clark was born in the Panama Canal Zone on July 14, 1914, the son of Arthur and Miriam Clark. His parents had emigrated from the island of Jamaica so that Arthur could work for the United Fruit Company. Despite the relatively stable financial condition of the family, Miriam Clark yearned for a better educational environment for their two children. When Kenneth was 4 years old, Miriam brought Kenneth and his sister Beulah to New York City. Arthur Clark remained behind.

Miriam and the children lived in a series of tenements in Harlem, with Miriam supporting the family as a seamstress. The family was poor, but Miriam was strong willed, with high aspirations for her children. She eventually became a shop steward for the International Ladies Garment Workers union. Her drive and energy had a continuing impact on her children's development. When school authorities wanted to send Kenneth to a high school to learn a trade, a typical recommendation for young Black males at the time, she insisted that he be allowed to attend a more academically oriented institution.

Kenneth proved to be a strong student, and after completing high school, he enrolled at Howard University in Washington, DC, considered to be among the very best of the historically Black colleges. Thurgood Marshall (1908–1993), the lawyer who would ultimately argue the case in which Clark's research was instrumental, and who would later become the first Black Supreme Court justice, was enrolled at Howard University School of Law at the time.

The chairman of the Department of Psychology at Howard was Francis C. Sumner (1895–1954), the first Black man to receive a doctoral degree in psychology in the United States. Sumner became one of Clark's most important influences. Kenneth completed his bachelor's degree in 1935 and immediately began studying for a graduate degree. In 1936, while completing his master's degree at Howard, he met his future wife, Mamie Phipps (1917–1983), who had been studying mathematics. Mamie was born in Hot Springs, Arkansas, the daughter of Harold H. and Katie Phipps. Her father was a physician and hotel manager, who had always provided well

Courtesy of Kate Clark Harris

▶ **Image 20.1** Kenneth and Mamie Phipps Clark

for his family. Kenneth's interest and passion for psychology was strong enough to influence Mamie to change her major to psychology. For the rest of his life, Kenneth acknowledged the crucial role that Mamie had played in his success.

After Kenneth received his master's degree in 1936, he returned to New York City to pursue a doctoral degree in psychology at Columbia University. (Howard University did not offer a doctoral degree in psychology at the time.) Kenneth traveled to Washington frequently to see Mamie, who was still in school at Howard. They were married in 1938. Later, Mamie also entered the psychology doctoral program at Columbia.

Mamie chose as her doctoral mentor Henry Garrett (1894–1973), who was academically distinguished but was known to have strong beliefs about the separation of races. Years later, they would meet again in a federal courtroom when they testified on opposite sides of a school segregation case (Clark, 1983). When Kenneth and Mamie graduated with their doctorates in 1940 and 1943 respectively, they became the first Black man and woman to receive doctoral degrees in psychology from Columbia University.

THE DOLL STUDIES

While still at Howard, Mamie had begun searching for a research topic for her master's degree. She came upon the work of Eugene and Ruth Horowitz (later Hartley) who had used drawings of Black and White children in their attempt to evaluate developing self-concept in children (Horowitz, 1939). With some modification, Mamie was able to adapt their work to suit her own research questions. The doll-play experiments would eventually involve many variations, but the initial procedure was simple. Black children were presented with two dolls, one Black and one White, and were asked a series of questions, such as: Which doll looks like you? Which is the good doll? Which doll would you like to play with?

▶ **Image 20.2** Kenneth Clark and the "doll play" study

Courtesy of Kate Clark Harris

The children had no difficulty identifying the doll that looked like them. Overwhelmingly, they chose the Black doll. But when they were asked which was the good doll or which doll they would like to play with, two-thirds of them chose the White doll. These results clearly suggested a poor self-concept regarding racial identification (Clark & Clark, 1939). The Clarks were able to expand the initial study and would eventually publish three articles based on their work. In one of them, they compared Black children from segregated schools to those from nonsegregated schools. Based on the results, the Clarks argued that educational segregation was an important contributor to poor self-concept in Black children.

THE ROAD TO THE SUPREME COURT

Rather than simply write about the difficulties facing the youth of Harlem, the Clarks decided to do something practical about it. After first attempting to have several agencies open their facilities to include Black children, they decided to create a facility of their own. In 1946, with financial help from Mamie's father, they opened the Northside Center for Child Development (originally the Northside Testing and Consultation Center). Over the years, it has provided a range of services including diagnosis and consultation, psychotherapy, crisis intervention, tutoring, and after school activities. Mamie was the director for 33 years. The center, open to children of all races, had as its original goal to provide the kinds of psychological and educational services that were often denied to inner-city children. It continues to provide services to underserved inner city youth to this day.

While still in school, Kenneth Clark met several individuals, in addition to Sumner, who had a significant impact on his later career. One of the most important was Otto Klineberg (1899–1992), a Canadian-born social psychologist and Clark's doctoral mentor at Columbia University. Earlier, Klineberg had conducted research that demonstrated the important role that culture played in the expression and assessment of psychological traits such as intelligence. His book *Race Differences* (1935) is considered a pioneering effort regarding racial differences in performance on intelligence measures. Clark was so impressed with Klineberg's work, it solidified his belief that social psychology could be an important agent for social change.

When Klineberg was asked to recommend a psychologist to participate in the Mid-Century White House Conference on Children and Youth (1950), he had no hesitation in suggesting Clark. It was his appearance at the conference that first brought Clark into national prominence. His paper titled "The Effects of Prejudice and Discrimination on Personality Development" would lead to another opportunity. In 1951, Robert Carter, who was representing the National Association for the Advancement of Colored People (NAACP) in its attempt to challenge school segregation laws, approached Klineberg. The NAACP planned to use a novel tactic—it intended to make as its central argument that segregation harmed the personality development of Black children. Carter and the NAACP had come to this argument on their own and were not certain if it would receive the empirical support they needed from psychologists.

Although Carter was hopeful that Klineberg would become their expert social scientist—indeed, Klineberg's books were the perfect background—Klineberg suggested that the paper Clark had prepared for the White House Conference might be exactly what they needed. Carter contacted Clark who gave him a copy of his paper. Clark later reported that Carter could not have been more enthusiastic. Clark immediately became the social science expert for the NAACP and testified in three court cases on desegregation over several years. The cases would eventually be merged with a fourth to become the class action suit known as *Brown v. the Board of Education*.

In addition to his testimony, Clark joined a committee of the Society for the Psychological Study of Social Issues (SPSSI), whose task was to prepare what became known as "the social science statement" for the court case. The statement contained several sections, the first of which was a summary of psychological research and theory about the impact of racial segregation on the development of Black children. The second section argued that desegregation would take place easily if the court established firm guidelines for its enactment. Written with psychologists Stuart Cook and Isidor Chein, but with Clark as the principal author, the document was eventually signed by 32 prominent social scientists and became an appendix to the *amicus curiae* (friend of the court) legal briefs regarding school segregation. It was generally agreed that Clark was the driving force behind the development of the statement.

Footnote 11 of the *Brown v. Board of Education* decision acknowledged the presence of psychological evidence, listing seven publications derived from the social science statement. Although it is sometimes said that the doll studies played the crucial role in the Supreme Court decision, they were not the only relevant publications. The first paper listed in Footnote 11 was the paper that Kenneth Clark had presented at the White House Conference. Although the court would later insist that the decision was based entirely on legal and moral grounds, the prominence of the psychological and sociological evidence suggested otherwise.

The unanimous Supreme Court decision was announced on May 17, 1954, with newly appointed Chief Justice Earl Warren reading the pronouncement. It was an occasion of enormous joy for many of those who participated, including the Clarks and Otto Klineberg. One of the curious details about the Supreme Court decision is that it appeared to be ignored by the larger psychological community. Despite the groundbreaking role the field of psychology had played in the decision, publications of the APA made no mention of it, which speaks volumes about the priorities and political face of the association at the time (Benjamin & Crouse, 2002).

A decade and a half later, members of the APA would elect Clark as their president, and in 1979, the association would organize a special symposium to honor the psychologists who participated in the Brown decision and the cases preceding it. Even though the association chose to ignore the Supreme Court decision in 1954, it could not ignore Kenneth Clark. He would continue his rise as one of the most vocal and visible critics of race relations in the United States.

AFTER *BROWN V. THE BOARD OF EDUCATION*

The Supreme Court decision did not immediately put an end to school segregation. To appease segregationists, the Supreme Court had tacked on a clause to the decision instructing states to integrate schools "with all deliberate speed." Many school districts found reasons to delay the implementation, and some groups tried to overturn it. Included among the challengers to the decision were some social scientists who argued that the evidence presented in the case was scientifically unsound. Further, they contended that the arguments used were nothing more than the personal beliefs of a well-intentioned but liberal minority.

Henry Garrett, Mamie Clark's former mentor, was among the challengers. In truth, there was something to their argument. None of the research cited included the kind of experimental study that would make a clear connection between racial segregation and the development of a poor self-concept among Black children. Proponents of the decision argued that separate was inherently unequal, regardless of science's ability to establish a causal relationship between segregation and self-concept.

Despite the many challenges, Clark's reputation as an expert on race relations continued to strengthen. In an attempt to show the public how cultural forces can lead to racism, he published *Prejudice and Your Child* (1955). His book challenged the status quo with its limited role for Blacks and pointed to the danger of stereotypes. He even included a chapter recounting his belief in the damage done to White children through discrimination of Blacks. Though not an instant success, the book slowly gained a following. A revised edition was published in 1963.

Despite Clark's increasing popularity, he continued to be tested by individuals resistant to civil rights. In fact, soon after the Supreme Court decision, he would meet with one of his greatest disappointments. The Kennedy administration appointed Clark to head up the Harlem Youth Project, a multimillion-dollar initiative. Unfortunately, the project became caught up in both the local and national political machinery of the day. If Clark retained total control of the project, it was likely that it would not be funded. If he gave up partial control, the purpose of the project would be lost. Seeing no possibility of the project achieving its original goals, and gravely disappointed, Clark resigned.

One positive outcome of his work on the project was the publication of *Dark Ghetto*, a controversial look at inner-city life (Clark, 1965). In it, Clark attempted to portray not only the plight of people living in poverty and slums but also the unique difficulties faced by Black Americans in the ghetto. His writing became less optimistic as he recounted systemic flaws in the social fabric. To his displeasure, some parts of the book were later quoted by members of the Black power movement.

Clark wrote that whereas most White people in poverty could see routes to greater success, many more Black people could not, stymied not only by the reality of their lives but by the expectations of others. Clark was critical of a social and political system that not only denied equal opportunity to all but often did so implicitly. He referred to it as a kind of "institutionalized pathology." He also directed some of his accusations at psychologists and their inability to accurately assess the intelligence of Black school children. Clark made no pretense that his work was one of a disinterested observer. Candid about the individual difficulties and faults of people in the country's ghettos, he became more and more a vocal advocate for the successful future of Black children in America.

As a Black man advocating for civil rights on a national scale, Clark became friendly with other Black leaders of the day, including Martin Luther King Jr., Malcolm X, and James Baldwin. In 1963, he arranged a television dialogue with the trio as they addressed the special racial problems faced by the nation. In 1967, he was instrumental in getting Reverend King to address members of the APA at their annual meeting.

THE AMERICAN PSYCHOLOGICAL ASSOCIATION

Until 1965 or so, Clark had not been a particularly active member of the APA. But in that year, he was asked to serve a term on the APA Executive Committee. The association had a somewhat mixed record on dealing with racial issues, preferring to put less controversial scientific issues first, but the strain between scientific priority and social relevance was becoming obvious. In Clark's view, social science had a responsibility to be relevant, to have an impact on people's lives.

Most organizational leaders were aware that there were few opportunities for Black psychologists in training or employment, and a committee was formed to explore possibilities for reform. APA's organizational sensitivity to racial issues was fueled by the social changes in the late 1960s, including the assassination of Reverend Martin Luther King Jr. and the race riots that followed. It was in that climate, in 1969, that Clark was nominated and elected to the APA presidency.

Clark was not entirely in agreement with some of the recent developments in psychology, including the creation of an Association of Black Psychologists (ABPsi). To him, the organization represented a separatist movement, and he was a staunch believer in integration. In his view, it was only through integration that a truly just society could be achieved. As a result of their differences, Clark was viewed with some suspicion by members of ABPsi. In addition to the distrust Clark was feeling from Black psychologists and some White psychologists, he also had to respond to a burgeoning movement of women psychologists. They, too, felt strongly that their needs were being ignored.

Clark addressed the problems directly in a meeting of the APA Board of Directors in December 1970. He recommended that APA establish a new board with responsibility for issues of social justice. This ultimately gave rise to the creation of the Board for Social and Ethical Responsibility for Psychology, which was finally approved by the APA membership in 1972. Its role was expanded well beyond inequalities related to women and Blacks and would go on to protect and advocate for groups ranging from Native Americans to returning veterans. Clark continued to monitor its activities for many years after its formation, and it would become one of his lasting contributions to APA (Pickren & Tomes, 2002).

THE FINAL YEARS

Clark retired from City College in 1975, but his retirement was hardly sedentary. He was named to a number of prominent positions, including an appointment as a member of the New York State Board of Regents (1975–1995). He continued to write and cofounded a consulting firm that addressed issues of affirmative action as well as other race-related problems. Mamie died in 1983, only a few years after retiring as director of the Northside Center. With her death, Kenneth had lost his closest collaborator and confidante.

Clark was displeased with the direction that Black freedom movements had taken. He didn't like the more aggressive, even violent, stance of groups like the Black Panthers. He was also outraged at some of the separatist attempts in the name of race relations, for example, the efforts to create racially separate college dormitories. In his view, that was not what the struggle for equality was about. Kenneth Clark died on May 1, 2005. He was 90 years old.

During his final years, Clark had grown increasingly pessimistic that his goals for racial equality would ever be attained (Keppel, 2002). In truth, the landscape of racial inequality had changed. Whatever his disappointment, his pioneering work helped to make America more sensitive to issues of race. His efforts to make institutional psychology, in particular the American Psychological Association, equally sensitive to all aspects of social justice, endure to this day.

REVIEW/DISCUSSION QUESTIONS

1. The *Plessy* Supreme Court decision argued for "separate but equal" accommodations. In what ways were schools for Black children not equal?

2. Were schools immediately integrated after the 1954 Brown decision? What were the barriers to integration?

3. What was the reaction of organized psychology to the Brown decision?

4. As Kenneth Clark grew older, he was less optimistic about race relations in the United States. What developments disturbed him? Were his feelings well grounded?

5. What were Clark's most important contributions?

6. How would you evaluate the state of race relations today, both progress and limitations?

CHAPTER TWENTY-ONE

CHALLENGING SOCIETAL NORMS ON HOMOSEXUALITY

The Story of Evelyn Hooker

In the current social climate, it may be difficult to appreciate the burden that gay men and women experienced in the United States in earlier decades. For many years, the gay and lesbian existence was largely a secret one, hidden from the general public. Individuals whose sexuality was exposed might experience not only significant embarrassment and legal difficulties but also the loss of a job. Police raids on gay clubs were commonplace.

Various methods were developed for attempting to change the sexual orientation of homosexual men and women, including such extreme techniques as electroshock therapy and lobotomies. During the 1950s, U.S. Senator Joseph McCarthy famously spoke of communists and homosexuals in the government as an example of the "horrors" he wanted to root out. He found many supporters. Before 1973, homosexuality was listed in the *Diagnostic and Statistical Manual of Mental Disorders* (DSM), a standard reference work published by the American Psychiatric Association, under various negative categories, such as *paraphilia.* By including it in the manual, homosexuality was officially considered deviant by the professional community of mental health workers.

The attitude toward homosexuality began to change in the latter part of the 20th century, a shift that was part of a larger cultural transformation that included the modern women's movement and the civil rights movement. The Stonewall Riots of 1969 are often identified as a turning point, signaling a new attitude among gay men and women themselves. In addition to the cultural shift, there were also a few individuals whose contributions were ahead of the curve. One of those individuals was psychologist Evelyn Hooker. She helped lay the groundwork for the movement that followed, ultimately becoming a much-honored icon of the modern gay movement.

Hooker's initial contribution was to conduct a piece of research that became a classic in the field of gender studies. Its effect was to challenge, in a decisive way, the prevailing view of homosexuality. Whereas homosexuality had previously been seen as pathological in and of itself, her study demonstrated that homosexuals were no more pathological than heterosexuals. And her initial study was only a starting point. Through additional writing and research by her and others, the classification system of homosexual behavior by mental health professionals came under greater scrutiny and was eventually changed. The ripple effect would later be seen from legal rulings on marriage and adoption to attitudes in the military. Her story is a prime example of the powerful effect that one person can have on an important social issue (Anonymous, 1992).

SETTING THE STAGE

Evelyn Gentry was born September 2, 1907, on a farm in North Platte, Nebraska, the sixth of nine children. Her mother had traveled west in a covered wagon. The family moved to Colorado when Evelyn was young, and she was initially educated in a series of one-room schoolhouses. As she approached high school age, her mother moved the family to Sterling, Colorado, the county seat, in part to ensure that Evelyn would be near the large and stimulating local high school. Evelyn's mother had left school in the third grade, but she valued education for her children and continually preached its virtues to Evelyn.

Evelyn was a bright and successful student, and after high school she entered the University of Colorado at Boulder, where she eventually majored in psychology. After completing a bachelor's and master's degree at Boulder, a favorite teacher, Karl Muezinger, encouraged her to study for a doctorate. Yale University was her first choice for a doctoral program, but she was denied a chance to go there. The chairman of the Psychology Department at Colorado had refused to write her a letter of recommendation. He was a graduate of Yale and believed his alma mater was no place for a woman. Instead, Evelyn applied to Johns Hopkins University and was accepted, but her encounter with gender discrimination stayed with her.

She received her doctorate in 1932 from Johns Hopkins in experimental psychology, with a dissertation on discrimination learning. Jobs were scarce during the Depression—especially for women—and she was fortunate to find a position at the Maryland College for Women, where she taught from 1934 to 1936. At the end of that period, she was diagnosed with tuberculosis and, with the help of friends, relocated to a sanitarium in California to recover. After nearly two years of recovery, she resumed part-time teaching at Whittier College in California.

During her long recuperation, Evelyn's interests had turned toward clinical psychology. In an effort to upgrade her credentials, she secured a fellowship to study at the Institute for Psychotherapy in Berlin for a year. While in Germany she lived with a Jewish family and was able to observe firsthand the rampant anti-Semitism there. It was another early life experience that sensitized her to the systematic mistreatment and marginalization of groups.

When she returned to the United States, Evelyn accepted a teaching position at the University of California, Los Angeles (UCLA) where she remained for 30 years. But she was not offered a regular position in the department of psychology. The chairman of the department thought there were too many women in the department already. Instead she was offered a position in their extension program, similar to an adult education program. Despite the decades she spent at UCLA, she would never hold a "regular" faculty position.

In 1941, she married Donn Caldwell, a freelance writer, and she settled into the life of an academic. Her reputation as a teacher grew and she derived a great deal of satisfaction from her work in the classroom. And it was through the classroom that the next important phase of her life began (Kimmel & Garnets, 2000).

SAM FROM

As Hooker later told the story, the idea for her study began with an undergraduate student named Sam From. She and Sam had become friendly, and although she was not initially aware that he was gay, he became comfortable enough with her to openly discuss his sexual orientation. During this period, when most homosexuals had to put on a public face of heterosexuality, there were also social gatherings consisting mostly of gays and lesbians where they could be more open about their sexual orientation. Sam invited Evelyn and her husband to attend some of these social gatherings with him, and she became acquainted with many of his friends.

One day in 1945, Sam posed a challenge to her. He insisted that she study gay men—that psychologists and other mental health workers consistently misrepresented them. Evelyn protested that she knew nothing about homosexuality. He insisted that she learn (Shneidman, 1998). It was a challenge that would change her life. (Unfortunately, Sam From died in an automobile accident in 1956, only months before the study that he had so strongly encouraged was published.)

The commonplace view of gay men and lesbians at the time was that their sexuality was, in fact, an outward sign of pathology, a deviant form of development. Sam From's argument was that homosexual men and lesbians were no more disturbed than the rest of the population. The problem, he argued, was that the members of their group who were typically seen by mental health professionals were a highly selective sample, often including people who were in hospitals or prisons as well as others who sought professional help. They were not a random sample of the gay population and therefore much more likely to show pathology than the general population.

Evelyn didn't argue with his thesis, but she was ambivalent about following through on his challenge. She knew nothing about studies in sexuality. How could she possibly test such a hypothesis? Where would she obtain a sample? In addition to these concerns, her personal life was in turmoil. In 1947, she divorced her husband and put aside any thoughts of a research project.

Evelyn married again in 1951 to Edward Hooker, a distinguished professor of English at UCLA. The marriage lasted 7 years, until his sudden and untimely death. She considered him to be the love of her life. After his death, she never remarried. But during the years of her marriage, Evelyn had become convinced that Sam From was right. Someone needed to study homosexuals in an objective way. A study had even begun to form in her mind.

THE STUDY

Her idea for a study had an elegant simplicity. She would compare a sample of "normal" homosexual men to a sample of "normal" heterosexual men on several psychological instruments. The idea was not to argue that homosexual men were paragons of mental health but rather that they were no more pathological than heterosexual men. Still, with all its simplicity, the study was a lot more difficult to implement than she had anticipated.

In 1953, she applied for a grant from the National Institute of Mental Health (NIMH). Her research idea so intrigued John Eberhart, the head of the grants division, that he came to UCLA to meet with her personally. At the end of their visit, he told Hooker that the division was prepared to give her a grant—though he cautioned that she might never receive it. The times were so perilous with witch hunts of communists and homosexuals that he couldn't guarantee there wouldn't be some kind of interference from bureaucrats along the way.

As it turned out, Evelyn received the grant. Not only that, but it was renewed until 1961, at which point she was given a Research Career Award. After Eberhart left NIMH, his position was taken over by Philip Sapir, who also became an ally in Hooker's research. She always remained grateful to Eberhart and later said that without the interest and help of Sapir, she probably would not have continued beyond her initial project (Hooker, 1993).

She chose three psychological instruments to use for her initial research: the Thematic Apperception Test (TAT), the Rorschach Inkblot Test, and the Make-a-Picture-Story (MAPS) test. All three are considered projective tests, that is, instruments designed to elicit projected feelings and thoughts from ambiguous stimuli. Many aspects of the instruments are debatable, including the theory underlying them and their scoring. None of the instruments are considered objective measures of personality, and this would later become one of the criticisms of Hooker's research.

Her selection of subjects also became a subject of controversy. Through her many contacts in the gay community, she was able to assemble a sample of gay men who had no significant heterosexual history and no history of pathology. None were in psychotherapy at the time of their participation in the study. Among the contacts she used were members of the newly formed Mattachine Society, a gay advocacy group. Critics would later argue that participants selected through such a group would hardly be representative of gay men at large.

And she had another problem. Where was she going to get her sample of heterosexual men? Once the nature of her research became known, recruitment became very difficult. Heterosexual men avoided visiting her office. In addition, UCLA insisted that she conduct the research on university property. But she knew if she did, it would be impossible to recruit participants. The privacy of the participants was paramount. She had to find a different way.

Luckily, her home was situated on an acre of property, with a garden study that was separate from the house. Once inside the gate, the privacy of her participants was ensured. She tape-recorded all of the sessions, including interviews and testing. After the sessions were transcribed, she erased the recordings. Only Hooker and her secretary had access to the material before it was transcribed.

The participants had put a great deal of trust in her and she was fastidious in honoring that trust. She even declined offers from potential coinvestigators because she didn't want to increase the risk of revealing the identity of her participants. She later wrote that she would have welcomed additional fellow workers, particularly because the times were so fraught with dangers from McCarthy-like thinking and she could have used the personal support, but she felt compelled to continue the study on her own.

Her interest in understanding the lifestyle of her participants took her beyond the simple act of interviewing and testing them. She had developed many gay friends, and they asked her to join them on some social occasions. Among other things, this meant going with them to parties and gay bars. Frequently she would be the only woman in attendance. Although she remained heterosexual her entire life, some of her gay fans would later consider her to be an "honorary homosexual."

Eventually, Hooker was able to gather her final sample of 30 heterosexual men and 30 homosexual men who had been matched on the variables of IQ, age, and educational level. After the personality measures were scored by experts on the tests—each test was scored by two judges—she pruned the data of obvious references to sexuality, such as male on male sexual stories in the TAT. She then asked three clinical experts to evaluate the responses of all the participants for overall adjustment. Finally, she presented the three clinical experts with the data in the form of 30 matched pairs. She asked two questions of the judges: (1) In each pair, which member is the better adjusted? (2) In each pair, which member is homosexual?

The responses of the judges were even more dramatic than she had hoped. The judges found the general adjustment of all the individuals in the study to be high. Perhaps most important, using the personality tests as their guide, the judges could not tell the difference between the two groups. Neither one struck them as more pathological than the other (Hooker, 1957).

PRESENTING THE FINDINGS

Evelyn presented her findings at a meeting of the American Psychological Association (APA) held in Chicago in 1955 and later wrote up her results as an article for the *Journal of Projective Techniques* (Hooker, 1957). The journal had a limited circulation, but professionals began to take notice of her research nonetheless. She continued to write articles for the journal on the subject of her research for several more years. Based on her research grants, she was eventually asked by NIMH to head a task force whose principal goal was to find ways to ease the social burden of gay men and lesbians.

One of the members of that task force was Judd Marmor (1910–2003), a psychiatrist, who would later become president of the American Psychiatric Association. He became convinced of the merits of her research and mission, and a strong supporter of her findings. Marmor was well respected and, through his leadership positions in the psychiatric community, was one of the individuals who would have an impact on the "official" mental health status of homosexuality.

The "bible" for most mental health workers has been the *Diagnostic and Statistical Manual of Mental Disorders* (DSM), published by the American Psychiatric Association, now in its fifth edition. It is a classification system that has enormous impact. Its descriptions have been used by a range of individuals and groups, from practitioners to insurance companies. In effect, the DSM has defined what mental illness is and what it is not. Until 1973, homosexuality was a mental illness—according to the DSM. After 1973, it was not. When a pivotal presentation regarding the classification of homosexuality was made to the DSM committee early in 1973 by psychologist Charles Silverstein, the work of Hooker was prominently featured.

Before the decision to modify the DSM was settled, a group of gay men and women met at the annual convention of the American Psychological Association (APA) and formed an Association of Gay Psychologists. Their first demand was that the board of directors of the APA convene a task force to consider the position of psychology on the issue. In 1975, the APA issued a statement expressing similar ideas to those of the American Psychiatric Association.

It is true that when the DSM was amended, there was still a classification for homosexuality that remained until 1987, but it was done with the recognition that some homosexual men and women might have difficulties related to sexual orientation. Homosexuality itself was considered within the range of normal sexual behaviors. This was a dramatic shift from the earlier position.

CRITICISMS

Hooker's work was not seen in a positive light by everyone. While some of the criticisms of her work were trivial, some of them would appear to have merit. The trivial ones included minor miscalculations and scoring errors in her report of the data. Her critics pointed to these errors as sloppiness on the part of Hooker and an indictment of her research. In fact, these errors, while unfortunate, did not change her findings in any significant way.

On a more substantial issue, her critics pointed out that Hooker was not trained as a clinical psychologist, although she later developed credentials in clinical psychology largely on her own. At the time of her initial research, she had virtually no experience with the personality assessment instruments she used, a crucial part of her research. Their administration and scoring can be complex and should not be undertaken by inexperienced individuals.

On the other hand, the individual who evaluated the Rorschach protocols after she finished with them was Bruno Klopfer, one of the leading experts on the Rorschach in the United States. The Make-a-Picture-Story test was scored by Edwin Shneidman, the psychologist who constructed the test. And the TAT was scored by Mortimer Meyer, also a clinician, with strong credentials in projective testing. If Hooker's own credentials in this area were not strong, she had put together an evaluation team of undeniable strength.

As mentioned earlier, the sample of gay men that Hooker used was hardly a random one, and she was particularly vague, even contradictory, about the selection of the heterosexual sample. Critics also pointed out that Hooker embarked on the research with a bias, hardly the dispassionate and objective figure that a scientist is supposed to be. She set out to prove that gay men were not pathological, and her intentions were clear from the beginning. Could her personal attitudes have had an effect on her results? Examples of experimenter bias in the social sciences are well known, so the answer has to be yes. But did they? The answer to that question is less clear.

It is worth noting that later studies, including those using more objective measures, have since validated her results. But it is unlikely that her work could have received the widespread acceptance that it eventually did without the interest and support of the granting agency, gay advocacy groups, and several professional groups. Even the journal in which she published her original results added an editorial note along with her publication. The note stated that the editors felt so strongly about the importance of her research that they pressured her to publish even though they characterized her results as perhaps "premature or incompletely documented." Their note was a rare event in the history of scientific publications.

THE FINAL YEARS

Evelyn's total output was not large by most measures of academic productivity, amounting to fewer than 20 articles. But their number is a poor measure of her impact and visibility. She retired from UCLA in 1970 but continued her private clinical practice. Not surprisingly, many of her clients were gay men and lesbians. She also continued her role as a charismatic and gracious host, entertaining many people in her home. By all accounts, she was a good friend and a fascinating conversationalist, well read, opinionated, and had a great sense of humor. One of the close friendships she developed during this period was with writer Christopher Isherwood.

Her success both personally and professionally became even more surprising when she revealed that she suffered from bipolar illness and sometimes had to use medication. Although she no longer conducted research, she remained in touch with a large group of people and never lost contact with the professional groups that had shown her so much support, particularly the American Psychological Association. But there were still more surprises to come.

In 1989, she received a letter from a trustee of a bank in Lincoln, Nebraska. She was told that one of the subjects in her original study, Wayne Placek, had established a trust fund to support research that would increase the understanding of gay men and lesbians and reduce the stress they experienced. Placek had designated Hooker to select the committee to decide how the funds should be distributed. When the fund was finalized 3 years later, it was valued at approximately a half million dollars. Today that fund is under the guidance and control of the American Psychological Foundation, and it dispenses annual grants for research related to gay and lesbian issues (Kimmel & Garnets, 2000).

Hooker received many awards in her later life, including the APA Award for Distinguished Contributions to Psychology in the Public Interest (1991). A documentary movie made of her life—*Changing Our Minds: The Story of Dr. Evelyn Hooker* (1992)—was nominated for an Academy Award (Schmiechen & Harrison, 1991). The University of Chicago established an Evelyn Hooker Center for Gay and Lesbian Mental Health.

Evelyn Hooker died on November 18, 1996, in Los Angeles at the age of 89. Her work helped to make the study of homosexuality a legitimate field for scholars. Most important for her, she lived to see her research play a role in removing the stigma associated with homosexual behavior and have a positive impact on the individual lives of many gay men and lesbians. There is little that would have made her happier.

REVIEW/DISCUSSION QUESTIONS

1. Describe the basic plan of Hooker's original study.

2. What were some of the difficulties Hooker faced in organizing her study?

3. Hooker's research was not without flaws. How valid are the criticisms of her original study?

4. Besides Hooker's research, what other forces contributed to the change in classification of homosexuality in the DSM?

5. Contrast the view of homosexuality today with the period during which Hooker began her study. What are some of the reasons for the change?

CHAPTER TWENTY-TWO

IN PRAISE OF LOVE
Harry Harlow and His Monkeys

By the early 1950s, Harry Harlow (1905–1981) was recognized as one of the leading experimental psychologists in the United States. His research was regularly funded by government grants, and his results were routinely quoted in textbooks. He was a popular speaker on college campuses and an active consultant. In 1958, he served as president of the American Psychological Association, a clear sign of his stature in the psychology community. In 1967, he received the National Medal of Science from President Lyndon Johnson.

Although Harlow's impact was on a variety of subfields in psychology, his research was almost entirely devoted to monkeys. Initially, he was concerned with how monkeys learned, and he made several important discoveries in that area. But then his research interests shifted. He began exploring the nature of love and affection using rhesus macaque monkey mothers and their offspring. Was it likely that monkeys could have anything important to say about the nature of maternal love? Was it even possible to explore a concept as vaguely defined as love? Harlow's answer was a resounding, "Yes!" Monkeys were not as complex as humans, but they had many of the same operating systems, or so Harlow argued.

The results of his experiments were both surprising and dramatic, and they encouraged him to explore related questions for the rest of his professional life. Eventually, however, his research came to be viewed as problematic, even unethical. This was particularly true of his later studies, when his treatment of the research animals became more severe. Some commentators equated it with torture. At the same time, an increasing sensitivity to animal experimentation was emerging, stimulated in part by Harlow's work.

FINDING A PROFESSION

Harry Harlow was born in Fairfield, Iowa, and raised in a close-knit extended family that included three brothers. He spent a year at Reed College in Oregon, beginning as an English major before he transferred to Stanford University. Throughout his life, he wrote poetry and loved puns and word play, evidence that his earlier interest in English had not disappeared entirely (LeRoy, 2008). While at Stanford, he discovered psychology. Harry remained at Stanford, receiving his doctorate in 1930 after three years of graduate study. His dissertation, using rats as subjects, supposedly soured him on using them for further research (Sears, 1982).

An incident reported while Harry was completing his doctoral work at Stanford provides some insight into the contemporary climate in higher education. Harry Harlow had actually been born Harry Israel. His formal mentor, Calvin Stone, an animal behaviorist, and the department chair, Lewis Terman, anticipated that Harry would have difficulty finding a job after graduation. There was no question about his intelligence or his drive. Their greatest concern was about his name—it sounded Jewish, and there was a strong anti-Semitic bias active in academia at the time (LeRoy & Kimble 2003).

In the usual telling of the story, Terman invited Harry to his office and told him of his concerns. He was certain that Harry was going to run into barriers when applying for an academic position because of his name. Harry protested that he wasn't Jewish. Terman responded that it didn't matter—people would think he was Jewish. As they reviewed possibilities for a name change, Harry mentioned "Harlow," a family name on his father's side. They both liked the name. And for the rest of his life, Harold Israel would be known as Harry Harlow. (Later, Harry's oldest son, Robert, chose to retain the name Israel.)

EARLY RESEARCH

Harlow was hired almost immediately after graduation by the University of Wisconsin, and it remained his professional home until his retirement. On arrival in Madison, Wisconsin, he was disappointed to find that the research laboratory he was promised had been torn down. However, with the help of his department chair, he was able to find a series of temporary quarters, eventually locating an abandoned building that the university let him use—as long as he didn't require too much in the way of additional support.

Harry immediately began modifying the building, eventually constructing an addition built mostly with the aid of students. Years later, the university turned over an abandoned cheese factory to him, along with money to fix it up. By the time he was satisfied with his research space, he had succeeded in establishing one of the most elaborate and successful primate research laboratories in the country. He was also fortunate in attracting a long list of energetic and creative graduate students. His first doctoral student was Abraham Maslow, a bright and committed student from Brooklyn. Maslow was equally fascinated with monkeys, at least initially, and valued his work with Harlow for the rest of his life. Later, Maslow would become one of the primary founders of the school of humanistic psychology.

Harlow's reluctance to use rats in his research led him to try out a variety of other animals, including cats and even frogs. According to one report, the wife of his department chair suggested he work with animals at the local zoo. It was small, she said, but there were animals there that he might find interesting. Harlow started working with an orangutan at the zoo, but the animal died before he could complete any substantive research. Rather than continue working with apes, he switched to monkeys. They were more complicated than he thought they would be, and they seemed to have distinct personalities. But as he worked with them, he became increasingly comfortable with them as his research animal of choice. He would continue to work with them for the rest of his professional life (Sears, 1982).

Harry's research on affectional systems in monkeys was not his first area of study with primates. Initially, he studied how they learned. In the process, he and John Bromer developed a standard device for testing monkeys known as the Wisconsin General Test Apparatus. Over the course of many experiments, he discovered learning sets, a method by which his animals "learned to learn." Initially, he found, his monkeys learned tasks on a trial and error basis. But after a while, they caught on to the principle involved in the learning tasks and were able to complete the tasks much more quickly. With this research Harlow was able to move the study of learning in a more cognitive direction and away from a strict behavioral position (Sidowski & Lindsley, 1989).

It was that experience that convinced him that the sequence of many behaviors—from nursing to visual exploration—were similar in human infants and monkeys. Even the development of fear and frustration seemed to develop in similar ways between the two species (Harlow, 1958). But there was something else he had learned. Monkeys don't learn just for food rewards. Their behavior was governed by many other nonphysiological drives, such as manipulation and curiosity. By the time Harlow was ready to investigate affectional systems in his monkeys, he already had three years of experience working with them.

Harlow often said that many of his research ideas were accidental, growing out of unplanned observations. That seems to be true of his most famous research. He had started a monkey colony, and because he was concerned about spreading disease among his rhesus monkeys, newborns were separated from their mothers soon after birth and were kept isolated under sterile conditions. The monkeys seemed to thrive in many respects. They were better fed and cared for, were disease-free, and even had a lower mortality rate. Harlow argued that the monkeys he separated from their mothers fared better than if they had remained with them. But it turned out they were also odd in other ways. For instance, they tended to be asocial and confused about breeding.

The design for his initial affection studies grew out of observations of the 60 monkeys he had separated from their mothers. Harlow had noticed the monkeys' attachment to the cloth diaper pads that lined the bottom of their cages. They would become very agitated when the cloths were removed for cleaning. How important were the cloth pads to the monkeys? What message were the monkeys sending?

Harlow decided to contrast the power of this "contact comfort" with the power of feeding. As part of the experiment, he would design and construct his own surrogate mothers (Harlow, 1958).

THE AFFECTION EXPERIMENTS BEGIN

In the 1950s, the theories of Clark Hull and Kenneth Spence dominated the field of learning. They argued that learning can take place only if a drive or need is being satisfied (LeRoy & Kimble, 2003). A child's love for his or her mother was commonly explained as a function of drive reduction. Since a mother is usually present when an infant's drives—such as hunger and thirst—are reduced, she becomes a secondary reinforcer. As a result, infants develop strong bonds of love and affection with mothers. In short, a child learns to love a mother because she satisfies his or her primary drives.

Harlow argued strongly against that position. His earlier research had made him sensitive to such simplistic views of behavior. Moreover, he felt that laws of learning were particularly weak in explaining the long-lasting love and affection that most people feel for their mothers. When behaviors are not reinforced, according to most learning theories, they drop out of the repertoire. In learning terms, they are extinguished. But love for a mother can last a lifetime, as most individuals would attest. For Harlow, there had to be something more than simple association and drive reduction to explain this complex emotion (Harlow, 1958).

For his affection experiments, Harlow created a pair of surrogate mothers. One was a wire mother, consisting of an elongated form made of wire mesh, with a head-like structure and a place for a bottle in the upper center of the figure. The second was a cloth mother consisting of a block of wood, also with a head-like structure but covered with sponge rubber wrapped in terry cloth. Harlow argued that the mothers were identical except for the comfort provided by the cloth. Both mothers provided heat through a light bulb under their bodies. Monkeys had access to both mothers in their cage.

In the initial experiment, four newborn monkeys were placed in separate

> **Image 22.1** A monkey with both surrogate mothers

cages with a feeding bottle on the wire monkey. Another four monkeys were placed in cages with the feeding bottle on the cloth mother. An obvious contrast between feeding and contact was established. If learning to "love" the mother was primarily due to drive reduction, the monkey should show signs of affection for the mother on which it had been fed. And one way for them to express this was through the amount of time they spent clinging to the surrogate mother.

The results were dramatic and not in favor of drive reduction theory. Monkeys fed by wire mothers spent little time clinging to them, other than the time spent feeding. They much preferred to spend their time on the cloth mother. Monkeys fed on the cloth mother, not surprisingly, spent almost no time on the wire mother. In short, monkeys preferred the mother with the most pleasurable contact comfort regardless of the source of feeding. Other variations were tried including a rocking mother and one with gradations of warmth. Nothing had as great an impact as the contact comfort. The effect was so great that Harlow concluded that the primary function of nursing as a variable of affection is to provide frequent close contact with the mother (Harlow, 1958).

For Harlow, the meaning of contact comfort represented the baby monkey's need for security. To demonstrate that further, he developed another test. Since mothers typically provide safety for their offspring in times of danger, he wondered how the monkeys would respond if they were exposed to something they viewed as dangerous. Which mother would they go to? Psychodynamic theorists had introduced the notion of a secure base, a place from which an infant could be comforted when frightened but also a place from which to explore. Would the monkeys use their surrogate mothers as a secure base? And which one would they choose?

Harlow introduced a variety of small wind-up toys to the monkeys' cages, their common attributes being movement and noise. On exposure to the clattering toys, the frightened monkeys immediately fled to the terry-cloth mother, regardless of the mother on which they had been fed. The source of feeding played no part in choosing the mother. Harlow maintained that the behavior of the monkeys when frightened was similar to babies raised with their natural mothers. Further tests in open fields, another source of possible anxiety for the monkeys, demonstrated the same phenomenon, additional evidence for the importance of contact comfort. Harlow had made an important breakthrough. However, his monkeys had some surprises in store for him.

SEX AND MOTHERHOOD

Harlow now had a group of monkeys in his laboratory who had been raised without typical mothering, having been separated from their mothers soon after birth. They seemed normal in some ways; they were physically healthy and disease-free. But they also exhibited some strange behaviors. They would rock back and forth, sit for long periods, unseeing, sometimes biting themselves. In addition to being raised with surrogate mothers, they had been socially isolated. As a result, they had difficulty interacting effectively with other monkeys (LeRoy & Kimble, 2003).

While the monkeys raised with wire surrogates exhibited the worst behaviors, all of the monkeys seemed to be affected. Surrogate monkeys may have been able to supply certain needs of the infant monkey, but they were far from supplying all of them. For one thing, the surrogate mothers were passive, offering no interaction. Real-life mothers might not always be hospitable to their children. They might even push their children away at times. But even if they did, they would still be providing their children with a social experience, and a real-world one at that.

The most dramatic examples of the limitations of monkeys raised with surrogates came when Harlow tried to breed them. He found that something was missing. His monkeys lacked the expertise to function sexually. The drive seemed to be there, but not the knowledge. Harlow characterized it by saying that their hearts were in the right place, but nothing else was.

Despite their inability to respond in a normal way sexually, Harlow was able to impregnate his monkeys, mostly by introducing some very aggressive male monkeys into their cages. Now he had a situation in which a group of monkeys who had been raised without natural mothers were being asked to mother their own children. How effective were they? Would they instinctively become good mothers?

In fact, the opposite was true. They were terrible mothers. The best response they could offer their young was to snub them. If they did not ignore them, they might push them away or bite at them. They might even kill them (LeRoy & Kimble, 2003). Something had happened to the monkeys by being deprived of natural mothering. Harlow recognized that the effect of the experiment on these monkeys was both severe and life changing. He soon gave up this line of research.

THE ISOLATION EXPERIMENTS

It's likely that Harlow's research interest in depression and despair had grown out of his personal experience, at least in part. Although seemingly a great success and widely recognized for his accomplishments, Harry sank into a clinical depression at what seemed to be the height of his career. He required several months of treatment, culminating in electroconvulsive shock therapy. There is some question whether he ever recovered completely from this depressive period. He never seemed quite the same after it (Blum, 2002).

Translating his interest in depression to research with his monkeys, he recognized that his motherless monkeys had been changed by their early experience. In fact, they exhibited many characteristics of severe mental disturbance. But separation had not produced the kind of severity he felt was true of genuine clinical depression. He decided to go even further.

Harlow placed monkeys in a windowless chamber; the only outside contact they had was with the experimenter's hands as food was introduced or the monkey cage was cleaned. They were observed through a one-way mirror. Monkeys isolated for even 30 days showed a high degree of disturbance. Those isolated for longer periods of time were almost hopelessly disturbed, unable to function when introduced to other monkeys and frequently becoming targets.

In another experiment, Harlow designed a chamber that was narrow at the bottom and wide at the top, with a mesh at the upper opening. Young monkeys who tried to climb to the top would be unsuccessful and slide back down instead. For them, isolation was virtually complete. Subjects were placed in the chamber for as little as a few days, but never more than 6 weeks. The impact was horrific. Previously happy and functional monkeys became abnormal. Virtually no monkey was able to escape the impact of isolation. When monkeys returned to their previous social existence, they brought their isolation with them. They were withdrawn and had great difficulties relating to other monkeys (Blum, 2002).

Now came the biggest challenges: How to repair the effects of such severe isolation? How to cure the depression? At first Harlow and his crew investigated the impact of drugs, particularly serotonin. It seemed to have a positive effect, but it was not enough. Eventually, they settled on the idea of using very young monkeys as therapists. Young monkeys can be very demanding when it comes to cuddling. After awhile, the young monkeys seemed to wear down the formerly-isolated monkeys, and the latter began to respond with a semblance of normality. Harlow was still working on ways to ameliorate their condition at the time of his retirement (Sears, 1982).

PERSONAL LIFE

As a young person, Harlow was described as shy but ambitious. Later, the most frequent word used to describe him was "eccentric," not only for his personal traits but also for the extraordinary amount of time he devoted to his work. He sometimes stayed at the laboratory working through the night and would finish by having coffee with the janitors in the early hours. He was also known for his fondness for alcohol, an interest that increased as he grew older (LeRoy, 2008).

In 1932, shortly after his arrival in Madison, he married Clara Mears, a teaching assistant at the university. Clara had been a subject in the famous Terman gifted study, referenced in Chapter 16 of this volume. Because of the nepotism policies in effect at the time, she was discouraged from continuing her doctoral study—they both couldn't be employed in the same department, and Harry would always be the first choice. She dropped out of her doctoral program and became a very successful dress buyer for a local store (Blum, 2002).

After 15 years of marriage and two children, Robert and Rick, they divorced. Harry soon found that the single life was not for him. Within a year, he married

Margaret Kuenne, a developmental psychologist who was on the Wisconsin faculty. She was also forced to resign her position because of the university nepotism rules still in force. However, Margaret and Harry continued to work closely together, with Margaret working in the laboratory and performing most of the duties on the *Journal of Comparative and Physiological Psychology*, which Harry supposedly edited. Margaret was eventually able to teach at the university, and shortly before her premature death, she was named a full professor.

Margaret and Harry were also the parents of two children. Although Margaret was sometimes described as cold and aloof around the laboratory, she seemed to be genuinely warm and affectionate toward her children, Pamela and Jonathan, and probably more shy than aloof. Margaret died of cancer when she was 52. Harry was devastated. However, he later reconnected with Clara Mears, his first wife, who was now a widow. They remarried within a year of Margaret's death and remained married for the rest of Harry's life. Not long after his remarriage, Harry developed early signs of Parkinson's disease; Clara was also having health issues. Reluctantly, Harry gave up his laboratory of more than 40 years and the couple moved to Arizona. He died in Arizona in 1981 at age 71.

CRITICISMS AND CONTRIBUTIONS

The fact that Harlow would even attempt to conduct research on love and affection was surprising. The Psychology Department at the University of Wisconsin was known for its statistical rigor and mainstream experimental research. Studies of vague concepts such as love and affection did not meet its usual model. In addition, the sample sizes that Harlow used were small, not large enough to lend themselves to the kind of statistics most experimental psychologists of the time treasured.

Ultimately, none of that seemed to matter. Once his research on the nature of love became public, he was hit with a blizzard of invitations, from both universities and public forums. He was tireless in pushing his research. But his work didn't proceed without criticism. His presentations were often laced with wit, but too frequently they involved what were seen as putdowns of women. Feminists criticized him for his beliefs about the nature of sex differences as well as what they saw as his overemphasis on mothering. Many women at the time were starting to break free of "the woman's place is in the home," whereas Harlow seemed to encourage it. What he really encouraged was the availability of consistent early nurturing for the young.

The criticisms of Harry and his work were generally mild during his lifetime. The stronger criticism came later and argued that Harlow knowingly caused his monkeys to suffer needlessly. Harlow even acknowledged that his monkeys had suffered, but he argued that the information he had gained helped alleviate the suffering of untold numbers of children. But this wasn't satisfactory to people in the animal rights movement. Even some of his supporters felt that he had gone too far with his isolation experiments. Harlow's blunt language didn't help. Almost everyone agrees that Harlow's experiments should never be repeated, not that there would be any need to.

In the end, Harlow revolutionized the field of animal learning and motivation (Sears, 1982), but he also contributed significantly to issues in child care and development. His emphasis on the crucial importance of early experience was not a new idea. Psychiatrists such as John Bowlby (1907–1990) had maintained for years that early mothering was crucial for successful development. Mary Ainsworth (1913–1999), a psychologist who had conducted cross-cultural studies on children, showed that securely attached children demonstrated more independence than other children, in direct contradiction to what John Watson had argued so many years before. Even ethologists, such as Nobel prize laureate Konrad Lorenz, had research that reflected on the topic. But Harlow supplied what many considered to be hard data.

Harlow's work encouraged others to explore the mother–child bond. He found that mothering matters, although it doesn't always have to come from the mother. And he demonstrated that early experience matters. In a curious way, Harlow's work made another important contribution to contemporary research. Through his writings on mother separation and isolation, he added to the growing concern about the treatment of laboratory animals and to the development of ethical guidelines.

REVIEW/DISCUSSION QUESTIONS

1. Why did Harlow choose to work with monkeys as his research animal?

2. Describe the basic design of the Harlow studies on love and affection. Explain the drive reduction approach to learning.

3. What was Harlow's belief about the fundamental nature of love? Is contact comfort the only important variable?

4. Could Harlow's research be conducted in the research climate of today?

5. What lessons for human development and behavior might be taken from the Harlow studies?

NOTE

The book by Deborah Blum (2002) cited in this chapter (see References) is a highly readable and detailed review of Harlow's life and work.

CHAPTER TWENTY-THREE

THE SHOCKING DR. MILGRAM

As a young man, Stanley Milgram was ambitious, creative, and assertive, with a playful nature that included occasional displays of cockiness. His selection of an academic career was consistent with his precocious intellect, and few doubted that he would make his mark in his chosen field. Because of his interest in sociopolitical issues, his choice of social psychology as his main academic interest appeared to be fitting and wise. Still, few people were prepared for the tumult that followed his most famous series of experiments—his "obedience to authority" research. Not only were his results surprising, they were shocking in more ways than one. In addition, they helped to shed light on one of the saddest chapters in human history, the Holocaust.

Critics were quick to question the appropriateness of Milgram's methodology. How far could an experimenter go in deceiving his subjects? Did the possible harm to his subjects outweigh the potential benefits of his research? Some have even questioned whether Milgram was completely honest in the way he presented his conclusions. As a result, more than a half century after it was conducted, the research remains controversial. But it is also fair to note that when Milgram conducted the experiments, many contemporary research safeguards had not yet been adopted. Any attempt at replication would almost certainly be denied by review boards. That said, there has been at least one modern effort to duplicate selected elements of the research.

BACKGROUND

Stanley Milgram was born in the Bronx, New York, on August 15, 1933, the second child and first son of Jewish immigrants from Eastern Europe. His parents recognized the intellectual precocity of their son very early. He excelled in grammar school and later at James Monroe High School where one of his classmates was Philip Zimbardo, who would also become a distinguished social psychologist.

In the fall of 1950, Milgram enrolled at Queens College in New York, part of the City University system. Not only did the college have an excellent faculty and reputation, it also had the additional advantage of being tuition free. Milgram took a range of courses, but his focus was primarily on political science and foreign relations. When he was in his junior year, his father died suddenly from a heart attack. Young Stanley predicted that he would also have an early death. Sadly, his prediction later proved to be correct.

Toward the end of Milgram's undergraduate studies, his interests began to shift toward psychology. However, applying to graduate school was going to be a problem since he had never taken a psychology course during his undergraduate years. Not surprisingly, when he applied to the Department of Social Relations at Harvard University (a combined program of sociology, anthropology, and psychology), he was rejected for lack of an adequate academic background. Milgram met the rejection head-on by completing six necessary courses during the summer of 1954. He was admitted to the graduate program at Harvard that fall (Blass, 1996).

Milgram arrived at Harvard during a particularly auspicious period—the faculty members were an unusually accomplished and creative group. He took full advantage of what they had to offer, forming a special and long-lasting relationship with Gordon Allport (1897–1967), one of the giants of psychology in that period. He was also drawn to the work of a visiting professor, Solomon Asch (1907–1996), for whom he was an assistant. Asch was best known for conducting experiments in social conformity, using lines of different lengths and employing confederates to help create social pressure on his experimental subjects.

Milgram modeled his doctoral dissertation on Asch's work but used auditory stimuli to conduct a cross-cultural comparison of conformity in France and Norway. Financing for both his research and living expenses was an ongoing problem, but he was eventually able to find various sources of support. Apart from the research itself, one of the benefits of his choice of a dissertation was to develop an ongoing love for France and French culture. His time in Europe also resulted in an international perspective that was reflected in many aspects of his later life (Blass, 1996).

▶ **Image 23.1** Stanley Milgram

Jan Rieckhoff/ullstein bild via Getty Images

When Milgram returned to the United States, he was slow to write up his dissertation. Finally, after spending a year working as a research assistant to Solomon Asch—who was then on sabbatical leave at the Institute for Advanced Study at Princeton—Milgram completed all the requirements for his doctoral degree. With course requirements satisfied and his doctoral degree finally in hand, Milgram was hired by Yale University as an assistant professor in 1960. By the time he arrived in New Haven to begin his new position, he had already decided on a plan for his own investigations. Ambitious as always, he intended for his initial research to establish his reputation early in his career. In that, he succeeded admirably, if not entirely in the way he had hoped (Blass, 2004).

THE EXPERIMENT BEGINS

Milgram's series of experiments are usually grouped under the title "obedience to authority." It is easy to see the link between the studies of Asch and Milgram's proposed work, but there was another link as well. Milgram's interest in obedience was strongly connected to the fate of many European Jews during World War II. His obedience research was his attempt to understand how the Holocaust happened. One of his most important questions was: How could so many seemingly ordinary citizens participate in such a heinous crime?

There was another related link, although it became more apparent a little later. In 1960, Adolf Eichmann, the Nazi general who had played such an important role in the death of millions of Jews during the Holocaust, was captured in Argentina and brought to Israel for trial. His major defense during the trial, which began in April 1961, was that he was "simply following orders." It was a defense that had been used by other Nazi war criminals during the Nuremburg trials immediately following World War II. Milgram's experiments resonated well with Eichmann's defense and could now be seen with implications beyond those that he had initially intended.

During his first semester at Yale, Milgram conducted a pilot study with undergraduates in an effort to determine how strong the "obedience to authority" phenomenon was. Both Milgram and his students were surprised at the strength of his results. He then made an application to the National Science Foundation (NSF) to support his proposed research. After a site visit by a team from the NSF, his request for 2 years of funding was approved. He recruited his initial subjects through newspaper ads in a New Haven newspaper and through mail solicitation. He used males for almost all of his obedience studies. The typical experimental arrangement is described in the following paragraphs.

When the recruit arrived at Yale's Linsly-Chittenden Hall, he was met by an experimenter who paid the participant recruits the agreed upon $4.50 for one hour of their time ($4.00 plus $0.50 carfare—remember, it was the 1960s!) Subjects were told they could withdraw from the experiment at any time. The experimenter then brought the recruit into a room with another participant. They were told that the experimenter was researching the relationship between learning and punishment. One of the participants was to be the "teacher," the other the "learner." The recruits drew slips of paper to determine who would take each role. The learner was then brought to a nearby room where he was hooked up to electrodes that were capable of giving him a shock. The experimenter described the shock as potentially painful, but not dangerous. The teacher was seated at an imposing control board in a different room with levers that displayed an escalating level of shock.

The control board contained some built-in information that was daunting. The intensity of the shock was clearly listed on the board, beginning with a 15-volt lever, progressing to 450 volts in 15-volt increments. At the upper end of the voltage there was a statement that read: "Danger: Severe Shock." Beyond that, the board simply listed a series of *XXX*s. The learner was required to give the correct response to one item from a group of items that he had been exposed to previously. Each time he gave a wrong answer, he would receive a shock, and the size of the shock was progressive, becoming greater and greater with each wrong answer. As the shock levels increased, the learner could be heard responding with growing signs of distress, shouting such things as "let me out of here" and "I refuse to continue." If the teacher hesitated to render the shock, he was told to continue and that the nature of the experiment required it. It appeared to be a cruel arrangement for both the teacher and the learner.

At the center of the experiment, however, was an important deception. No shock was being administered. The control board was fake, and the "learner" was a confederate in the experiment. The behavior being measured was not memory or learning but the extent to which the teachers were willing to shock the learners simply because they were told to do so. Roughly 65% of the teachers continued to administer the shock even though the learner could be heard crying out in pain or saying that his heart was bothering him. (The responses of the learner had all been prerecorded.) The subjects expressed discomfort at continuing the shock, but the bulk of them followed the instructions nonetheless.

By the time Milgram completed his experiment, a total of 780 subjects had participated under more than 20 different experimental conditions. The

▶ **Image 23.2** Milgram's shock machine

results held up under many variations, although there were some notable exceptions. For instance, the proximity of the learner to the teacher reduced the effect. Thomas Blass, who is the acknowledged authority on Milgram's work, has stated that the degree of compliance was not the central issue for Milgram. Rather, Milgram was concerned with the varying conditions that would have an impact on compliance (Blass, 2009).

The percentage who complied surprised nearly everyone, and according to a later follow-up, most of the recruits were convinced the shock was real. The participants were ordinary citizens, under no physical coercion to continue. Moreover, they were paid at the outset, with the assurance that the money was theirs even if they quit the experiment. Milgram had made a point to recruit participants from all levels of the social strata. They represented the range of "everyday" people. Yet most obeyed the instructions they were given, ignoring the cost to the learner.

In the end, that was the major lesson of the obedience studies. Most individuals think of themselves as living by certain internal moral principles that guide their behavior. But Milgram's studies demonstrated that there are other unseen forces that impact behavior, obedience to authority being one of them. His studies demonstrate that most individuals, under the right circumstances, would be willing to engage in such unacceptable behavior. The environment, or context, can be more powerful than any inner principles to which an individual may subscribe. It is a striking finding that speaks to the very heart of the human condition. Blass (2009) offered additional ways of viewing the study. He points out that in order for the compliance to take place, the subject must accept the authority of the experimenter. He must also shift the responsibility for his behavior to the experimenter.

In June 1962, Milgram wrote a letter to the chairman of the Psychology Department at Yale to say that his experiments were completed. Milgram was 28 years old at the time. The early 1960s had been a busy time for Milgram. Beyond his new position and his research, his personal life also changed dramatically. Early in 1961, he had met Alexandra (Sasha) Menkin at a party in New York City. She was a college-educated former dancer from much the same background as his. They were married in December of that year. In 1964, she gave birth to their daughter Michele and in 1967 to a son, Marc. Despite his devotion to his work, Milgram found great joy in his children and often made time to be with them. But if his domestic life was undergoing a great change, so was his professional life.

CRITICISMS OF HIS RESEARCH

Even before his initial report of the research was published, the ethics of his experiments came under fire. The American Psychological Association received a complaint about his study and deferred accepting his membership application until his experimental ethics could be investigated. He was later admitted to the association, but the early criticism would not be the last.

Critics considered his work to be unethical because Milgram caused his participants to think they were harming a fellow human being. Since the potential harm to the participant was perceived to be significant, they believed the research should not have been conducted at all. Milgram had always been concerned with the ethics of his experimentation, probably more so than other experimenters of his day. In his doctoral dissertation, he had debriefed his participants, asking them a series of questions about the research. Were they sorry they agreed to participate? Would they participate in it again? And so on. Debriefing was not a common practice at the time.

In the obedience studies, most of the participants were debriefed following the experiment. Not only were they told the nature of the experiment, they also met with the "learner" to show that no damage had been done. It is undeniably true that many of the subjects were upset by their behavior, but they seemed to understand that the deception was necessary. Milgram sent the participants a follow-up questionnaire asking about their feelings regarding the experiment. Most expressed no long-lasting negative effects from their participation. Milgram kept a notebook, recording his private thoughts, including some misgivings about his experimental deception. Later, he would become more confident that the deception was essential to the experiment.

Milgram's first publication on the topic took place more than a year after completing his research (Milgram, 1963). Three more articles on various aspects of the research soon followed. Almost immediately his research became a topic for public discourse. Newspaper articles appeared both in the United States and in Europe. Some simply reported the work; others were more critical.

One of the most critical reports came from Diana Baumrind (1927–2018), a well-known developmental psychologist, who published her criticism in the *American Psychologist*, the flagship journal of the American Psychological Association (Baumrind, 1964). She was particularly concerned about the long-term effect that involvement in the study might have on the participants. Milgram was annoyed that the journal had not notified him in advance that the article was being published so that he could offer a simultaneous defense, but he responded to her comments later anyway (Milgram, 1964).

Milgram had planned to write up all of his obedience studies in book form, including material that had not appeared previously in print. The book finally appeared under the title *Obedience to Authority: An Experimental View* (Milgram, 1974). As expected, it contained several variations on the obedience research that had not been published before, as well as a theoretical basis for his work, something that had not appeared in any of his previously published works. A large number of reviews appeared, both nationally and internationally, generating even more controversy than the original introduction of his research.

People have sometimes argued that Milgram's results were time bound, that is, a product of a particular era in the United States. In 2009, Jerry Burger, a psychologist at Santa Clara University, published what he referred to as a partial replication of the Milgram study (Burger, 2009). He modified several of the more offensive parts of the experiment, cutting off the attempted shock at a relatively early level, and took special care to ensure the well-being of the participants. His results indicated that the degree of compliance was approximately the same as in the original Milgram experiments.

A detailed criticism of Milgram's obedience studies appeared in a book by Gina Perry, a psychologist and author based in Melbourne, Australia. She wrote that she originally intended *Behind the Shock Machine* (Perry, 2012) to be about the lives of the participants in the study, and indeed she interviewed a number of them. However, as she delved further into the audio recordings and questionnaires in the archives at Yale, she developed a host of questions about the study itself, including both the way it was conducted and the way it was reported. (The individual subject identities will not be made available until 2039.)

The first item that Perry questioned was the response to a postexperiment questionnaire that Milgram had sent to the participants. He indicated that the vast majority (84%) were glad to have taken part in the experiment. In her judgement, that was a surprisingly high value. After her interviews, she was convinced the true value was much lower. In fact, many of the participants she interviewed were still angry decades later and spoke of the strong negative impact of the experiment on them.

In addition, she concluded that Milgram had used ambiguous wording in his book and articles regarding the supposed debriefing. Most subjects were not told the full story of the experiment and left the site of the experiment believing they had shocked an individual, a blow to their self-concept. Perry also wrote that Milgram had minimized the impact of the subjects who saw through the experimental setup and were convinced that no shock had taken place. Finally, she alleged that Milgram was selective in his published accounts, eliminating or downplaying conditions that conflicted with his overall thesis.

AFTER THE OBEDIENCE STUDIES

In the period immediately following the obedience studies, Milgram created a series of educational films in social psychology and eventually became seriously absorbed in filmmaking as a way of expressing his interests. Appearances on television followed. In 1976, a television play loosely based on his work was presented. He agreed to speak at various professional meetings and was asked to write a chapter for the prestigious *Handbook of Social Psychology* (Milgram & Toch, 1969). In short, he became a psychologist celebrity not only with the public but among his colleagues as well.

Although a large part of Milgram's reputation was based on the "obedience to authority" studies, he had other productive and creative ideas that would later enliven the field. Two of them became particularly famous—the "lost letter" technique and his "small world" study, popularly known as "six degrees of separation." The lost-letter technique had originated at Yale before he left for his position at Harvard and had emerged through discussion in one of his graduate classes. The initial study proceeded in the following fashion. Innocuous letters ostensibly about arranging a meeting were distributed in envelopes around New Haven by being dropped on sidewalks, left in telephone booths, and placed on car windshields with a note attached saying, "found near your car." The critical variable was the address on the front of the envelope indicating for whom the letter was intended.

Based on the address, it appeared that the letters were being sent to one of four different entities—the Communist Party, the Nazi Party, a medical research group, and a private individual. Actually, all the envelopes shared the same post office box number in New Haven, which had been rented beforehand. Not surprisingly, most of the returned letters were those for the medical group and the private individual. The letters addressed to the Communist and Nazi Parties were least likely to be mailed.

Milgram concluded that the methodology could be a sensitive measure of attitudes. Presumably, the majority of the citizens of New Haven were not in favor of either the Nazi or Communist parties. It was a better measure than a simple questionnaire because it required something more substantial than marking a point in a scale—it required an action. Milgram would continue to use the technique to evaluate a range of attitudes and contexts, particularly political attitudes and other attitudes that people would be less likely to acknowledge publicly.

The "small world" study did not originate with Milgram—it had been discussed by other nonpsychology researchers earlier—but he was the first to translate it into experimental terms and to demonstrate some of its quantitative simplicity. His research reflected a social phenomenon experienced by many individuals in which surprising connections are found among people. His technique involved a folder that he hoped would end up in the hands of a person identified as the target.

Folders were given to random individuals, who were encouraged to pass them on to someone whom they considered closer to the target. They were instructed that they could pass it only to a person close to them, that is, someone with whom they were on a first-name basis. That person was then asked to pass it on to another person with whom they were also on a first-name basis, and so on. Each link was intended to get the folder closer to the intended target. There were cards in each folder that were used to track the route of the folder. When the target was finally reached, the folder, with the evidence of its route, was returned to Milgram. He was then able to determine how many connections were necessary to reach the target.

When people were originally asked to estimate the number of connections necessary to have the folder reach a complete stranger, the estimates were usually quite high, some as high as 100. Although Milgram did not get a strong return on his effort, the average number of connections necessary to reach the target was approximately six, a surprisingly low number, hence the label "six degrees of separation" that is so often attached to the research. Among the billions of people in the world, Milgram was able to demonstrate an amazing level of connectedness and do it with such surprising simplicity. The notion of a small world was indeed apt (Milgram, 1967).

THE MOVE TO THE CITY UNIVERSITY OF NEW YORK

Milgram's original contract with Harvard was for three years, and it was renewed for another year, but he was not yet on a tenure line. When a tenure line became available, he had several supporters, but the position eventually went to someone else. It was a great disappointment to him. He and his wife Sasha had grown to love Harvard and the Cambridge area as well. The effect of his not being granted tenure would linger for many years and have an impact on his self-esteem.

He received offers from several universities, but not from those he preferred. His obedience research had made him a controversial researcher, and it is likely there was faculty resistance to his hiring. One of his requirements for a new position was that the university be located in a thriving urban area. He eventually accepted an offer from the City University of New York (CUNY) beginning in the fall of 1967. If CUNY did not have the prestige of some of the universities he hoped for, at least it was in New York, the home of many friends and relatives. Moreover, he was hired as a full professor, a jump in rank as well as in salary. CUNY would remain his home for the rest of his professional life (Blass, 1996).

The Graduate Center at CUNY only recently had been formed out of several separate colleges in the New York City system. Its newness gave Milgram a measure of freedom that he would not have experienced at older universities. He developed new courses, particularly in the area of urban psychology. CUNY would eventually become a leader in that field. He continued to create experimental situations to document various aspects of life in New York City. He researched the impact of television and even helped produce a low-budget film on New York City life.

A Guggenheim fellowship allowed him to spend a year in Paris with his family, where he indulged in another original creation of his—developing a psychological map of the city. During his year in Paris, he was able to visit other European cities, as well as to include a trip to Israel where he was offered, and declined, a position at Hebrew University. At home, he was a frequently chosen dissertation mentor and one who would continue to support his former students well into their careers.

FINAL YEARS AND SUMMARY THOUGHTS

Milgram had been diagnosed with high blood pressure at a relatively young age, but there had been no other indications that he was in poor health. He suffered his first heart attack in 1980, while still in his 40s. A second heart attack followed a year later. Tests indicated that he had significant arterial blockage and that bypass surgery was not a good option. He took time off from teaching, but his condition and the required medication weakened him. Even his personality began to change. By all accounts, he became more mellow. Eventually, he was able to return to work, but his health problems continued. He had his fifth and fatal heart attack on December 20, 1984, soon after completing a dissertation oral exam for his final doctoral student. He was 51 years old.

Among the descriptions that were frequently mentioned about Milgram were not only his originality but also his playfulness and apparent joy in the process of discovery. He could be cocky, a trait that seemed to emerge in his days at Harvard. He was often described as having a prickly personality, impatient with small talk, and sometimes engaging in behaviors that could be described as bizarre. He was known to use amphetamines and cocaine occasionally, which may account for some of his erratic behavior (Blass, 2004). But overriding all of this was his generally recognized genius.

Despite his energy and creativity, nothing in his later career would match the impact of Milgram's obedience studies. They established him as a psychologist of note early in his career, just as he had hoped. But he grew to resent his almost complete identification with the obedience studies. He felt his other contributions were of equal worth and deserved more recognition. Still, the impact of the obedience studies lingers.

Business students are advised to be careful of the role that authority may play in their decisions, even when those decisions may be clearly ethical. Citizens of authoritarian regimes come to have a better understanding of the dynamics taking place in their home countries. Blass (2004) has documented the influence of the obedience studies on many individual lives. The power of authority is striking within any kind of hierarchical social structure.

As for the decades-old study, it remains controversial even today. Was it really a study of obedience? Can such artificially constructed encounters be generalized to real life situations? Are the data truly representative of the individual differences among subjects? Do the results hold up cross-nationally? And how far can social scientists go in search of answers to their questions? The obedience study of Stanley Milgram has made other social scientists reflect on their methodology as well as the meaning of their work. Yet, when all is said and done, the study remains a vivid commentary on the power of authority.

REVIEW/DISCUSSION QUESTIONS

1. What is the basic design of the Milgram "obedience to authority" studies?

2. Would his methodology be acceptable today? How far can an experimenter go in deceiving his subjects?

3. Did the possible harm to Milgram's subjects outweigh the potential benefits of his research?

4. Would the results of Milgram's experiment vary depending on the gender of the subject? The proximity of "learner" and "teacher"?

5. How powerful is personality compared to context in determining behavior?

6. How important was the era in which the study took place? Would Milgram get the same results today?

NOTE

Over several decades, Thomas Blass has gathered extensive personal and professional information about Milgram and has published widely on him and his work. Readers who wish to explore the work of Milgram in greater depth are advised to seek out Milgram's original writings as well as the writings of Dr. Blass.

TWENTY-FOUR

THE MURDER OF KITTY GENOVESE

In 1964, approximately 700 people were murdered in New York City. Catherine (Kitty) Genovese, a 28-year-old bar manager, was one of them. But the immediate report of her death did not cause a great outcry. It was just another sad tale among many sad tales in the big city.

However, a newspaper account 10 days later catapulted her death into a story of national importance. *The New York Times* reported that 38 individuals had witnessed her murder but made no effort to help her. No one intervened; no one called the police. In short order, her death became a symbol of the coldness and insensitivity of city dwellers. News of the murder—and the silent 38 witnesses—spread throughout the nation, even the world. Ultimately, her death would generate dozens of articles and news stories, several books, as well as a documentary. Most of the reports focused not on her death but on the behavior of the observers.

Two academic researchers, John Darley and Bibb Latané, explored another aspect of her death. Rather than simply criticizing the nonresponsive observers, they proposed that the behavior of the witnesses could be explained by a social psychological phenomenon they labeled the *bystander effect*. They posited that individuals had not responded that night because there was a diffusion of responsibility based on the number of witnesses. In simple terms, they argued that when there are multiple observers, individuals feel less responsible, leaving it up to others to act (Latané & Darley, 1968; 1970).

The Genovese murder, along with the bystander effect, became staples of textbooks, particularly in introductory psychology and social psychology courses. But the story also began to change. In the years that followed, questions arose about Genovese's death, particularly about the so-called bystanders. A comprehensive article, published in *American Psychologist* in 2007, questioned the way the story of her murder was told. On the 50th anniversary of her death, two books raising even more questions and providing additional details about the events surrounding her death were published (Cook, 2014; Pelonero, 2014). The story of the 38 witnesses looked much different from what was first reported.

THE MURDER

Catherine (Kitty) Genovese was an attractive and independent 28-year-old, a bartender and the manager of Ev's Bar in Hollis, Queens. She was respected, even loved, by her boss and patrons alike. She lived in an apartment in Kew Gardens, another Queens suburb 10 miles away, that she shared with another woman, Mary Ann Zielonko. Only later would her family and many of her friends realize that the two were involved in a romantic relationship.

On the day of her murder, March 13, 1964, Kitty closed the bar at approximately 3 a.m., got into her bright red 1963 Fiat, and drove home on the Grand Central Parkway. She could not know that Winston Moseley, a man with a good job and a family, was on the prowl that night looking for someone to kill. He had spotted her coming out of the bar, followed her in his car, and watched as she parked the Fiat in a lot at the railroad station near her apartment. As she left the parking lot and started walking the short distance to her home at 82-70 Austin Street, he began to follow her. She became aware of him and quickened her pace. He immediately quickened his.

When Moseley caught up with her, he grabbed her and stabbed her twice in the back. She struggled and cried out, awakening neighbors. A man from the apartment house across the street shouted, "Leave that woman alone." He later said he didn't realize that Genovese had been stabbed. He thought the couple was engaged in a lover's quarrel. Bailey's Tavern was nearby and quarrels in the street were frequent. As it turned out, the bar had closed early that night and the street was empty.

NY Daily News Archive via Getty Images

▸ **Image 24.1** Kitty Genovese at Ev's Bar

Moseley reacted to the shout, afraid that the neighbors could identify him. He fled the scene, running back to his car. Genovese was wounded, but not fatally. Slowly she got up and began walking in the direction of her apartment. Weakened by the stabbing, she couldn't make it all the way. Instead, she found refuge in the vestibule of an apartment entrance two doors short of her own. As she tried to regain her strength, Moseley, still in his parked car, sat waiting, wondering if anyone had called the police. Minutes passed. When no police arrived, Moseley decided he was safe.

Moseley left his car and began searching for Genovese, walking back along Austin Street, eventually checking the vestibules to each of the apartment entrances. It didn't take long for him to find her. When he did, he stabbed her again, this time even more brutally. And he raped her. An upstairs neighbor, Karl Ross, opened his door, aroused by the noise. But when he looked down the stairway and saw what was happening, he said nothing and immediately closed his door. By the time the police arrived, Moseley had fled. Genovese was still alive but died on the way to the hospital.

THE INITIAL REPORT

The murder of Kitty Genovese was out of character for the quiet borough of Queens, New York—at the time, it was considered the safest borough in New York City. Still, the murder would not have been seen as remarkable if it had not been for the newspaper story that followed. Abe Rosenthal, the city editor for *The New York Times* was having lunch with Police Commissioner Michael Murphy days after the murder. They discussed the crime, and Murphy casually remarked that there had been 38 witnesses to the murder but that no one called the police or tried to intervene. Rosenthal knew immediately that he had a story. He assigned a reporter, Martin Gansberg, to investigate the murder. Gansberg spent 3 days interviewing neighbors. On March 27, the *Times* printed a front-page story that included the following statement:

> For more than half an hour 38 respectable, law-abiding citizens in Queens watched a killer stalk and stab a woman in three [sic] separate attacks in Kew Gardens. . . . Not one person telephoned the police during the assault; one witness called after the woman was dead. (Gansberg, 1964, p. 1)

The newspaper account soon took on a life of its own. Other newspapers and magazine articles reprinted it and used it to denigrate city life. It was not only Winston Moseley who took the life of Kitty Genovese, they argued, it was the big city itself—cold, distant, and unwilling to help anyone, even when it came to saving a human life. Toward the end of 1964, Rosenthal published a book retelling the events of that night with the same thesis regarding the unwillingness of city dwellers to get involved (Rosenthal, 1964/1999). Later accounts would attribute the development of the 911 emergency system to the death of Genovese.

SOCIAL SCIENTISTS AND THE "BYSTANDER EFFECT"

Bibb Latané and John Darley, both social scientists, read about the murder and interpreted the behavior of the 38 witnesses in a different way. In the unwillingness of the neighbors to respond, they saw a social-psychological phenomenon. Eventually they would devise a series of experiments to test their hypothesis. The conclusion they reached has become known as the *bystander effect*, and the robustness of the phenomenon has been demonstrated time and time again. When people are in a group, responsibility is diffused. A person who might act if he or she were alone will not feel the same responsibility when in a group, deferring to others to initiate action. The researchers concluded that is what happened in the case of Kitty Genovese. The bystanders held back, expecting others to intervene or call the police.

Textbook writers took note of the phenomenon and the gruesome story that gave rise to it. The bystander effect became commonplace in virtually every introductory psychology and social psychology book for years to come, several of them describing the murder in great detail. A novel, a television story, and a movie would also appear based roughly on the events of that night. Years later, a documentary would be created, with Genovese's younger brother Bill as the central character.

THE PARABLE OF THE 38 WITNESSES

Several authors raised questions about the murder over the years, but their inquiries were mostly about small details of the case. However, three British social scientists wrote an article exploring the case in greater depth. Published in *American Psychologist*, a leading professional journal, their article refuted many of the so-called facts surrounding Genovese's death. They argued that the evidence simply did not support the claims about the witnesses to the murder. They referred to the typical telling of the story—the way the *Times* told it—as a "parable" (Manning, Levine, & Collins, 2007).

The Manning et al. article did not question the bystander research itself, which they considered valid and well researched. Rather, their doubts were built around three assumptions related to the murder: (1) that there were 38 witnesses, (2) that the witnesses actually observed the murder, and (3) that the witnesses did not act. The authors drew their evidence from several different sources, including statements by Winston Moseley—the murderer himself—during his trial. Both he and several witnesses gave evidence that contradicted some of the supposed facts. A local lawyer and amateur historian, Joseph De May Jr., who devoted a good deal of time and energy to unearthing the truth about the murder, also reached a different conclusion about the circumstances surrounding the murder.

Manning et al. began by arguing that the evidence did not support the contention that there were 38 eyewitnesses. No one could name all of them; no list has ever been made available. Many local residents may have heard something that night, but there was no indication that they thought the sounds were anything more than unruly bar patrons. At Moseley's trial, only three eyewitnesses testified to actually seeing Genovese and her assailant in the street, but they did not realize that a murder was taking place. At least, that's what they testified. Instead, they observed what appeared to be an altercation of some kind between a man and a woman. None of them saw the stabbing. Most importantly, after one neighbor shouted, "Leave that woman alone," Moseley left and Genovese got up and slowly walked away. (There were two other eyewitnesses who saw Genovese and her murderer that night, but the prosecution chose not to have them testify, believing their testimony would not be helpful.)

Another point of difficulty with the usual story was the location of Genovese's apartment. The entrance was in the back of her building. When she rounded the corner toward her apartment, she was no longer in sight of any of the known eyewitnesses, all of whom lived in the nine-story Mowbray Apartments across the street. As Genovese struggled to get to her home and entered the vestibule of a nearby apartment instead, she would have been visible to practically no one. (There was one exception.) It was here that Moseley found her when he returned, and it was here that the second fatal stabbing and rape took place. It would have been impossible for any of the eyewitnesses who testified to have observed this second deadly encounter. How, then, were there 38 witnesses?

The police report said that there were actually 49 people who saw or heard something (Cook, 2014), although there were 38 entries in the report. Perhaps this was the source of the number. (One of the early published reports refers to 37 witnesses.) Undoubtedly, there were residents who heard something that night, but to characterize them as witnesses to a murder was a gross misrepresentation. Whatever the number of residents who heard or saw something, most of them did not believe they saw anything resembling a murder. None of them could have seen the two incidents that resulted in the death of Genovese. It appears that only two people actually saw and likely understood the horrible event that was taking place that night.

Joseph Fink, the assistant superintendent of the Mowbray Apartments, apparently saw the first stabbing in the street from inside his apartment. Rather than take any action, he did nothing and retired to his room. Karl Ross lived at the top of the stairwell where the final confrontation between Moseley and Genovese took place. After hearing sounds of the struggle, he opened his door, looked down at the scene below, then closed his door again, deciding not to intervene. Accounts vary as to his motivation. Ross was apparently drunk that night. He was also a gay man afraid that the police would not treat him kindly. Instead of reporting the incident, he first called a friend who told him not to get involved and then called another neighbor (Pelonero, 2014).

Eventually, Sophia Farrar, a friend and neighbor of Kitty was phoned and told about the ongoing assault. She went immediately to the stairwell to comfort Genovese, ignoring the fact that the killer might still be lurking there. Thankfully, Moseley had gone. Farrar proceeded to cradle Genovese in her arms until the police arrived. Genovese was still alive when she was taken away by ambulance but died on the way to the hospital. Ross left the neighborhood soon after the murder and was not seen locally again.

The final question posed by Manning et al., and perhaps the most important one, is why no one responded to the attack or called the police? The answer appears to be that many people did respond. The report was in error. The man who shouted at Moseley during the first attack intervened enough to scare Moseley away although, as it turned out, only temporarily. Several people later insisted that they called the police. Samuel Hoffman, a retired police lieutenant who lived in the Mowbray Apartments, was one of them. In later years, others have verified that calls were made. There may have been some reluctance on the part of the police to respond to the calls since the bar on Austin Street had been the subject of frequent disturbances. Sophia Farrar certainly intervened by going immediately to the stairwell to try to help Genovese. In short, the thesis that 38 witnesses observed the crime and chose not to respond is deeply flawed.

▶ **Image 24.2** Winston Moseley

WINSTON MOSELEY

Genovese's murderer remained at large for only a few weeks after the murder. Winston Moseley attempted to rob a house in Corona, Queens, a few miles from the site of the Genovese murder. A local man saw him carrying a TV and realized that Moseley did not belong in the neighborhood. He rightly concluded that Moseley was in the process of robbing an apartment. According to one account, the neighbor opened the hood of Moseley's car, disabled it, and called the police. So much for the indifference of the big city! After Moseley was arrested, a wise police captain noticed the scabs on his fingers. He also realized that Moseley's general appearance matched that of Genovese's murderer. It didn't take long before Moseley confessed.

As it turned out, Moseley had a wife, two young children, five German shepherds, and a full-time job. He and his wife, Betty, owned a four-bedroom home in South Ozone Park in Queens. When his IQ was tested, it was found to be 135, well above average. (Later testing would result in a lower score, but still above average.) In many ways, Moseley appeared to be a model middle-class citizen. But appearances were deceiving.

In the period leading up to the murder, Moseley had become moody. Always fastidious about his appearance, he had become lax. His wife had begun to have some concerns about him. But she worked a night shift as a nurse and didn't have many opportunities to discuss his changing habits with him. Moseley had a difficult background, including a mother who abandoned him when he was 8 years old, although she later returned when he was an adult. The man he thought was his father was not his biological father. And the murder of Genovese was not the only example of his pathology.

As the police questioned Moseley further, they discovered that he had murdered another woman, in an even more ghastly way, only a few weeks before. Because Moseley was Black, some people had speculated that there may have been a racial aspect to the Genovese crime. But the other woman he murdered, 24-year-old Annie Mae Johnson, was Black, reaffirming his statement that he simply had an urge to murder someone that night. The race of the person was irrelevant to him.

Moseley was eventually convicted of first-degree murder and given the death penalty. However, his sentence was changed on appeal to a life sentence. Assigned to Attica prison in upstate New York, he injured himself in order to be sent to a hospital. He escaped while at the hospital and held a family hostage for several days before he was captured again. But that would be his last time outside of a prison. He successfully studied for a bachelor's degree while incarcerated and, after many years, applied for a parole on the basis that he had undergone a significant change in prison. He was turned down. In all, he made 17 appeals for a parole, all of them rejected. In the end, he was the longest-serving prisoner in the New York State prison system. Moseley was 81 years old when he died on March 28, 2016, still in prison.

THE AFTERMATH

Not surprisingly, the Genovese family suffered terribly because of the murder. Kitty's father, Vinny, had previously moved the family to New Canaan, Connecticut, out of fear that New York City was becoming too violent. Of the five siblings, only Kitty chose to remain behind, promising her parents that she would find a safe place to live in the city. Her siblings tried to shield their mother, Rachel, from many of the details of the murder. After her death, they found a stack of newspaper clippings that she had secretly kept about the murder.

Kitty's younger brother, Bill, also suffered greatly. He was only 15 years old when Kitty died. In an attempt to make some sense of her death and to do something positive, he later joined the Marines. While in Vietnam, he lost both legs in a land mine explosion. Still, he persisted in trying to understand the death of his sister. In 2015, a film was released titled *The Witness*, produced and directed by James Solomon. It documents the efforts by Bill Genovese to clarify aspects of his sister's death. It included his unsuccessful attempts to speak to Winston Moseley in prison, although he did get to speak to Moseley's son, a minister.

Mary Ann Zielonko, Kitty's companion and lover, had the difficult task of identifying the body on the morning of the murder. Before the police zeroed in on Moseley, Zielonko realized that she had been a suspect in the murder. Although Kitty's family had more or less accepted Zielonko as their daughter's companion, after Kitty's death they marginalized her, putting her in the background throughout the funeral and burial in Lakeview Cemetery in Connecticut.

FINAL THOUGHTS ON THE GENOVESE TRAGEDY

The story of Kitty Genovese became a symbol of the coldness and indifference of people who live in today's cities, unwilling even to respond to a person who was dying. But it was a story that was based on a lie. People did respond. How was it possible that such an erroneous account would be believed by so many people? The power of the media provides one answer. As other researchers have noted, we tend to believe things that are told to us in an authoritative way, and newspapers have been a powerful source of information. They seem less powerful today. And given the ubiquity of social media, it is doubtful that such a tragedy could play out in the same way.

The power of context also played a major role in the events that day. As the well-researched bystander effect has demonstrated, the behavior of people is strongly influenced by many aspects of their environment, including the number of people present. How many of the observers who saw something—not necessarily a murder—would have reported it if they thought they were the sole observer?

Many current textbooks, particularly in introductory and social psychology courses, continue to tell the story with varying degrees of accuracy. Most reflect a more toned-down version of the 38 witnesses (Griggs, 2015). But what are we to learn from the heartbreaking story of Kitty Genovese? Not to trust the media would be a simple answer. But the larger one may be our responsibility to each other as human beings. As Manning et al. pointed out, the story of the 38 witnesses is really a parable whose lesson is to remind us of our responsibility to each other.

REVIEW/DISCUSSION QUESTIONS

1. Why was the original reporting of the murder so erroneous? How many witnesses were there?

2. How did a more accurate story eventually become known? Is the story reported correctly today?

3. Despite the inaccuracy of the original story, does the phenomenon of the bystander effect still hold true?

4. Why have so many of the founding stories of psychology been distorted? Is this equally true for other disciplines?

INTRODUCTORY PSYCHOLOGY KEY TOPIC APPENDIX

1. Introducing Psychology and Its Methods. Ch. 6 (Clever Hans); Ch. 11 (Freud); Ch. 12 (Münsterberg); Ch. 13 (Calkins); Ch. 18 (Burt).

2. Behavioral Neuroscience: Ch. 3 (Phineas Gage).

3. Lifespan Development and Its Contexts. Ch. 2 (Wild Boy); Ch. 16 (Genius Study); Ch. 22 (Harlow).

4. Sensation and Perception. Ch. 9 (Rorschach).

5. Consciousness and Sleep. Ch. 4 (Hypnosis and Hysteria).

6. Learning and Memory. Ch. 8 (Pavlov); Ch. 10 (Montessori); Ch. 15 (Little Albert).

7. Thought, Language, and Intelligence. Ch. 6 (Clever Hans); Ch. 7 (Galton); Ch. 14 (Goddard); Ch. 16 (Genius Study); Ch. 18 (Burt); Ch. 19 (Nim Chimpsky).

8. Personality. Ch. 3 (Phineas Gage); Ch. 9 (Rorschach).

9. Social Psychology. Ch. 1 (Salem Witches); Ch. 20 (The Clarks); Ch. 21 (Hooker); Ch. 23 (Milgram); Ch. 24 (Genovese).

10. Motivation and Emotion. Ch. 1 (Salem Witches); Ch. 15 (Little Albert); Ch. 22 (Harlow).

11. Health, Stress, and Wellness. Ch. 1 (Salem Witches): Ch. 17 (Minnesota Starvation); Ch. 23 (Milgram).

12. Psychological Disorders. Ch. 5 (Anna O.); Ch. 9 (Rorschach); Ch. 11 (Freud).

13. Treatment and Interventions. Ch. 2 (Wild Boy); Ch. 4 (Hypnosis and Hysteria); Ch. 5 (Anna O.); Ch. 11 (Freud).

REFERENCES

Chapter 1

Caporael, L. R. (1976). Ergotism: The Satan loosed in Salem? *Science, 192*, 21–26.

Demos, J. (2008). *The enemy within: 2,000 years of witch hunting in the Western world.* New York, NY: Penguin Group.

Hill, F. (2002). *A delusion of Satan: The full story of the Salem witch trials.* Cambridge, MA: Da Capo Press.

Norton, M. B. (2002). *In the devil's snare.* New York, NY: Knopf.

Schiff, S. (2015). *The witches: Salem, 1692.* New York, NY: Little, Brown.

Spanos, N. P., & Gottlieb, J. (1976). Ergotism and the Salem Village witch trials. *Science, 194*, 1390–1394.

Chapter 2

Bettelheim, B. (1967). *The empty fortress.* New York, NY: Simon & Schuster.

Candland, D. K. (1993). *Feral children and clever animals.* New York, NY: Oxford University Press.

Itard, J. M. G. (1962). *The wild boy of Aveyron.* New York, NY: Century-Appleton.

Lane, H. (1976). *The wild boy of Aveyron.* Cambridge, MA: Harvard University Press.

Shattuck, R. (1980). *The forbidden experiment: The story of the wild boy of Aveyron.* New York, NY: Farrar Straus.

Yousef, N. (2001). Savage or solitary? The wild child and Rousseau's man of nature. *Journal of the History of Ideas, 62*, 245–263.

Chapter 3

Damasio, A. R. (1994). *Descartes' error: Emotion, reason, and the human brain.* New York, NY: Putnam.

Damasio, H., Grabowski, T., Frank, R., Galaburda, A. M., & Damasio, A. R. (1994). The return of Phineas Gage: Clues about the brain from the skull of a famous patient. *Science, 264*, 1102–1105.

Macmillan, M. (2002). *An odd kind of fame: Stories of Phineas Gage.* Cambridge: MIT Press.

Macmillan, M., & Lena, M. L. (2010). Rehabilitating Phineas Gage. *Neuropsychological Rehabilitation, 20*, 641–658.

Wilgus, J., & Wilgus, B. (2009). Face to face with Phineas Gage. *Journal of the History of the Neurosciences, 18*, 340–345.

Chapter 4

Crews, F. (2017). *Freud: The making of an illusion*. New York, NY: Henry Holt.

Ellenberger, H. F. (1970). *The discovery of the unconscious: The history and evolution of dynamic psychiatry*. New York, NY: Basic Books.

Ellenberger, H. F. (1993). *Beyond the unconscious: Essays of Henri F. Ellenberger in the history of psychiatry* (M. S. Micale, Ed.; F. Dubor & M. S. Micale, Trans.). Princeton, NJ: Princeton University Press.

Owen, A. R. G. (1971). *Hysteria, hypnosis and healing: The work of Jean-Martin Charcot*. New York, NY: Garrett Publications.

Wyckoff, J. (1975). *Franz Anton Mesmer: Between God and devil*. Englewood Cliffs, NJ: Prentice Hall.

Chapter 5

Borch-Jacobsen, M. (1996). *Remembering Anna O.: A century of mystification*. (K. Olson, trans.). New York, NY: Routledge.

Breger, L. (2009). *A dream of undying fame: How Freud betrayed his mentor and invented psychoanalysis*. New York, NY: Basic Books.

Breuer, J., & Freud, S. (1957). *Studies on hysteria*. (J. Strachey, trans.). New York, NY: Basic Books.

Ellenberger, H. F. (1970). *The discovery of the unconscious*. New York, NY: Basic Books.

Freud, S. (1910). The origin and development of psychoanalysis. *American Journal of Psychology, 21*(2), 181–218.

Ellenberger, H. F. (1993). *Beyond the unconscious: Essays of Henri F. Ellenberger in the history of psychiatry* (M. S. Micale, Ed.; F. Dubor & M. S. Micale, Trans.). Princeton, NJ: Princeton University Press.

Rosenbaum, M., & Muroff, M. (Eds.). (1984). *Anna O.: Fourteen contemporary reinterpretations*. New York, NY: Free Press.

Rosenzweig, S. (1992). *Freud, Jung, and Hall the king-maker: The expedition to America (1909)*. St. Louis, MO: Rana House Press.

Chapter 6

Candland, D. K. (1993). *Feral children and clever animals*. New York, NY: Oxford University Press.

Fernald, D. (1984). *The Hans legacy*. Hillsdale, NJ: Lawrence Erlbaum Associates.

Heinzen, T. E., Lilienfeld, S. O., & Nolan, S. A. (2015). *The horse that won't go away: Clever Hans, facilitated communication, and the need for clear thinking*. New York, NY: Worth.

Kressley-Mba, R. A. (2006). On the failed institutionalization of German comparative psychology prior to 1940. *History of Psychology, 9*, 55–74.

Pfungst, O. (1911). *Clever Hans, the horse of Mr. Von Osten: A contribution to experimental animal and human psychology*. (C. L. Rahn, trans.). New York, NY: Henry Holt.

Sebeok, T. A., & Rosenthal, R. (Eds.). (1981). *The Clever Hans phenomenon: Communication with horses, whales, apes, and people*. New York: New York Academy of Sciences.

Chapter 7

Brookes, M. (2004). *Extreme measures: The dark visions and bright ideas of Francis Galton*. New York, NY: Bloomsbury.

Fancher, R. E. (1985). The intelligence men: Makers of the IQ controversy. New York, NY: W. W. Norton.

Forrest, D. W. (1974). *Francis Galton: The life and work of a Victorian genius*. New York, NY: Taplinger.

Gillham, N. W. (2001). *Sir Francis Galton: From African exploration to the birth of eugenics*. New York, NY: Oxford University Press.

Terman, L. M. (1917). The intelligence quotient of Francis Galton in childhood. *American Journal of Psychology, 28*, 209–215.

Chapter 8

Fancher, R. E., & Rutherford, A. (2012). *Pioneers of psychology* (5th ed.). New York, NY: W. W. Norton.

Kimble, G. A. (1991). The spirit of Ivan Petrovich Pavlov. In G. A. Kimble, M. Wertheimer, and C. L. White (Eds.), *Portraits of pioneers in psychology*, (pp. 27–40). Washington, DC: American Psychological Association.

Todes, D. P. (1997). From the machine to the ghost within: Pavlov's transition from digestive physiology to conditioned reflexes. *American Psychologist, 52*, 947–955.

Todes, D. P. (2000). *Ivan Pavlov: Exploring the animal machine*. New York, NY: Oxford University Press.

Todes, D. P. (2014). *Ivan Pavlov: A Russian life in science*. New York, NY: Oxford University Press.

Windholz, G. (1997). Ivan P. Pavlov: An overview of his life and psychological work. *American Psychologist, 52*, 941–946.

Chapter 9

Ellenberger, H. F. (1993). *Beyond the unconscious: Essays of Henri F. Ellenberger in the history of psychiatry* (M. S. Micale, Ed.; F. Dubor & M. S. Micale, Trans.). Princeton, NJ: Princeton University Press.

Erdberg, P., & Weiner, I. B. (2007). Obituary: John E. Exner Jr. (1928–2006). *American Psychologist, 62*, 54.

Kessler, J. W. (1994). Obituary: Marguerite R. Hertz (1899–1992). *American Psychologist, 49*, 1084.

O'Roark, A. M., & Exner, J. E. (1989). *History and directory: Society for Personality Assessment fiftieth anniversary* (Separate Issue). London, UK: Routledge.

Searls, D. (2017). *The inkblots: Hermann Rorschach, his iconic tests, and the power of seeing*. New York, NY: Crown.

Wood, J. M., Nezworski, M. T., Lilienfeld, S. O., & Garb, H. (2011). *What's wrong with the Rorschach: Science confronts the controversial inkblot test*. San Francisco, CA: Jossey-Bass.

Chapter 10

Gutek, G. L., & Gutek, P. A. (2016). *Bringing Montessori to America: S. S. McClure, Maria Montessori, and the campaign to publicize Montessori education*. Tuscaloosa: University of Alabama Press

Kramer, R. (1988). *Maria Montessori: A biography*. New York, NY: Da Capo Press.

Lillard, A., & Else-Quest, N. (2006). Evaluating Montessori education. *Science, 313*(5795), 1893–1894.

Lillard, A. S. (2017). *Montessori: The science behind the genius* (3rd ed.). New York, NY: Oxford University Press.

Standing, E. M. (1962). *Maria Montessori: Her life and work*. New York, NY: The New American Library.

Chapter 11

Evans, R. B., & Koelsch, W. A. (1985). Psychoanalysis arrives in America: The 1909 psychology conference at Clark University. *American Psychologist, 40*, 942–948.

Freud, S. (1910). The origin and development of psychoanalysis. (H. W. Chase, trans.). *American Journal of Psychology, 21*, 181–218.

Hale, N. G., Jr. (1971). *Freud and the Americans: The beginnings of psychoanalysis in the United States, 1876–1917*. New York, NY: Oxford University Press.

Koelsch, W. A. (1987). *Clark University 1887–1987: A narrative history*. Worcester, MA: Clark University Press.

Rosenzweig, S. (1992). *Freud, Jung and Hall the king-maker: The expedition to America (1909)*. St. Louis, MO: Rana House Press.

Chapter 12

Benjamin, L. T., Jr. (2000). Hugo Münsterberg: Portrait of an applied psychologist. In G. A. Kimble & M. Wertheimer (Eds.), *Portraits of pioneers in psychology, Vol. IV* (pp. 113–129). Washington, DC: American Psychological Association.

Boring, E. G. (1929). *A history of experimental psychology*. New York, NY: D. Appleton-Century.

Hale, M., Jr. (1980). *Human science and social order: Hugo Münsterberg and the origins of applied psychology*. Philadelphia, PA: Temple University Press.

Moskowitz, M. J. (1977). Hugo Münsterberg: A study in the history of applied psychology. *American Psychologist, 32*, 824–842.

Scott, W. D. (1903). *The theory and practice of advertising*. Boston, MA: Small, Maynard.

Spillman, J., & Spillman, L. (1993). The rise and fall of Hugo Münsterberg. *Journal of the History of the Behavioral Sciences, 29*, 322–338.

Chapter 13

Benjamin, L. T., Jr., (2006). *A history of psychology in letters* (2nd ed.). Malden, MA: Blackwell.

Calkins, M. W. (1909). *A first book in psychology*. New York, NY: MacMillan.

Calkins, M. W. (1915). The self in scientific psychology. *American Journal of Psychology*, *26*, 495–524.

Calkins, M. W. (1930). Autobiography of Mary Whiton Calkins. In C. Murchison (Ed.), *History of psychology in autobiography* (Vol. 1, pp. 31–62). Worcester, MA: Clark University Press.

Furumoto, L. (1980). Mary Whiton Calkins (1863–1930). *Psychology of Women Quarterly*, *5*, 55–68.

Furumoto, L. (1990). Mary Whiton Calkins (1863–1930). In A. N. O'Connell & N. F. Russo (Eds.), *Women in psychology: A bio-bibliographic sourcebook* (pp. 57–65). Westport, CT: Greenwood Press.

Scarborough, E., & Furumoto, L. (1987). *Untold lives: The first generation of American women psychologists*. New York, NY: Columbia University Press.

Chapter 14

Goddard, H. H. (1912). *The Kallikak family: A study in the heredity of feeble-mindedness*. New York, NY: Macmillan.

Goddard, H. H. (1914). *Feeble-mindedness: Its causes and consequences*. New York, NY: Macmillan.

Goddard, H. H. (1942). In defense of the Kallikak study. *Science*, *95*, 574–576.

Herrnstein, R. J., & Murray, C. (1994). *The bell curve: Intelligence and class structure in American life*. New York, NY: Free Press.

Smith, J. D. (1985). *Minds made feeble: The myth and legacy of the Kallikaks*. Rockville, MD: Aspen Systems Corporation.

Smith, J. D., & Wehmeyer, M. L. (2012). *Good blood, bad blood: Science, nature, and the myth of the Kallikaks*. Washington, DC: AAIDD.

Zenderland, L. (1998). *Measuring minds: Henry Herbert Goddard and the origins of American intelligence testing*. Cambridge, UK: Cambridge University Press.

Chapter 15

Beck, H. P., Levinson, S., & Irons, G. (2009). Finding little Albert: A journey to John B. Watson's infant laboratory. *American Psychologist*, *64*, 605–614.

Fridlund, A. J., Beck, H. P., Goldie, W. D., & Irons, G. (2012). Little Albert: A neurologically impaired child. *History of Psychology*, *15*, 302–327.

Harris, B. (1979). Whatever happened to little Albert? *American Psychologist*, *34*, 151–160.

Jones, M. C. (1924). A laboratory study of fear: The case of Peter. *Journal of Genetic Psychology*, *31*, 308–315.

Powell, R. A., Digdon, N., Harris, B., & Smithson, C. (2014). Correcting the record on Watson, Rayner, and Little Albert: Albert Barger as "Psychology's lost boy." *American Psychologist*, *69*, 600–611.

Watson, J. B. (1913). Psychology as the behaviorist views it. *Psychological Review*, *20*, 158–177.

Watson, J. B., & Rayner, R. (1920). Conditioned emotional reactions. *Psychological Review*, *3*, 1–14.

Chapter 16

Clynes, T. (2016, September). How to raise a genius. *Nature, 537*, 152–155.

Feldman, D. H. (1984). A follow-up of subjects scoring above 180 IQ in Terman's genetic studies of genius. *Exceptional Children, 50*, 518–523.

Friedman, H. S., & Martin, L. R. (2011). *The longevity project*. New York, NY: Hudson Street Press.

Lubinski, D. (2016). From Terman to today: A century of findings on intellectual precocity. *Review of Educational Research, 86*, 900–944.

Shurkin, J. N. (1992). *Terman's kids: The groundbreaking study of how the gifted grow up*. Boston, MA: Little Brown.

Terman, L. M. (1926). *Genetic studies of genius. Vol. 1. Mental and physical traits of a thousand gifted children*. Stanford, CA: Stanford University Press.

Terman, L. M., & Oden, M. H. (1959). *The gifted group at mid-life*. Stanford, CA: Stanford University Press.

Warne, R. T. (2019). An evaluation (and vindication?) of Lewis Terman: What the father of gifted education can teach the 21st century. *Gifted Child Quarterly, 63*, 3–21.

Chapter 17

Guetzkow, H., & Bowman, P. H. (1946). *Men and hunger: A psychological manual for relief workers*. Elgin, IL: Brethren Publishing House.

Kalm, L. M., & Semba, R. D. (2005, June). They starved so that others could be better fed: Remembering Ancel Keys and the Minnesota experiment. *Journal of Nutrition, 135*, 1347–1352.

Keys, A., Brožek, J., Henschel, A., Mickelsen, O., & Taylor, H. L. (1950), *The biology of human starvation (Vols. 1–2)*. Minneapolis: University of Minnesota Press.

Maslow, A. (1943). A theory of human motivation. *Psychological Review, 50*, 370–396.

Tucker, T. (2006). *The great starvation experiment: The heroic men who starved so that millions could live*. New York, NY: Free Press.

Chapter 18

Burt, C. (1958). The inheritance of mental ability, *American Psychologist, 13*, 1–15.

Fancher, R. E. (1985). *The intelligence men: Makers of the IQ controversy*. New York, NY: Norton.

Fletcher, R. (1991). *Science, ideology and the media: The Cyril Burt scandal*. New Brunswick, NJ: Transaction.

Hearnshaw, L. (1979). *Cyril Burt, psychologist*. Ithaca, NY: Cornell University Press.

Jensen, A. R. (1991). IQ and science: The mysterious Burt affair. *The Public Interest, 105*, 93–106.

Joynson, R. B. (1989). *The Burt affair*. London, UK: Routledge.

Kamin, L. J. (1974). *The science and politics of IQ*. Potomac, MD: Lawrence Erlbaum Associates.

Mackintosh, N. J. (Ed.). (1995). *Cyril Burt: Fraud or framed?* New York, NY: Oxford University Press.

Chapter 19

Candland, D. K. (1993). *Feral children and clever animals*. New York, NY: Oxford University Press.

De Waal, F. (2016). *Are we smart enough to know how smart animals are?* New York, NY: W. W. Norton.

Hess, E. (2008). *Nim Chimpsky: The chimp who would be human*. New York, NY: Random House.

Linden, E. (1986). *Silent partners: The legacy of the ape language experiments*. New York, NY: Ballantine Books.

Terrace, H. S. (1979). *Nim*. New York, NY: Knopf.

Terrace, H. S., Pettito, L. A., Sanders, R. J., & Bever, T. G. (1979). Can an ape create a sentence? *Science, 206*, 891–902.

Chapter 20

Benjamin, L. T., Jr., & Crouse, E. M. (2002). The American Psychological Association's response to *Brown v. Board of Education*. *American Psychologist, 57*, 38–50.

Clark, K. B. (1955). *Prejudice and your child*. Boston, MA: Beacon Press.

Clark, K. B. (1965). *Dark ghetto: Dilemmas of social power*. New York, NY: Harper.

Clark, K. B., & Clark, M. P. (1939). The development of consciousness of self and the emergence of racial identification in Negro preschool children. *Journal of Social Psychology, S.P.S.S.I Bulletin, 10*, 591–599.

Clark, M. P. (1983). Mamie Phipps Clark. In A. N. O'Connell & N. F. Russo (Eds.), *Models of achievement: Reflections of eminent women in psychology* (pp. 267–276). New York, NY: Columbia University Press.

Horowitz, R. E. (1939). Racial aspects of self-identification in nursery school children. *Journal of Psychology, 7*, 91–99.

Jackson, J. P., Jr. (2006). Kenneth B. Clark: The complexities of activist psychology. In D. A. Dewsbury, L. T. Benjamin Jr., & M. Wertheimer (Eds.), *Portraits of pioneers in psychology, Vol. VI*, (pp. 273–286). Washington, DC: American Psychological Association.

Keppel, B. (2002). Kenneth B. Clark in the patterns of American culture. *American Psychologist, 57*, 29–37.

Klineberg, O. (1935). *Race differences*. New York, NY: Harper & Brothers.

Philips, L. (2004). Antiracist work in the desegregation era: The scientific activism of Kenneth Bancroft Clark. In A. S. Winston (Ed.), *Defining difference: Race and racism in the history of psychology* (pp. 233–260). Washington, DC: American Psychological Association.

Pickren, W. E., & Tomes, H. (2002). The legacy of Kenneth B. Clark to the APA. *American Psychologist, 57*, 51–59.

Chapter 21

Anonymous. (1992). Awards for distinguished contributions to psychology in the public interest. *American Psychologist, 47*, 498–503.

Hooker, E. (1957). The adjustment of the male overt homosexual. *Journal of Projective Techniques.* *21*, 18–31.

Hooker, E. (1993). Reflections of a 40-year exploration: A scientific view on homosexuality. *American Psychologist, 48,* 450–453.

Kimmel, D. C., & Garnets, L. D. (2000). What a light it shed: The life of Evelyn Hooker. In G. A. Kimble & M. Wertheimer, *Portraits of pioneers in psychology, Vol. IV* (pp. 253–267). Washington, DC: American Psychological Association.

Schmiechen, R. (Director), & Harrison, J. (Producer). (1991). *Changing our minds: The story of Dr. Evelyn Hooker* [Motion picture]. San Francisco, CA: Frameline.

Shneidman, E. S. (1998). Evelyn Hooker (1907–1996). *American Psychologist, 53,* 480–481.

Chapter 22

Blum, D. (2002). *Love at Goon Park.* Cambridge, MA: Perseus Books.

Harlow, H. (1958). The nature of love. *American Psychologist, 13,* 673–685.

LeRoy, H. A. (2008). Harry Harlow: From the other side of the desk. *Integrative Psychological and Behavioral Science, 42,* 348–353.

LeRoy, H. A., & Kimble, G. A. (2003). Harry Frederick Harlow: And one thing led to another . . . In G. A. Kimble & M. Wertheimer (Eds.), *Portraits of Pioneers in Psychology, Volume V* (pp. 279–297). Washington, DC: American Psychological Association.

Sears, R. R. (1982). Harry Frederick Harlow (1905–1981). *American Psychologist, 37,* 1280–1281.

Sidowski, J. B., & Lindsley, D. B. (1989). *Harry Frederick Harlow 1905–1981: A biographical memoir.* Washington, DC: National Academy of Sciences.

Chapter 23

Baumrind, D. (1964). Some thoughts on ethics of research: After reading Milgram's "Behavioral study of obedience." *American Psychologist, 19,* 421–423.

Blass, T. (1996). Stanley Milgram: A life of inventiveness and controversy. In G. A. Kimble, C. A. Boneau, & M. Wertheimer (Eds.), *Portraits of pioneers in psychology, Vol. II* (pp. 315–331). Washington, DC: American Psychological Association.

Blass, T. (2004*). The man who shocked the world: The life and legacy of Stanley Milgram.* New York, NY: Basic Books.

Blass, T. (2009). From New Haven to Santa Clara: A historical perspective on the Milgram obedience experiments. *American Psychologist, 64,* 37–45.

Burger, J. M. (2009). Replicating Milgram: Would people still obey today? *American Psychologist, 64,* 1–11.

Milgram, S. (1963). Behavioral study of obedience. *Journal of Abnormal and Social Psychology, 67,* 371–378.

Milgram, S. (1964). Issues in the study of obedience: A reply to Baumrind. *American Psychologist, 19,* 848–852.

Milgram, S. (1967, May). The small world problem. *Psychology Today, 1*, 60–67.

Milgram, S. (1974). Obedience to authority: An experimental view. New York, NY: Harper & Row.

Milgram, S., & Toch, H. (1969). Collective behavior: Crowds and social movements. In G. Lindsey & E. Aronson (Eds.), *The handbook of social psychology (2nd ed., Vol. 4*, pp. 507–610). Reading, MA: Addison-Wesley.

Perry, G. (2012). *Behind the shock machine*. New York, NY: The New Press.

Chapter 24

Cook, K. (2014). *Kitty Genovese: The murder, the bystanders, the crime that changed America*. New York, NY: W. W. Norton.

Gansberg, M. (1964, March 27). 37 who saw murder didn't call the police. *New York Times*, p. 1.

Griggs, R. A. (2015). The Kitty Genovese story in introductory psychology textbooks: Fifty years later. *Teaching of psychology, 42*, 149–152.

Latané, B., & Darley, J. M. (1968). Group inhibition of bystander intervention in emergencies. *Journal of Personality and Social Psychology, 10*, 215–221.

Latané, B., & Darley, J. M. (1970). *The unresponsive bystander: Why doesn't he help?* New York, NY: Appleton-Century-Crofts.

Manning, R., Levine, M., & Collins, A. (2007). The Kitty Genovese murder and the social psychology of helping: The parable of the 38 witnesses. *American Psychologist, 62*, 555–562.

Pelonero, C. (2014). *Kitty Genovese: A true account of a public murder and its private consequences*. New York, NY: Skyhorse.

Rosenthal, A. M. (1999). *Thirty-eight witnesses*. Berkeley: University of California Press. (Original work published 1964).

INDEX

U.S. academic psychology, unification of, 139

See also Little Albert case study; Watson, John B.

Bekhterev, Vladimer, 76

Bell, Alexander Graham, 97

Bell curve, 64

The Bell Curve, 137

Benbow, Camilla, 156

Bernheim, Hippolyte, 35, 40–41

Bettelheim, B., 18

Bias:
  confirmation bias, 53, 171
  experimenter bias, 204
  role of, 58–59
  selection bias and, 155

Bigelow, Henry, 24, 25, 30

Binet, Alfred, 41–42, 83, 84, 104, 132, 149

Binet-Simon Scale, 132, 149

Binet-Simon Scale/Stanford Revision, 135, 149

Binswanger, Ludwig, 85

Biological determinism, 173, 174

Bishop, Bridget, 7

Blacklisting, 153

Blass, Thomas, 220, 225

Bleuler, Eugen, 81, 83, 85

Board for Social and Ethical Responsibility for Psychology, 196

Borch-Jacobsen, M., 51

Boring, Edwin Garrigues, 119

Bowlby, John, 18, 215

Braid, James, 37

Brain function. *See* Gage's brain trauma; Phrenology

Breuer, Josef, 44, 45–46, 48, 106

Brill, Abraham Arden, 105

Bromer, John, 209

Brown v. Board of Education of Topeka (1954), 193, 194

Brožek, Josef, 162, 169

Burger, Jerry, 222

Burt, Cyril Lodovic, 171
  background of, 172–173
  changing attitudes, clearing his name and, 176–177
  controversial research results of, 174–176

educational/psychological testing, interest in, 172, 173

eleven-plus examinations, tracking system and, 173

fraudulent data, validity issues and, 171, 175–176

heredity vs. environment argument and, 171, 173–174

intelligence, differences in, 171, 173

knighthood of, 173

media coverage and, 172, 175, 176

political ideology, potential role of, 172, 177

professional standards, violation of, 171

quantitative analytic approach and, 172–173

school psychologist, employment as, 173

twin studies of, 173–174, 177

unproven guilt of, 177

vilification of, 171–172

See also Modern era psychology

Butler, Joyce, 184

Bystander effect, 227, 230, 234

Calkins, Mary Whiton, 121
  Clark University education of, 123, 125
  early life/education of, 121–122
  Harvard University education of, 123, 124–126
  later work of, 127–128
  legacy of, 128–129
  paired-associate method and, 126, 128
  psychology research laboratories, lack of, 123
  psychology research laboratory, establishment of, 125
  psychology, study of, 122–124
  Radcliffe College, founding of, 127
  self-psychology, promotion of, 127, 128
  Smith College education of, 121–122
  unofficial doctoral examination and, 126
  Wellesley College appointment and, 122, 125, 127, 128
  women in higher education and, 121
  See also Early era psychology

Candland, D. K., 15, 57

Caporael, L. R., 9, 10

Carter, Robert, 192, 193

correlation coefficient, development
of, 66
data collection, questionnaire method
and, 64–66
eugenics, interest in, 60, 63–64, 67, 68
experimental psychology, precursor of, 68
explorer's notes of, 62
final years of, 67
fingerprints, identification tool of, 66
heredity, work on, 64–66
human evolutionary context and, 67–68
intelligence measurement and, 60, 61,
64, 65
International Health Exhibition,
participation in, 65–66
knighthood of, 173
legacy of, 67–68
nature vs. nurture debate and, 65, 68
precociousness of, 60–61
psychology, impact on, 60
racism of, 62–63
religion, exploration of, 66–67
Royal Geographic Society and, 62, 63, 66
statistical tools, development of, 64–66
travel/adventure, inclination for, 61–62
variability/individual differences,
interest in, 68
See also Early era psychology
Galvanic skin response, 116
Gansberg, Martin, 229
Gardner, Allen, 180, 182
Gardner, Beatrix, 180, 182
Garrett, Henry, 191, 194
Gender studies. *See* Hooker, Evelyn
Geniuses, 148, 149
See also Intelligence measurement;
Terman, Lewis Madison
Genovese. *See* Kitty Genovese murder
Gestalt school, 77
Gifted and talented individuals, 137, 148
See also Terman, Lewis Madison
Gillie, Oliver, 175, 176, 177
Glover, Goody, 4
Goddard, Henry H., 130–133
applied psychology, interest in, 131
Binet-Simon Scale, administration of,
132, 149
Clark University education of, 131

death of, 137
defective genes, negative family
characteristics and, 131, 133, 134
Ellis Island arrivals, evaluation of, 136
feeblemindedness, causes of,
131–132, 133
gifted and talented, interest in, 137
intelligence, biological factors in, 132,
133, 134
Martin Kallikak families, study of,
133–135
Martin Kallikak study, criticisms of,
134–135, 136, 137
mental retardation, terminology for,
132–133, 149
nature vs. nurture debate and, 131,
134, 135
Ohio Bureau of Juvenile Research
appointment and, 136
Ohio State University appointment
and, 136
prevention/management aspects,
interest in, 132
Training School for Feebleminded
Boys and Girls and, 130, 131,
132, 133, 136
See also Kallikak, Deborah
Griggs, William, 4–5
Guetzkow, Harold, 167

Hall, G. Stanley, 102, 103, 105, 106, 108,
109, 115, 123, 125, 131, 149
Hallucinatory experiences, 7, 10–11
Hans. *See* Clever Hans/wonder horse case
study
Harden, Edward, 97
Harlem Youth Project, 194, 195
Harlow, Harry, 18, 207
academic career of, 207–208
affection experiments, initiation of,
210–211
affectional systems research and, 207,
209–210, 214
anti-Semitic bias and, 208
behavioral sequences, monkey-human
infant similarities and, 209
contact comfort vs. feeding, relative
powers of, 210–211